D0163512

Eminent Rhetoric

Eminent Rhetoric

Language, Gender, and Cultural Tropes

ELIZABETH A. FAY

Series in Language and Ideology
Edited by Donaldo Macedo

BERGIN & GARVEY
Westport, Connecticut
London

Library of Congress Cataloging-in-Publication Data

Fay, Elizabeth A.
    Eminent rhetoric : language, gender, and cultural tropes /
Elizabeth A. Fay.
       p. cm.—(Series in language and ideology, ISSN 1069–6806)
    Includes bibliographical references and index.
    ISBN 0–89789–309–3 (alk. paper)
    1. Women—Language. 2. Rhetoric—Political aspects. 3. Sexism in
language. 4. Language and culture. I. Title. II. Series.
P120.W66F39 1994
401'.41—dc20   93–43408

British Library Cataloguing in Publication Data is available.

Library of Congress Catalog Card Number: 93–43408
ISBN: 0–89789–309–3
ISSN: 1069–6806

First published in 1994

Bergin & Garvey, 88 Post Road West, Westport, CT 06881
An imprint of Greenwood Publishing Group, Inc.

Printed in the United States of America

The paper used in this book complies with the
Permanent Paper Standard issued by the National
Information Standards Organization (Z39.48–1984).

10 9 8 7 6 5 4 3 2 1

Copyright Acknowledgments

The author and publisher are grateful to the following sources for permission to reprint
material:

Elizabeth Fay, "Anger in the Classroom: Women, Voice and Fear." *Radical Teacher* 42, part II
(Fall 1992): 13–16.

Elizabeth Fay, "Thoughts on the Gendering of (French) Tongues." *Semiotica* 98, 3/4 (1994):
443–48.

Contents

Series Foreword

This book is a powerful testimony of how language is the only means through which we come to consciousness. Thus, "the purposeful manipulation of language to gain political ends" is part and parcel of the ideological mechanism designed to muffle the emergence of submerged voices of cultural subjects who, by virtue of their race, gender, class, and ethnicity, are not treated with the dignity and respect they deserve. The emergence of a multiplicity of cultural voices has struck the white patriarchal nerve, leading Pat Buchanan to urge his fellow conservatives "to wage a cultural revolution in the nineties as sweeping as the political revolution of the eighties." This cultural revolution is indeed moving forward with rapid speed, ranging from Pat Buchanan's call, to our national and patriotic impulse to keep Mexicans out by building a large wall along the U.S. border with Mexico, to Pat Robertson's onslaught against cultural diversity and feminism—blaming the equal rights amendment for encouraging "women to leave their children, practice witchcraft, destroy capitalism, and become lesbians."

Eminent Rhetoric: Language, Gender, and Cultural Tropes not only succinctly demonstrates how language makes social inequalities invisible but it also painfully describes how we have been subjected to a pedagogy of lies that distorts and falsifies realities while giving us "the illusion of individual freedom, ownership of our own thoughts and decisions."[1] This pedagogy of lies creates a "reality" within which we accommodate ourselves to living "within a big lie" that tranquilizes us if we adhere to the web of falsehood but makes us feel guilty and uncomfortable should we attempt to live in truth.[2] It is a process, Elizabeth Fay argues, through which "ideology works on us, co-opts us into being its believers and its agents." For example,

during the Gulf War, to not wear the yellow ribbon constituted an unpatri-
otic act. As a sign, the yellow ribbon structured a reality that brooked no
debate. To not wear it meant not supporting our troops. The yellow ribbon
did not enable us to question our government's motive for the war while
still supporting the destiny and safety of our troops. Hence, the yellow
ribbon, as a sign, became an ideological straight-jacket that left very little
room for the existence of multiple thoughts and positions, all the while
making us feel not only in total control of our position, but also very proud
of it.

Like signs, words have the same ideological power. Elizabeth Fay convincingly states that since the debate over language is not merely linguistic
but ideological, the white patriarchy often celebrates a particular discourse
while discrediting other forms of language. According to Olivier Reboul,
discourses are very often anchored in "shock-words, terms or expressions
[that] when produced by themselves, due to their strong connotations,
provoke a reaction no matter what sentence within which they are in-
serted."[3] In other words, these terms, expressions, and words have a
positive association, almost independently of their meanings. For example,
in the present educational reform debate, the word "choice" provokes a
positive effect that forces us to leave its meaning across different contexts
unexamined. Who would be opposed to the freedom to choose a particular
school? Almost everyone would support the right to choose. However, the
subtext that underlies "choice" is that although it is theoretically possible,
not all of us have the same privileged position from which we can exercise
our right to choose. That is to say, middle- and upper-class white families
have means to support their choice of schools, such as their ability to
provide alternative transportation, their history of participation in their
children's educational process, and other privileges accorded to them
solely by virtue of their race and class position. An African-American
family may enjoy the same class privileges, but the race factor makes the
matter of choice immensely more troublesome to the extent that the prob-
able host schools may not roll out the welcome carpet to their children due
to the structure of racism. For poor non-white families, the educational
choice concept is enormously more problematic. Because they do not
possess the cultural capital that would enable them to support their choice,
they will often remain without choice, abandoned in inner-city schools with
little resources and decrepit buildings.

The power of ideology is so insidious that the unanalyzed association of
shock words such as "choice" is often accepted by the very people who will
be adversely affected by it. Thus, many poor people, including poor people
of color, are led away by the illusion that the shock word "choice" creates.
Unfortunately, the very ideology that anchors its discourse on positive-ef-
fect shock words also prevents us from having access to the subtext which
often contains a meaning opposite to the illusory "reality" created by shock

words. It is for this very reason that conservative educational reformers who promote "choice" as a panacea will not tolerate a counter-discourse that points to the false assumption inherent in the educational choice proposal. For the right to choose to be equally exercised, we would have to live in a classless, race-, gender-, and ethnic-blind society. Since we know that this is not the case, the only way we can rationalize our support for educational choice is to stay at the level of the positive effect of the shock word which often obfuscates the true reality.

Shock words, terms, and expressions do not only produce positive effects. According to Olivier Reboul, shock words can also "produce by themselves negative effects that disqualify those who use these shock words."[4] Thus, the use of words such as "oppression," "radical," and "activist" often provoke a negative effect that prevents a thorough analysis of the reality encoded by these terms. In other words, if "oppression" is not allowed as part of the debate, there will be no need to identify its perpetrator "oppressor." In the same vein, the dominant discourse uses the presence of these taboo words to dismiss the counter-discourse that challenges the falsification of reality so as to prevent the understanding of the mechanisms used as obstacles to the development of spaces for dialectical relationships. I am reminded of the former dean of the College of Arts and Sciences at my university who, when pressured by the central administration to get the college more involved in education and teacher preparation, asked the chair of the English department to appoint a liaison with the Graduate School of Education. However, he cautioned her to avoid nominating someone "radical." Thus, radicalism is a shock word that triggers a negative effect and all those involved in work that is *a priori* considered by the dominant discourse as radical are dismissed as political and therefore not scientific and are prevented from taking part in the discussion, particularly if the overall agenda is to maintain the *status quo*. In a like manner, to denounce racism with strong conviction is often considered radicalism. A moderate position is to acknowledge that racism exists but not the need or urgency to do anything that would change the very structures that produce racism.

The term "reform" in conjunction with education produces a positive effect to the extent that it announces change in a system that has been determined to be working ineffectively but without threatening the core values of the system or the people who run it. In this sense, "reform" produces a positive effect in that it tranquilizes people who consciously recognize that some cosmetic changes must occur while adhering to those same values and mechanisms that created the need for reform in the first place. In contrast, the term "transformation" is a taboo word, in that it produces a negative effect by announcing a total and radical change of the system which has been identified as not working. In the political sphere, politicians use taboo words as an effective means to control the population and dismiss any challenge presented by a counter-discourse. For example, Michael Dukakis' challenge to Republican conservatism was totally neutralized by George Bush when he associated Dukakis with liberalism. No debate about the possible promise and values of liberalism was necessary or allowed. All Bush had to do was to call Dukakis a liberal and the little movie in peoples' heads played in the proper ideological context, did the rest.

This is why Bob Dole, the Republican Senator, confidently sent a letter full of falsehoods to his fellow Republicans, pointing out that "the liberal Democrats are literally dancing in the streets here in Washington. They now *control* the White House, the Congress, the Federal bureaucracy, the media, academia, and the entertainment industry. And while the liberal Democrats wish to force their dangerous agenda on America . . . we Republicans are stuck in a destructive debate over 'who lost the White House.' "

Senator Dole hid his falsification of reality behind the overuse of the word "liberal" in his letter that enables it to function as taboo shock words, such as "socialist," "communist," and "Marxist," among others. These shock words have the same negative effects and are often successfully used for ideological control.

Another pernicious mechanism used by academics who suffocate discourses different from their own is the blind and facile call for clarity. Such a call often ignores how language is used to make social inequality invisible. A graduate student of mine pointed out to me in class that while she agreed politically with almost all the issues raised by me, she could not understand why I use such complex and sometimes inaccessible language when I write. Her position points out that one can read a high level of political clarity and yet be undermined by other forms of ideology that insidiously betray the political positions that one may take. For example, two ideological forms come to mind: taste and style. If we consider taste to be outside the ideological symbolic evaluation systems, we can easily understand how someone is able to deconstruct the ideology of oppression while at the same time insisting that the only way to achieve such a goal is through a discourse that involves what they characterize as language clarity.

When I was writing the book *Literacy: Reading the Word and the World*, which I co-authored with Paulo Freire, I asked a colleague whom I considered to be politically progressive with a keen understanding of Paulo's work to read the manuscript. Yet, during a discussion we had of the book, she asked me, a bit irritably, "Why do you and Paulo insist on using this Marxist jargon? Many readers who may enjoy reading Paulo may be put off by the jargon. I was at first taken aback, but proceeded to calmly explain to her that the equation of Marxism with jargon did not fully capture the richness of Paulo's analysis. In fact, Paulo's language was the only means through which he could have done justice to the complexity of the various concepts dealing with oppression. For one thing, I reminded her, "Imagine that instead of writing the *Pedagogy of the Oppressed*, Paulo Freire would have written the *Pedagogy of the Disenfranchised*." The first title utilizes a discourse that names the oppressor while the latter fails to do so. If you have oppressed you must have an oppressor. What would be the counterpart of disenfranchised? The *Pedagogy of the Disenfranchised* dislodges the agent of the action while leaving in doubt who bears the responsibility for such action. This leaves the ground wide open for blaming the victims of disenfranchisement for their own disenfranchisement. This example is a clear case in which the object of oppression can be also understood as the subject of oppression. Language such as this distorts reality. And yet, mainstream academics seldom object to these linguistic distortions that disfigure reality. I seldom hear academics on a crusade for "language clarity" equate mainstream terms such as "disenfranchised" or "ethnic cleansing," for example, to jargon status. On the one hand, they readily accept "ethnic cleansing," a euphemism for genocide, while, on the other hand, they will, with certain automatism, point to the jargon quality of terms such as "oppression," "subordination," and "praxis," among others. If we were to deconstruct the term "ethnic cleansing" we would see how it prevents us from becoming horrified by Serbian brutality and horrendous crimes against Bosnian Muslims, such as the killing of women, children, and the elderly. The mass killing of women, children, and the elderly and the raping of women and girls as young as five years old take on the positive attribute of "cleansing" which leads us to conjure a reality of "purification" of the ethnic "filth" ascribed to Bosnian Muslims, in particular, and to Muslims the world over, in general.

I also seldom heard any real protest from these same academics who want "language clarity" when, during the Gulf War, the horrific blood bath of the battlefield became a "theater of operation," and the violent killing of over one hundred thousand Iraqis, including innocent women, children, and the elderly, by our "smart bombs" was sanitized into a technical military term, "collateral damage." I can go on and on giving such examples to point out how academics who argue for language clarity not only seldom object to language that obfuscates reality, but often use that same language as part of the general acceptance that the standard discourse is a given and should remain unproblematic. While these academics often acquiesce to the dominant standard discourse, they aggressively object to any discourse that fractures the dominant language, on the one hand, and on the other, makes the veiled reality bare so as to name it. Thus, a discourse that names it becomes, in their view, imprecise, unclear, and wholesale euphemisms such as "disadvantaged," "disenfranchised," "educational mortality," "theater of operation," "collateral damage," and "ethnic cleansing" remain unchallenged since they are part of the dominant social construction of images that are treated as unproblematic and clear.

xii • Series Foreword

For me, the mundane call for language simplicity and clarity represents yet another mechanism to dismiss the complexity of theoretical issues, particularly if these theoretical constructs interrogate the prevailing dominant ideology. It is for this very reason that Gayatri Spivak correctly points out that "plain prose cheats." I would go a step further and say: the call for clarity not only cheats, it also bleaches. Elizabeth Fay's *Eminent Rhetoric: Language, Gender, and Cultural Tropes* is an eloquent and pointed response to all those who are willfully entrapped by the illusion that language is neutral and equally available to all people. She convincingly not only demonstrates that language is eminently political, but also challenges us to deconstruct the ideology that shapes and maintains language manipulation, unless we want to remain prey to the ever-increasing "blindsiding" of the white-male dominated academic and political discourses.

Donaldo Macedo

NOTES

1. O. Reboul. *Lenguage e Ideologia* (Mexico: Fondo de Cultura Economica, 1986), p. 117.
2. Ibid., p. 117.
3. Ibid., p. 116.
4. Ibid., p. 117.

Acknowledgments

Inspiration for this book came from many places, from the painful 1992 electoral campaign to the stimulating debates and discussions I enjoyed at talks given at The Queen's University, Belfast and Molloy College, and especially at a 1992 NEH Summer Seminar at Johns Hopkins directed by Jerome Christensen. Much inspiration came from my mother's thoughtful provocations, and some of the most important ideas in this book are, or probably are, or might as well be hers. Closer to home were the contributions and enthusiasm of Chuck Meyer, who also read endlessly for me.

Eminent Rhetoric

Chapter One

Introduction: A Tropology

One of the oldest rhetorical insights has it that, in the domain of the uncertain, things overlap and shade into one another and that to commence and deploy a discourse bearing on that domain is, consequently, a radically contingent act. Moreover, such contingency is unavoidable.

Bender and Wellbery, viii

Eminent domain: a right of a government to take private property for public use by virtue of the superior dominion of the sovereign power over all lands within its jurisdiction.

Webster's Ninth New Collegiate Dictionary
(Springfield, MA: Merriam-Webster, 1984)

Eminent Rhetoric is a direct response to a phenomenon that recurs among the students, friends, women's groups, and colleagues I converse with: the appearances of sudden and inexplicable walls when the conversation turns to politics, feminism, human rights, or theories of subjectivity and consciousness. In other words, when we touch on issues that verge on both the private individual and the public institution, we get into trouble, instantly. These are issues that take personal loyalty to a high point, leaving logical argument far afield.

Although initiated by it, this book is not precisely concerned with this phenomenon, which is more complicated than the simple contentiousness between a staunch liberal and a staunch conservative. The book focuses instead on where these deep loyalties come from, especially in woman; how they are created; and why we cling to them when so often we are their victims. These are questions regarding ideology, about which we have some very clear ideas and theories. Despite the many books that explore ideology, politics, and power systems, we cannot be as clear about how ideology works on us, co-opts us into being its believers and its agents. As I listen to what women say—women of all ages and from different nations, races, and ethnic backgrounds—I hear words and phrases I remember from political speeches, newspaper headlines, the evening news. I also recognize certain tonalities in what is said, certain hardnesses and walls being raised over issues such as taxation, welfare programs, sexual harassment, women in high-ranking positions, gays in the military. What I do not hear, however, is a certain politicized use of words: the phrases and images get absorbed and reused, but not the rhetoric with which those words were first conveyed. The thesis of this book is that rhetoric—as the purposeful manipulation of language to gain political ends—is the unacknowledged weapon of ideology, and that women are the greatest target and the greatest victims of a political rhetoric that is most often used to support and reinforce the masculine power hegemony. Moreover, certain rhetorical tropes can be isolated, identified, and made recognizable so that women can protect themselves against the political manipulation of their minds, loyalties, and hearts against their own well-being.

I have organized the analyses and discussion of these rhetorical tropes into four arenas of the current cultural scene, each of which deeply affects women's lives: education, literature and film, the media, and feminist thought. I might have separately treated certain social phenomena, such as politics, war, and economics, but instead elected to integrate these all the way through because they seem to me inseparable. Rhetorical tropes and figures of speech are available to all of us both as users and receivers; they are part of everyday language usage and can be read in innumerable places and manifestations.

To talk of rhetoric as analyzable and as politically motivated requires more than a taxonomy of types, such as the list of tropes provided here; it also requires a perspective from which to think about language and rhetoric. Language as it is used in conversation is less static than linguists have previously thought. In *Talking Voices: Repetition, Dialogue, and Imagery in Conversational Discourse*, Deborah Tannen uses the term "constructing dialogue" to describe how speakers improvise dynamic and integrative discourse by employing rhythm, repetition of words and phrases, cliché, and creative uses of images (98–133). Rhetoric, in the political sense that will be used in this book, is a conscious deployment of these dynamic strategies to make the rhetorical speaker the only one being heard, to produce a noninteractive discourse, to inspire the audience with which the speaker identifies, and to silence the receiver of the rhetoric against which the speaker positions himself.

Thus, this book is about words and women's relation to them. The relation is a complex one, invoking at the same time women's embodiment of certain linguistic conceptions, and the state's conception of women as bodies without language. Hamlet understands the everyday politicization of words quite clearly, as he reveals in his library intercourse with the king's counselor:

Polonius What is the matter, my lord?

Hamlet: Between who?

Polonius: I mean the matter that you read, my lord.

Hamlet: Slanders, sir. (II.ii.195–98)

Hamlet's answers invert rhetoric to hide meaning as a protective device, as well as to smoke the old man out in insinuating that his counsel is mere rhetoric. And when Hamlet later warns Ophelia to "Get thee to a nunnery," he is both getting her out of the way of harmful, politicized words (slanders) and making war on that which her body represents: the "whoring" and "incest" of his mother's marriage to his scheming uncle. Nunnery in Renaissance England can mean both a religious cloister and a brothel; religion can mean both the state religion and sexuality.

When Freud analyzed Hamlet's distress, he concluded that it was not due to the difficulty of seeking out the truth about his father's death in a political situation where every rhetoricized word has two or more contrary meanings. Instead, Freud saw in Hamlet's turmoil a parlance with incestuous desire and the confusion over familial and sexual definitions and boundaries. That is, Freud took the linguistic and semiotic difficulty of the Danish court—a social dysfunction—and translated it into a psychological and sexual problem—an individual, mental, and emotional dysfunction. This confusion on the analyst's part of the private with the public, the individual with the social, is a substitution common to our culture. Even more common is the substitution of a social ill for an individual female ill, usually in order to project the larger ill onto the female body as a sophisticated form of scapegoating. Hamlet draws Freud's attention because his indecision marks him in the modern world as effeminate, and therefore available to theories about the female psyche and body. Freud's analysis of hysteria as a predominantly female disorder is another example of this ideological practice, in which words are disregarded so that the body may be reinterpreted as ill. Such confusion stems from a refusal to take the woman's words at face value, a condition Freud and Hamlet both suffer from; Hamlet believes nothing Ophelia or his mother says in a paranoid world where everything is deceit. Pat Robertson also understood this when he announced at the 1992 Republican Convention that the equal rights amendment "encourages women to leave their children, practice witchcraft, destroy capitalism, and become lesbians." The illogic of such a statement does not matter when the world is depicted in so paranoid and vulnerable a way.

Hamlet's relations with women and language—as seconded by Freud—are useful to us because they demonstrate a prominent rhetorical act or trope used by those seeking to control others, especially women: *appositive thinking*. Robertson's claim demonstrates another, *hystericization*. In this book we will examine six tropological moves by which gender relations become constituted, implemented, or supported by rhetorical usages. These rhetorical acts are more than political uses of language: they are *enactive*, actualizing behavioral attitudes from the structure of the linguistic trope itself. Hystericization is the act of declaring an author and her text hysterical, but at the same time it produces a hysteria in the namer himself. In the act of naming he becomes hysterical because he realizes or enacts the danger he has just put words to. Social critics and politicians are the two groups of individuals most committed to the use of cultural tropes as a kind of crowd control or ideological tool. The significant advantage of cultural tropes is that they, like classical tropes, attain a transparency through repetition so that we as audience do not even recognize their presence. And like classical tropes, cultural tropes use words to enact affective responses that disengage our logic from our emotions. The classical trope "hyperbole," according to Longinus, provokes the auditor's apprehension to the point that he figuratively runs away with himself, is carried away by his emotive response. Yet he stays in his seat. Hystericization, on the other hand, has a more literal application in that it does carry us away, causing us to block birth-control clinics or rampage through South Central Los Angeles. Without recognition we cannot disinterest ourselves from cultural tropes: we cannot discern where political agendas depart from our own interests, or when blame issued from a politician's or critic mouth is due or undue.

Additional tropes discussed in the following chapters include *blindsiding*, *conduct books*, *conspiratorial thinking*, and *literalization*; these occur less often and are less destructive than *appositive thinking* and *hystericization* because they are more recognizable. These tropes will be defined shortly, but first there is the question of naming. I have had to term each figural device discussed where no name as yet exists. For instance, appositive thinking, which is a substitutive trope, comes close to the figure of speech known as *catachresis*, a classical trope in which the wrong word is purposely used for paradoxical effect ("taloned justice"). However, catachresis clearly positions itself as a negative indicator of how the reader is to respond; as a cultural trope, appositive thinking must not mark its positioning intention, so that one term is unremarkably blended over into the other, and the auditor unquestioningly accepts the juxtaposition as the same difference. For instance, by this device power equals abuse: Pat Robertson's definition of political rights for women as equal to those of men is that equal rights would destroy feminine instincts and morality, and turn women into haters of men, children, and American culture.

To repeat, the claim I want to make for cultural tropes as opposed to classical figures such as catachresis, metaphor, or simile is that they provoke a thought pattern in the auditor that traces the pattern of the verbal play. These tropes therefore entrench a kind of cultural and political thinking that helps stabilize institutional power. Figures of speech can be used by speakers toward such a goal, but the uses of figures are so multiple that no single intention can be attributed to their application. On the other hand, the reason that political tropes remain both singular and pervasive must be that they are unacknowledged. To acknowledge and name them here is an obviously political move; more to the point, if nominalization incurs power, then women need to participate more in naming the world around them, particularly as it impinges on and is directed toward them. This is even more important when men's naming process has not yet recognized those parts of the male-driven language system directed toward women or encompassing the social experience of women as well as other non-dominant groups.

This said, the tropes are:

Appositive thinking is a term that seems to me to aptly describe a particular kind of dangerous logic. In sentence structure, apposition is a figure of speech in which two terms are parallel and coterminous but by definition never touch. I use appositive thinking when rhetoric is used to force the terms to cross over so that they identify each other, with one term falsely standing for the other.

Hystericization describes the process of denominating something as hysterical, whether it be a person, a text, or a social movement. I argue that although hysteria is perceived to be a woman's illness and therefore the mark of effeminacy or uncontrolled femininity, it is not "natural" to the female psyche or body; rather, it is put upon women by men as in Freud's jointly authored study on hysteria, a book by two male doctors about their female patients. Its value is that hystericization enables those uneasy about some threat to project their unease as disease onto women. And *conspiratorial thinking* is the term I apply to rhetoric that is already hystericized, but which goes beyond hystericization to paranoia.

In *blindsiding*, the speaker usually tries to convince his audience to agree with his proposal, yet the proposal is usually one detrimental to that audience. Therefore the speaker must raise a screen over the potential harm by discoursing about a related but irrelevant issue which he then calls by the name of the issue he wants agreement on. When Senate Republicans wanted to continue protection of tax exemptions for the wealthy against President Clinton's proposed tax revisions, they discussed the issue as general taxation increases and renamed it "fiscal responsibility."

Literalization provides such a screen by treating the fictional as reality. We casually employ this trope when we confuse actors with their film roles, treat serial episodes as seriously as real life drama, or view real life drama as if television. One commonplace version of literalization that we knowingly enter into is the romance story, for instance. But when literalization is used toward a specific political end that sways our opinions and fears, it becomes a dangerous ploy.

Conduct books or *conduct-book thinking* is the trope involved with going beyond mere socialization to actually controlling women's behavior. It is nakedly prescriptive and norm-making, but when rhetorically clothed it appears merely descriptive, as do all the cultural tropes discussed here. As a master's student, I once received a paper comment suggesting that I did not possess the acumen to continue in graduate school, and that it would save me and my professors a great deal of trouble if I dropped the program at the end of the semester or sooner. Three years later I learned from a woman friend who did drop out that, as far as she could determine, any woman enrolled in the seminars taught by this professor received the same carefully worded comment. *Conduct-book thinking* asserts one behavioral code as correct by pointing to another as unnatural and disturbing.

RHETORIC AS SYMPTOM

Before defining these language devices further, it is important that we realize that the political bombast of Polonius and any other political or social leader is never just empty words. Words harm through powerful symbolic and imaginative processes, and they do so insidiously precisely because we think they are ephemeral and immaterial. But as any preacher and president knows, words are the greatest weapon available; at the same time, words can backfire worse than any other lethal weapon because their ability to make meaning is neither precise nor absolute. Ironically, we know how powerfully words can affect us but we rarely give that knowledge credence; our daily lives are too filled with "words, words, words" to pay much attention. The purpose of this book is to point out recognizable patterns in word usage so that paying attention can be easier on a daily basis.

Rhetorical tropes that consistently emerge in politicized language and which have long been recognized include classical figures of speech: metaphor, allegory, hyperbole, metonymy, synecedoche. While these terms occasionally surface in the following chapters, the main focus will be on a different order of tropes which have not been determined or acknowledged by rhetoricians. They have been historically present but not recognized as *rhetorical* weapons used against a specific portion of society: women. I have determined these "tropes," or metaphorical ways of organizing thought and speech, to be specifically masculine constructions although women often use them, sometimes against other women. Generally, however, women have thought of weaving, birthing, and web-making metaphors by which to imagine their world rather than tropes of containment and control. Their language is full of allusions rather than displacements, and connections rather than synecdoches (synecdoches substitute a word denoting the part for a larger term, or vice versa).

At the same time, women had to create images to describe the ways that male power impinges on their lives. Divisions in the family nexus began to be imagined as walls being erected between the woman and another person important to them. It is also the image that has allowed people living in the last two centuries to associate gender with separate space: public and private spheres. Through the image of division, keeping women in their homes appears to be a "law of nature" rather than a manmade rule and thus becomes acceptable and even affirming for many women under patriarchy. However, young girls often use wall and border images to create a continuity between themselves and others, rather than to cut themselves off from their communities. I am therefore less interested in this book in how women use language to defensively imagine their worlds, since female images do not manipulate the language in the way that the tropes I discuss do; such images will occasionally enter the discussion for descriptive but not analytic purposes. Unlike images, tropes do manipulate the language, and they do so by performing the same operation on thought process as they do on word construction. A trope works invisibly to enact on the audience what is not really heard. This is the manner in which rhetoric is intended to persuade audiences, and it is the purpose of the political and legal speeches addressed to constituencies and juries. But when we respond without analyzing the language that has swayed us, we put our future in another's hands.

Thus in a recent article in *U.S. News and World Report* on gays in the military, it is not surprising to find examples of appositive thinking in a subject about blurring boundaries. The reporter quotes a soldier as saying, "In combat you have to rely on every single guy at any moment, at any time. . . . And if you're in combat and you mistrust somebody, it's over. You want to have that cohesion. And if you lose that cohesion, that's your life" (Auster and Borger, 26). Another soldier commented, "The military is not an ordinary job. . . . We work together but we actually live together" (26). In a discussion on the topic "Does [lifting the ban] help me or hinder me in winning at war?" the discussion has suddenly veered away from socialization—training soldiers to work well together in artificial circumstances as white, blacks, men and women—to a discussion about Nature. The apposition, a crossover from nurture to nature, rests on the assumption that men cannot control their sexuality, that heterosexual men will naturally be inclined toward rape in times of war and therefore need access to brothels. The soldiers fear that homosexual men will harass, seduce, or rape their fellows because of their greatly increased access. It appears that the military hierarchy believes this too, and women's precarious inclusion in the military can be revoked when this belief becomes too powerful, as it nearly did after the Gulf War. Nonetheless, women are more securely socialized as part of the group when the nature argument can be thrust on gays. In all the argument over the ban on gays, there is little heard about the socialization versus nature issue despite the hard evidence that gays have served well and honorably. We might ask, were they socialized to behave as soldiers, did they only have sex with consenting (gay) partners? There is little discussion of how gays experience military service and little attention paid to the discussions of how heterosexuals perceive the gays in their outfits. Nor is much attention paid to the hard evidence that rape in war is from the heterosexual population. It is only what the military command believes that is attended to. It is because the military hierarchy believes its heterosexual troops to be only superficially socialized (natural men) that it puts the onus of nature on those groups it has been forced to assimilate (black men, women, and now gays and lesbians). By doing so the hierarchy makes the "natural" or uncontrollable group appear an exaggerated nature, an unnatural being which is cast as a version of the enemy invading the ranks. Heterosexual soldiers appear the socialized or civilizing force in comparison; however, if their ranks are invaded, they will be denatured and thus demoralized. This is appositive thinking because the crossover is nearly invisible in the language itself, and yet the crossed ideas are replicated in the reader's mind and retained as fact: gay troops will molest and rape their straight tentmates, who then will be so emasculated they cannot fight. Tropes are in this sense performative: appositive thinking ties one's reasoning into knots.

Pejoration like blindsiding, is another variant on appositive thinking; it is widely practiced and was particularly evident in President Bush's rhetorical practice. A device linguists do recognize and study, it is the process of defaming a word so that it now connotes a negative valence instead of its original positive meaning. The best example of this during Bush's presidency is *liberal*, a term Bush pejorated in the 1988 presidential campaign in order to gain a rhetorical stronghold over both his Democratic opponent and a recalcitrant House. But what the president was more successful at than influencing Congress was disheartening the nation. Many liberals had come to wonder in the last four years how it is possible that everything they believed in could have taken on such a fouled resonance. Their wonderment stems from the fact that tropes work invisibly and succinctly; at the same time they can look like something else fairly easily. Thus Bush's use of pejoration looked too much like hysterical grandstanding to be easily recognized. And while hysteria is not difficult to spot, its related trope, hystericization, is.

Hysteria, as it will be used in this book, will have a specialized meaning which will be in contrast to the term *hystericization*. It is a precursor condition to the act of hystericization, and as such, *hysteria* will infer a sociological rather than a clinical meaning: hysteria is the term used by men to describe ultra-feminine behavior which exceeds the bounds of femininity into illness.[1] The process allows the one who names to deny his own insecurity by turning it into the name which he places on the body of another. This is the very process by which witches get made, as well as hysterics and even dizzy blondes. It is also the process by which men are labeled as effeminate and therefore unfit or even a bit crazy; George Bush suffered from this stigma when the media labeled his speech patterns as "hysterical" during the campaign, insinuating his unfitness for the presidency. Some public personalities have found it effacacious in gaining media attention to portray themselves as hystericized, thus providing an interesting flipflop on the power relation of the namer and named. In other instances, the namer has been female and the named male; although this version might seem to hold interesting possibilities, it usually follows the male model so that the namer can deny her fear by projecting on the named hysteric. In all of these variations on the normative model, the important relation is a gendered assertion of power by which the masculinized participant discredits or silences the speech and language of the feminized participant. Hystericization turns out to be not only a pervasive trope in the current cultural scene, but one that is discoverable throughout our social, literary, and religious history.

The other tropes that will occur in the analyses of different arenas of language use in this book are less important to developing a defensive strategy of reading or listening to those deploying language. "Conspiratorial thinking" is a trope that can be used to point to conspiracy plots, and when used in this way it resembles hystericization. But it can also be used to create and incorporate conspiratorial counterplots, as depicted in the film *JFK* or played out in the Iran-Contra scandal. This trope is more easily recognizable than the others, but it works even more powerfully to construe a paranoid feeling in the listener or reader that reciprocates the trope itself.

Blindsiding, like pejoration, is another variant of appositive thinking. Whereas appositive thinking can be quite subtle and clever, blindsiding has more of the feel of being plowed into. And while it is quite effective, it wears thin if used too often; it is best saved for patriarchal discourse and electoral campaigns where the assumption is that the listener or audience lacks the requisite intelligence for rhetorical sophistication. The following example is perhaps so unsubtle as to seem empty of rhetoric, but it seems to me a common and clear use of this trope. In writing about her life, seventy-nine-year-old Frances DeVore recalls that not all that long ago things were still difficult for her as a woman reporter: "I would have been afraid to complain. I knew I made less money than the men. But that changed one day when the publisher explained to me that they (I was the only female) made more money because they had families to support. I just looked at them. All were single. I was divorced with four children" (7C). DeVore's publisher used the argument that men have to earn more because they support two or more people while women only support one. That is, all men work because they are married, and to be fair they are treated as if married even when they are not. By the same token all women work because they are not married, since married—and divorced—women will be provided for by those men who are paid more, and since single women are expected to quit their jobs when they marry. The blind is the focused attention on marital status and its humiliating implications (single women are single because they cannot get married); the blow to the head is that under patriarchy the publisher could demoralize his male employees if he paid his female employees equally—particularly because they usually work harder and for less, but (it is believed) produce inferior results.

Conduct books reflects the need to influence such results, and the behavior that goes with it produces another rhetorical figure. The literal conduct books were pamphlets or books written by both men and women on how to be good housewives, good mothers, and good daughters.[2] These books generally argue that women's behavior is integrally linked to their own morality and to the morality of the nation. Therefore, when an author writes a book for a purpose other than the conduct book yet assumes the same anxiety over women's behavior and morality and thus national safety, the tropes involved are conduct book tropes. These tropes are particularly abundant in nineteenth- and twentieth-century medical and psychoanalytic literature, and in educational treatises throughout the last five centuries. They are particularly prevalent today in treatises on cultural literacy in which the author is anxious to control the conduct of the young.

Literalization was egregiously employed in Dan Quayle's bid for electoral attention during the 1992 campaign. When the vice-president sought to imply that the fictional Murphy Brown was a literal character, or that her fictional acts mirrored or were literal acts, he used literalization. Like appositive thinking, literalization performs a crossover in our reasoning by which the fictitious becomes actual, literally true. The benefit to the rhetorician is that literality, like reality, is hard to argue against, it just *is*. Authors create fiction, Hollywood produces sitcoms, but the literal is like Nature— inarguable. So when Quayle said Murphy Brown's pregnancy was "just another lifestyle choice," his use of literalization made it possible for him to elide an enormous amount of very real fact had she been a real person: her lover refused to marry her or to stay, she could afford a child, she would probably never marry, this was her last chance to have a baby. Had he discussed Murphy Brown as a *scripted* character, he would not have been able to dismiss the plot difficulties so easily.

Quayle's literalization aided his political intent because his point was not about this woman, fictitious or real. He was attempting to conflate her experience with the young black unwed mothers of southern California in order to blame the "breakdown of American society" on Hollywood; his speech was neither to Hollywood producers nor to the black community, but to a white, conservative audience. His argument was that black teen-aged girls watch *Murphy Brown* and then emulate the *star* (not the character) without having her yuppie privileges. The literalization involved—comic character to real woman—is an argument a children's rights watchdog group has successfully used to improve children's television viewing. The argument there is that children imitate the violence in animated cartoons. However, a large difference exists between a teen-aged or even adult television audience and a child audience. Quayle's literalization should have produced guffaws, but the effect of this trope is so forceful that it did not; in addition, it prevented his audience and the nation's newspaper readers from realizing that Quayle belongs to the very privileged, yuppie elite that he accused the fictional Murphy Brown of representing.

As may be apparent from the above examples, these tropes are most often visible as political scare tactics or propaganda, and least often recognizable in our everyday talk. But they blend in with, and even dominate, our other meaning-making strategies because they are effective and powerful tools of persuasion. Rhetoric at its most powerful affects emotions rather than reason to such a degree that it can even turn our thinking off as we respond to the rhetor's pleas or demands. A skilled rhetorician combines emotion with reason, using the one to enhance the other, but more and more our political figures have succumbed to the lure of emotionalism as a tool to accomplish their hidden goals. An unthinking group response to a powerful leader's demands can only harm subsets of that group, since the leader increases his own possessions and privileges when others have lost theirs.

So far, this list of tropes hints at the intention of the person who elects to use them, but it is important to think more concertedly about this person and their politico-rhetorical agenda. To determine a politician's principles, or his or her ideological "take" on an issue, we must be able to "read" their rhetoric and recurrent vocabulary as much as we "read" their alliances and predictable stands. A politician's vocabulary keys us in to their particular position, so that we know when they are ungrounded, free-falling through a variety of liberal and conservative postures, and not open-minded so much as hystericized. And it is the fear of the loss of ground—or of appearing irrational and effeminate (the word *wimp* has been used in this sense)—that some politicians act out a literal manliness by declaring war, refusing asylum to refugees, playing the sportsman for the press. Open-mindedness without principle might lead to being persuadable rather than persuasive regardless of rhetorical usage, but an equally hystericized manliness (the refusal to be persuaded) which is without ground can be even more dangerous.

In thinking about the rhetor, we might consider some subtler issues. Hystericization plays on a reactionary fear of the future by redefining the ideology of past events. Until George Bush's 1988 presidential campaign, for instance, the term *liberal* had a meaning variously related to Johnson's

"Great Society," Kennedy's Peace Corps, protest against the Vietnam War, the rights movements of the 1970s, and welfare state legislation. With Bush's campaign platform, *liberal* underwent pejoration and moved from a positive (if "bleeding heart") connotation to a corrupted connotation. Bush sees liberals as welfare statists, and implies liberals legislate the care of others only in order to enrich themselves through diverting funds. Pejoration and its accompanying appositive thinking, as illustrated in the re-creation of *liberal* as a dirty word, is a classic form of reactionary response. Its use is not just symbolic but performative; columnist Ellen Goodman writes that people's current characterization of themselves as conservative despite liberal undertakings and attitudes "is a legacy of the years between 1980 and 1992. First we learned that the country was more traditional than many of us believed.Then we became convinced that the country was more conservative than it is" (A17).

It should be no surprise, then, that President Bush's adroit use of language, like that of his immediate predecessor, is a conscious rhetorical strategy. A purposefully developed sophism, it usefully furthers ideological ends: the intention to make over the country in the dominant party's image, and to harm sections of the population in order to do so. But unlike classical sophism, both Reagan and Bush rhetoricized language in ways that made their political goals appear natural ones; when Reagan blamed the recession in available jobs on women in the work force, for instance, he was iterating a highly believable notion about women's natural place, the division of a feminine private sphere from a masculine public sphere, and the natural greed of women which makes them view childrearing as sacrifice unless reminded of their moral duty. Because Reagan and Bush are clear on what they believe about the nature of women, their politicized language is more than sophical because it *is* interested. Vested interest cannot be cynical; it must involve emotionalism in order to persuasively convey its intent. Thus the Reagan-Bush rhetoric is consistently emotional—verging on hysterical—when something as large as women in powerful positions is at stake. However, as receivers and direct addressees of this rhetoric, women can either be persuaded to accept the party line, or they can feel targeted by it. Both responses are desirable to the reactionary rhetor, but the third way women can respond is not: to see through the tropology.

SCREENS

Because we are the addressees of the rhetor's words, we need to consider how we are meant to respond to rhetoric as well as how we respond to all language as political. Being in the world is always a negotiation; this is the imperative that women are socialized to operate by and men are taught to deny. Negotiation is about positionality and stance, performance and mask.

More importantly, it is about wearing contradictions or choosing which contradictions to wear.[3] Traditional Western ideology forces us to hold on to a stance, a static self-identity, yet we simultaneously negotiate "being" in relation to the shift of community from private to public identities. We experience and yet have no language with which to express "being" as mobility. It can become a mobilization or it can turn to suppression, but we understand the shifts that happen as something else. Or we understand someone else's "being" as something else: for instance, Anita Hill's experience with the abjection and subjection of harassment was viewed as an ongoing hysteria, and a warped relation with reality and her community. Senators and reporters attempted to understand her utterances as truth statements and could not ameliorate the rift between the conflicting versions of the past as presented by Hill and supporters, and Thomas and supporters. When only one truth can stand, then the statements of all those subversive to the hegemonic power will be unacceptable because they are othered. The question of how to fight this one truth arises, and terrific battles are fought over the possible solutions: multiculturalism, postmodernism, post-structuralist theories, and particularly feminism itself. Interestingly, the most powerful and persuasive rhetors are the archconservatives who desperately want to preserve the old order and its one truth. And these rhetors use language so authoritatively, precisely because they belong to the privileged members of that old order or have recently been admitted to its ranks. Yet their strongest claim is always that it is the liberals who misuse language, who abuse eloquence for their own ends. This is because rhetors know that what they say is true is more impressive than what actually is true, especially if the reality needs to be analyzed before being recognized. This is why women, whose needs as a group are so often promoted by the liberal camp, need to defend against rhetorically conservative evaluations of those needs. One way to defend is to imitate the ongoing project of French feminism to "take back the language" by redefining everyday words to create new meanings within old systems of thought. Or, as with this book, we can participate in the process of naming, which helps to redefine the way we had understood our world. But some feminists argue that language is inherently and inescapably patriarchal, and that until we escape language in its patriarchal form altogether, we cannot rethink anything.

But is it likely that by going outside the linguistic meaning system, feminists can make significant achievement possible? Graphics, for instance, have been proven to be a more efficient meaning-conveyor, and a more effective pathway into the brain. Art therapy operates from the knowledge that the unconscious can express itself without the conscious censorship that comes from language use, and without the need for disguised codes. Because of this accessibility, images, particularly in film, have been shown to be strong ideological tools, both for governmental and cultural politics.

Feminist artists believe that more real progress may come from works of art, film, and drama than from individual court cases. It is through language that the film media convey salvation, while the visual only convey a silenced love that would have ended in damnation; this is because for women's stories and art produced in a male economy, the world remains strikingly male. Whereas women's novels and films tend to deal with the reality of speaking in male-controlled spaces and arenas, men's revisions of these texts reassert a rhetoric of heroic aggression and the satisfaction of revenge. But French feminists feel that women can also revise male scripts, reciprocating the male turn, by reappropriating social myths about women. For instance, Catherine Clément and Hélène Cixous view the mythic types of sorceress and hysteric as marking "the end of a type—how far a split can go" (6). If Circe is the man-obsessed sorceress, Medea is the sorceress with a man's strength, and Cassandra the hysteric whose words go unheard, and her truth laughed away. Medea tells "herstory" but male historians ignore her text; Cassandra tells "hystery" and historians tape her mouth.

In some ways *Eminent Rhetoric* is also about why hysteries never get told, and are instead transformed into histories about the men involved. Patty Hearst was tried for revolutionary activities, but she was scapegoated by both the right and the left for her father's sake; MaryBeth Whitehead went to trial as a surrogate mother, but the court's ruling was about male property and paternal rights; William Kennedy Smith's rape trial became a popularity contest between the genial Smith and "ice princess" lawyer Moira Lasch.

The confusingly gendered stories these trials have produced are easy to misread because they sit at the split between history and hystery, between rhetoric and visual images. And if the visual screen is the more efficacious communicator, it can be too easily belied by language which makes its own meaning dominate that of images. The visual is powerful only in terms of the linguistic message it underwrites; against the linguistic the visual embodies feminine silence. For that reason *Eminent Rhetoric* focuses specifically on the interplay between language and women's social presence or embodiment. A second reason to focus on language-specific arenas is, as mentioned above, because hysteries are too often men's stories disguised as women's: hystericizations of history.

Alternately, the visual gives over too easily to a split image between media and Medea. Writing for the British magazine *The Spectator*, essayist Auberon Waugh recently criticized the separation of the Prince and Princess of Wales. Noting that "I have heard many women express [the view] in London" that the Prince was "two-timing" the Princess "from day one," Waugh comments,

How are they all so sure that Wales was two-timing from the very start? A much more likely scenario, it seems to me, is that the Prince and his paramour decided to lay off the hanky-panky on his marriage, but to *remain friends*. It was only when the "shy and lovely girl who has won the hearts of millions" (*News of the World*) showed signs of becoming a manipulative anorexic, given to hysterical mood-swings, that the older couple were driven back into each other's arms. (8, emphasis is Waugh's)

Despite having "heard many women express [the view] in London," Waugh asks "How are they all so sure that Wales was two-timing from the very start? A much more likely scenario, it seems to me, is. . . ." His speculation beats out theirs simply because he paints a more "likely scenario"; his screen beats theirs. And it does so not because his visual image is more efficient: certainly not, with its roundabout explanation, and its accusatory accusations. It does so simply because he is doing the interpreting using the language of a powerful rhetor.

Waugh quotes Nigel Dempster as describing Lady Diana soon after her wedding as having "become a fiend. She has become a little monster" (8). Diana Spencer is perceived as having been transformed by her royal marriage into a monstrous Medea figure. The tall young woman is "little," and she is "anorexic" and "hysterical" and moody. By concentrating on her body, these men reduce Lady Diana paternalistically and hysterically to a monster because they allow her no mind, only animal instincts: pet dogs manipulate, children throw tantrums.

Diana's story, her hystery of transformation from privileged young woman to princess of the realm, is hystericized, vilified, and silenced; Waugh translates her resistance to the role that the media and public provide for her into unnatural and monstrous bodily acts. At the same time, the patronizing and bestializing rhetoric that dehumanizes her makes the Prince a prince of men and a maker of human history. His "hanky-panky" is completely normal, something he gave up in a dignified way by "*remaining friends*" with his mistress. The emphasis given to "friends" and the use of the term "paramour" romanticize their natural and generous relationship. Charles's real romance has had to give way to the false, gothic romance of his marriage ("Although her wise old step-grandmother, Dame Barbara Cartland . . ."). Naturally, he "was driven back" into his mistress's arms. Charles's affair is his courtly privilege, but Diana is the witch disguised as the princess, the "Princess Monster," the Medea who will bring down the nation. Waugh's concern in his piece, indeed, is that the New Britain will look like Diana instead of Charles, a screen image instead of a maker of words.

When Medea is a villainous witch rather than a powerful woman who casts her own spells, then we are not hearing of a woman's tale. Clément and Cixous argue that women must take their turn at "putting myths into words" in order to also have a chance at telling this "history that is not over" (6). According to Hegel's theory, history ends with the resolution of social antithesis; when we are no longer becoming but are one class with one sense of ourselves, then the historical process ceases. This is the sense that Francis Fukuyama takes up in his book *The End of History and the Last Man*, which will figure in chapter five. But Clément and Cixous see that Hegelian history, like Marxist class, is a masculine construct, a "history" told in men's words that leaves out hysteries. Or rather, it displaces women's story onto an hystericized and wordless space. But to say the "history that is not over," as opposed to "history" or "the end of history," is to question the rhetoric of history itself. At the same time, refiguring hystery into a history-that-is-not-over means to determine a hermeneutics of the self that is both male and female, multiple, and variable. It requires an understanding of ourselves as textual subjects whose sense of self is liable to linguistic and visual markers, but also a comprehension of ourselves as readers and thinkers within the codes that threaten to seduce and remodel us. When we are masterful readers, cultural texts—including those that incorporate us, such as landmark court cases or significant political decisions—can operate less effectively to construe consent as ours. One way to move toward such a goal is to use the reading practice developed by rhetoricians to scrutinize the tactical implementation of words; this reverses the reader's role from receiver to active engager of the rhetor's intent. This is the first step in translating hysteries into history-that-is-not-over.

SCRUTINY

In *Rhetorical Power* (1989), Steven Mailloux proposes a "rhetorical hermeneutics" in which rhetoric is "the political effectivity of trope and argument in culture" (xii). A hermeneutics—the study of interpretation as a methodology—is a more rigorous approach to some of the questions we have been asking here, one which assumes an ability to control the potentialities of language at both the literal and metaphoric or imagistic levels. But as Mailloux makes clear, while we can never be fully in control of our language use—of how others will understand and reconceive it—being conscious of language's innate multiplicity allows us to purposefully cross-examine the rhetorical levels of others' speech. Cross-examination is a legal act, but it is also an act of rhetorical interpretation that offers a model for a methodical scrutiny.

Scrutiny is the act of reading itself as a *production* of meaning rather than a *perception* of meaning. Readers normally assent with the writer of a text when they begin to read because they are engaged in information gathering, leaving the process of argumentation to the writer. But by questioning the account of an event the reader no longer fully consents to the writer's meaning, and in questioning the text gains new meaning through an interactive production of meaning. This time the meaning may be more conflicted and less authoritative, but it is also more productive.

Mailloux posits three stages in the reading of and thinking about rhetoric. Hermeneutic activity, he notes, devolves into the *theoretical moment*, in which we attempt to discover the "meaning" or correct interpretation of a speech act; the *rhetorical exchange*, in which differing and opposing interpretive possibilities are debated; and the *institutional setting*, where the debate occurs according to professional, cultural, and social conventions and discourse expectations (4). These three moments operate both within the ritualized space of governmental halls, and within our homes, workplaces, or classrooms. They are affected by media intervention, government decrees, and a host of contemporaneous public events which color our perception of the event and the ways in which it gets rhetoricized. In addition, the rhetorical moment can be manipulated to account for or to hide gender, positionality, cultural dominance, and contingencies by disguising the rhetorical exchange as a discourse of one, of self-same rather than opposition or difference.

Nevertheless, what Mailloux calls "the theoretical urge," the desire to "discover the correct interpretation," can be so powerful that truth is assigned one's own interpretation by the claim that the meaning lies in the text or speech act, only waiting to be discovered by the trained reader. When the claim is that meaning is not imposed on the text by a critic, but is instead "coerced by the texts themselves" (J. Hillis Miller, quoted in Mailloux, 4n), then we have the will to pronouncement for the group as if by the group. That is, a level of rhetorical exchange is reached whereby one critic's or reader's unique ability to find meaning disguises party line—whether that line is political or cultural. The political party line is what is commonly referred to as "ideology," or the clear pursuit of power through the value system, gender system, and methodology of a particular political body. The cultural party line is less easy to recognize, but is sometimes referred to by terms such as Antony Easthope's coinage, "social phantasy." In social phantasy consensual fictions such as romantic love, aesthetic values, racial supremacy, and domestic harmony come to be seen as dependent on gender hierarchy without any overt platform being promoted.[4] The declarations of individual and outspoken readers can effectively create and continue the cultural party line in the same way that political party leaders work to sustain party ideology.

Both forms of interpreting reality—the political and the cultural—help to form a national and regional group identity that informs how we understand ourselves and others. And in fact, both modes are interdependent because the political uses the cultural in order to contextualize and personalize its methods and goals. No presidential candidate wins voter confidence without a critical mix of the two, which is why Bill Clinton cultivated the Elvis touch while George Bush depended on his war service as a young man. Both are romantic appeals to cultural phantasies of seductive icons, and the candidate hopes to evoke an emotional identification through the cultural that will shore up the abstract parts of his message.

Using Mailloux's three moments to read the situation and a typology of tropes to elicit an historically specific interpretation, rhetorical scrutiny can allow us a toegrip in fundamentalisms that seek to skew our social and political attitudes toward rights issues. For instance, when Colorado's Coalition for Family Values argues that gay rights should not be recognized by law because gays are not a minority, and therefore do not qualify for legal protection either in the workplace or in the home, their position initially sounds plausible. But when the group concedes that their purpose is to prevent gays from "swelling the ranks of their species by recruiting from children" (NPR newsbroadcast, April 12, 1992), we find a trope that blindsides our reason by claiming that homosexuality is taught rather than discovered, induced rather than inherent, not different enough yet far too different for comfort.

Likewise, issues of free speech offer difficult interpretive moments. For example, the 1992 annual parody issue of the *Harvard Law Review* lampooned an article published posthumously in an earlier issue of the review by Mary Joe Frug, a feminist law professor who was murdered near her home in 1991. The editorial board, made up of top law students preparing for prestigious careers, made the decision to parody her work at the same time that the police were seriously considering that she was slain by a student infuriated by her feminist advocacy for legal theory.[5] As a woman law professor, and even more as a feminist scholar, Professor Frug was marked among Harvard Law School faculty as different; the lampooning students further scapegoated her with "Manifesto of Post-Mortem Legal Feminism," by "Mary Doe, Rigor-Mortis Professor of Law." Yet the students were supported by faculty, including Alan Dershowitz, under the First Amendment in a moment of political blindsiding.

Free speech provides a blanket argument for rights issues; the argument is that we cannot question the freedom of all speech because if we begin to pick away at a freedom, it crumbles in any instance. But this argument assumes a masculinist logic in which a right is an all-or-nothing arrangement provided by legal proclamation. The blindside is that "freedom of speech" tells us not to dig deeper because the essential right must be preserved: pornography is protected under the same right. But when speech harms, how free is it? And how private or public is our pain? Or, how responsible are the lawyers who protect our thought and its products? Such events construct a doublebind around us, pulling in opposite and perhaps unresolvable directions. It is helpful to construe ourselves as readers of these texts rather than as implicit victims, although we should make no mistake that misogyny targets each one of us in the end. If we can detect the blindside, locate the institutional setting that structures the discourse patterns, and determine the opposing positions—then it is possible to counter the forces that seek to keep us passively in our place.

LANGUAGE GAMES

We need to think more clearly about how language works in this mix of political and cultural transmission of ideology. N. Y. Marr, a Russian linguist working during the Russian Revolution, managed despite the repressive party line to posit a clear understanding of the formation of language within a material society.[6] Language usage, according to Marr, evolves concurrently with the material technology of a culture, and both are subject to the political ideologies and social phantasies dominating everyday life and labor. That is, language is neither the direct reflection of a "natural" or given reality, nor is it the exclusive tool of a powerful hierarchy. The last assumption, for Marr, is unnecessarily self-victimizing, while the first is romantically naive and liberally self-deceiving. However, Marr's theories are not widely known, and because we do not understand the interrelation of language and electronic innovations, or language and an economically oriented politics in our society, we tend to give credence to both assumptions. Instead, we should be looking hard at the language of laws passed in Washington because of hard lobbying; and when presidential candidates perch on a neo-Nazi platform, we need to examine closely the tenets their backers applaud. When cable news can report events as they occur or interview diplomats during a political crisis, allowing politicians to do away with telefaxes or phone calls in order to communicate,[7] then language is modified to serve new communicative modes. This not only means that jargon or neologisms find their way into daily speech or that political doubletalk overwhelms us, but that our language use itself finds new applications. To understand this is to also understand that with the daily, even hourly evolution of language in today's society, fundamental ideologies and phantasies, which serve to constrain us as well as to comfort us with their familiarity in an increasingly uncomfortable world, do not devolve into cliché or ridiculed sentiments of yesteryear or even yesterday. The speed of these changes, however profound they may or may not be, is fueled by telecommunications. Television is a technology exclusively directed toward drama, phantasy, and virtual reality, though it sells itself as reflecting (rather than refracting) our experience itself. When Senate hearings were closed sessions, our reception of their documentation occurred through obviously secondhand modes: newspapers, evening news spots, and magazine summaries. It was easier to realize, although not always crystal clear, that secondhand information passes through several hands and their attached biases, and so we needed to suspend judgment. But the perception that we are experiencing firsthand, unedited news events, which we have with cable news coverage, makes it more difficult to see how manipulatable language is, or that truth is multiple and subjective.

But once we become aware how the medium of transmission affects the politico-cultural generation of a "truth" by affecting the way language gets used and manipulated, we still need to know how to decode what we hear and read. Decoding can be better understood as scrutiny, or an attentive consideration of all messages encoded in an event, and not just the denotative statement of the main participants. Yet scrutiny does not require a mastery of the contextual, historical, fact-ridden field surrounding a spoken or written text. To think that without mastering a body of knowledge we have no right to speak or even think means that for most incidents we can only respond emotionally. When an extremely bright graduate student confesses that she does not have enough knowledge of the field to assess an assigned reading, I am left to ponder how the blatant political interpretations contained in the book could have escaped her. True, she marked several of these statements in the reading, she was not blind to their presence, but she did not know how to take them, and so she took them at face value. Masterful pronouncements are comfortable, and students have been trained to seek this comfort. But it is this mark of mastery which warns us that an ideological move is about to take place, because nothing is ever "clearly," "obviously," "unquestionably" this or that, but such language is easy to accept as true. And when we do accept such propositions, we have consented to be passified as readers and as thinkers.

Scrutiny works by marking the ideas put forth under the larger gestures of mastery and assertion. For instance, Reagan remarked in a 1982 speech on the recession that unemployment levels were not really related to the recession: "it is the great increase of the people going into the job market, and—ladies, I'm not picking on anyone but . . . because of the increase in women who are working today" (Faludi, 67). Under the marker of paternal concern is the code of reactionary inversion, the assertion of an untruth. As Susan Faludi points out, while Reagan pointed the finger at women and away from his economic policies, women were gaining employment at 1.56 percent of the overall annual rate. In addition, 77 percent of new jobs during this period were service jobs which paid below or at the poverty level, jobs for which men offered little competition (67–68). By pointing the finger, Reagan could ignore the facts: that women's salaries were not a privilege but a necessity both in single-parent homes, and in middle-class homes where double incomes had become imperative; that men's salaries were no longer enough because of leveraged buyouts, rising housing costs, farmed-out manufacturing, tax breaks for the wealthy, rising military expenditures; and that these are recurrently the conditions under which women's rights are attacked as effeminizing men's ability to support their families and therefore recognize their manhood (Faludi, 68).

Bush, too, understands the politics of the finger. If Reagan saw misogyny as the best strategy for shifting blame concerning unemployment rates, Bush found an even more reactionary target in xenophobia with Japanese trade practices. On a trip to Japan to "talk tough" and force the Japanese parliament to concede trade policies that favor the United States, Bush touted big business by bringing with him the actual persons whose multi-million-dollar salaries are responsible for part of the auto industry's woes. By pointing the finger, he was able to ignore the fact that while Japanese cars sold in this country are often largely made of American parts or put together with American labor, American cars are often largely made from foreign parts and can hardly be termed domestic products. Bush was able to veil the fact that he desperately needed a homefront Gulf War to regain the "tough man" status on which he believed his platform and popularity to rest. If his debate with Geraldine Ferraro included the joys of "kicking a little ass," and if the point of the Gulf War was to engage Saddam Hussein in "kicking ass," then clearly the trip to Japan was predicated on similar tactics, tactics which kept Bush at a banquet "toughing out" his stomach flu and allowing American millionaire CEOs to insult Japanese dignitaries.

But what is "kicking ass," and why should we find meaning in such a phrase? Scrutiny is not only the process of locating markers that signal the different cultural consensual codes at work: it also involves identifying the organizing metaphors. In the case of Ferraro, there is a body violence which connects woman to war in the most egregious sense. Hussein will be humiliated by being made to feel womanly, that is, weak and dominated, for his ass will be kicked. Ferraro will be defeated in such a way that the Democratic party will be womanized, made ineffectual, soft and bleeding-hearted, turned into the very "wimp" Bush himself was accused of being. Bush will be a war hero in either case, since to "kick ass" is an identifying military term. It is a term we should have heard and affixed meaning to before now, for by choosing that metaphor over ones of nation or unity or peace, Bush proclaimed his attitude toward women, their rights, their children, and their status as citizens. In less than one day after the April 4–5, 1992, march on Washington by more than 500,000 women and men to support the upholding of Roe vs. Wade, Bush signed a friend-of-the-court brief filed by the Justice Department to reverse the 1973 Supreme Court decision. This, too, is kicking ass. But it is not news.

Media outlets such as broadcast news shows, news magazines, and investigative reporting programs highlight the special importance of "news" in our information-driven society. We normally assume the news is factual, objective, and as much of the truth as is currently known. But the media depends on language, and even if reporters and anchors do not have the same goods to sell as political rhetors, for instance, they still engage copiously in rhetoric because it enhances reportage. More importantly, rhetoric helps the media form opinions, and as I argue in chapter four, the media is highly invested in *making news* as opposed to reporting newsmaking stories.

Time magazine, for example, devoted one cover story to two feminist books that were published within a few weeks of each other, Susan Faludi's *Backlash* and Gloria Steinem's *Revolution from Within*. The article, "Fighting the Backlash against Feminism" (title on the cover, "The War Against Feminism"), asks, "Will the shortage of young women in the movement cause feminism to fade away because it can't replenish its troops?" (Gibbs, 54). The rhetoric of the title and of this lead question provokes an image of feminism as a militarized adversary whose "troops" are deserting, and which are not being replenished with new recruits. The metaphor purposefully plays off of the term "backlash,"which itself represents the argument implied in Faludi's subtitle that "a war is being waged against American women." Posed against "backlash" are the words "replenish," and "fade." The first is an unmistakably maternal term, the second a term unmistakably associated with old maids or unfulfilled sexual promise. The female military body must replenish itself with young as a maternal act or she will die, a spinster—or a witch. Women concerned only with their own rights are witches; or at least, this is the *natural* conclusion to be drawn.

The article itself, written by a woman reporter, is not adversarial to the feminist debate, but the title and lead question are designed to provoke that response from readers disinclined to read about feminism if it is favorably portrayed. This is a progressive example of how the media seek to change minds almost subliminally, manipulating images just under the level of conscious awareness. However, this strategy is less effective than the tropes outlined above because its purpose is less clear. The article is neither completely for nor completely against feminism or the feminist movement; it straddles the issue not because it is objective but because it only aims to give both sides of the issue. Neither objective nor partisan, the article cannot actually take advantage of a trope's purposeful pitting of sides and skewed outcome of argument.

RHETORIC AS HISTORY

The ambivalence over sexual difference exhibited in the *Time* article is part of a general equivocation over the distribution of power and prestige through the layers of society—or at least the promise of such a distribution. Intellectuals are drawn toward theorizing how the coming multiplication (multicultural, postmodernist) of social values and the sign systems that represent and communicate those values will affect the human condition as we know it.

Language is one of the most visible vehicles and targets of such change, and theorists have devoted themselves to assessing the relation between consensual language exchange—the language systems of community and social being—and hegemonic language use—politicized language or rhetoric. It is helpful to consider one theorist of rhetorical systems and their ideologies, Paul de Man, in order to clarify that theory itself is not free from either historical implication or rhetoric. Like politicized talk that pretends to be rhetorically free or neutral, rhetorical theory employs a discourse similarly held to be objective or neutral. The sincerity of the first looks like the scientificity of the second, both offering a clear field from which to speak about other, nonneutral things. But like politics, theory is historically situated and driven. This point is an important one to make here, both in terms of the goals of this book and in thinking about theories of language and rhetoric. For it is when one thinks to transcend rhetoric, history, and politics that we are drawn toward totalizing theoretical models that privilege the masculine.

Paul de Man worked to produce a body of knowledge about the trajectory of classical rhetorical usage by considering each trope and figure as containing its own ideological purpose; historical periods favor particular figures of speech depending on the forces at work in constructing a subjectivity characteristic of the time. However, these figures are also transhistorical, *forms* that one detects in a text rather than artifices of the author: it is "precisely when the highest claims are being made for the unifying power of metaphor, [that] these very images rely in fact on the deceptive use of semi-automatic grammatical patterns" (de Man, 16). But reading rhetorically allows us to comprehend that when cognitive patterns we all share occur at crucial junctions in the text, what we understand as individual talent covers over an ideological move by "us[ing] resemblance as a way to disguise differences." To read thus is to desubjectify our reading, to read scientifically. "Such a reading puts into question a whole series of concepts that underlie the value judgments of our critical discourse: the metaphors of primacy, of genetic history, and, most notably, of the autonomous power to will of the self" (16). Transcendent and hegemonic metaphors are discoverable because the critical self perceives clearly and arhetorically, rather than "naively" and subjectively.

Although in his theory de Man argues against the ahistorical and transcendent "metaphorical mystification" of literature, "a vast thematic and semiotic network . . . that structures the entire narrative," he understands both his own discourse and his own life quite differently. De Man dehistoricized both his life and his art by creating and managing a theory of literature and rhetoric that defends itself against history by reducing that history to figures and tropes, metaphor and allegory. In a post-structural universe, the argument goes, history cannot be adequately represented by chronicles, annals, records, or media coverage because language itself (the medium of reportage) is symbolically rather than "realistically" representative. For de Man, history is unknowable except on an individual and therefore highly idiosyncratic and biased basis; in addition, what the individual "knows" about the past is distorted by the lens of memory, others' accounts, time lapse, and the internal language we use to represent experiences to ourselves. To all of this is added the struggle and collusion between conscious and unconscious over what will be remembered and what will be stored in other, seemingly less harmful ways (repressed). De Man's repression of his wartime pro-Nazi journalism within his deconstructive theory of language (his insistence that history does not exist in any linguistically recuperable sense) contains a kind of blindsiding thinking characteristic of the attempt to understand what happens in universal (and therefore necessarily mythic) terms.

The problem de Man addresses is the proposition that language is the tool that mediates how we understand the difference between external and internal experience, history and consciousness. The circulation of felt sense, ciphers, emotions, facts, imaginings, conversations, and reportage produces a speculative economy that moves within and between individuals to, in turn, produce a shared or communal ideology. Such a group-generated idea-system reigns in individual participants or speculators in its economy by assuring them that this particular vision, this speculation, is the correct one for making sense of the inner/outer conflict that they feel. This conflict, this encounter with the Real, the unknowable, the unsayable, History, can be known and said according to the rules of the group game (monarchy, democracy, patriarchy, liberalism, communism); this is the promise that keeps participants playing, speculating, politicking, consenting.

When these are the stakes—the control of history and thus the future through a consensual account of being and nothingness—then theorizing language becomes exponentially important. Indeed, philosophers have always concerned themselves with explaining the mysteries of our linguistically oriented being. With the possibility extended by twentieth-century world wars and cold wars of not existing at all—of leaving nothing of ourselves to future generations, of being lost to the void—the tenuousness of linguistic economies has struck philosophers to the core. Consequently, postwar thought has concentrated on either configuring speech as self-defining and liberatory, or defending it against the engulfing tides of phenomenal history.

Theories of language that resist history insist that those which heroically presume to reproduce history—those that embrace referentiality—are duplicitously or self-consciously naive. Derogated as liberal and humanist, these latter theories are master narratives that center meaning around the individual and his historical centeredness. Individuation is metaphorized to describe the interaction of external and internal experience in such a way that world wars tell victory stories; not surprisingly, these are American-based theories derived from traditional views about the transparency of language and its efficacy as a representational vehicle. The former theories, those that resist theory and interpose themselves between a modern and a postmodern sensibility, understand language in the nonindividualist terms created by world war, holocaust, and exile. For them, the individual-as-metaphor is an invidious blinder to the nonconsensual aspect of the human (or inhuman) condition. Thinkers like de Man construct critical syntaxes that put the horror of historical choice strictly within the terrain and even jurisdiction of the literary. This position allows the critic to understand historical imaginings as having no agency, while it gives complementary force to literary universes. In either case, linguistic structures become the real thing, the solid that absorbs light thus blinding us to all but its storytelling—no transparent vehicle but the thing itself.

In de Man's syntactical world, metaphor and metonymy are the allegorical figures that tell us stories about ourselves, about being and nothingness. They stand in for rhetoric and grammar in the sense that metaphor/rhetoric allows for choices and creativity while metonymy/grammar "undermines" rhetoric with its "semi-automatic grammatical patterns" so that "[a] literary text simultaneously asserts and desires the authority of its own rhetorical mode" (Elliott, 729). But in drawing from this suppositive framework the claim that history as an aspect of the literary text is therefore a rhetorical effect (i.e., what makes Shakespeare's figurative and literal language choices different from those of Winston Churchill), de Man keeps "history safely at home" (Elliott, 729). De Man's metaphor/metonymy distinction differs from the primary definitions used here throughout in that metaphor represents freedom (however illusory) while metonymy—groundedness, associationism, cultural structure and system—represents human bondage in all the senses intended by W. Somerset Maugham. I have been referring to metaphorical or figurative speech as rhetoric here, but the more pervasive meaning throughout will be that of the blinding sense of deliberate political storytelling, a sense opposed to the liberatory potential of language.

To see how it is possible for two such different ways of constructing meaning to occur through rhetorical use, we must understand *all* rhetoric as ideological *and* performative in the sense of demanding a response of the audience to the ideology at stake. In each chapter that follows, I analyze the rhetoricized language particular to a highly ideological arena of social formation according to the six rhetorical tropes enumerated above. These chapters place us squarely in the history de Man so desires to elide. However, the slippage between arenas means that the discussions of each chapter overlap and intrude on other chapters. And, although nearly every arena can be characterized by the trope peculiar to its ideological purpose, each arena employs every trope in our list as well as the traditional list of rhetorical figures such as metaphors, metonymies, symbols, and so on.

I cannot be more adamant in saying that it is not the intention of this book to provide isolated examples of how these performative tropes work as if they could be clinically specified and removed from the cultural scene. The point is to discover these tropes at work within the cultural scene, in order to analyze the extent of their contribution to that scene to which they are integral. Recognition and analysis suggest the possibility of shifting the power of tropological discourse from blocking audience cognition to heightening it through an interactive speech model. If *Eminent Rhetoric* does not explicitly address such a goal, it does most certainly embrace it.

NOTES

1. Hysteria is a neurosis or "conversion reaction" in which the person responds to a stressful event by developing physical symptoms that are not traceable to a physical cause. The victim and family members do not recognize the illness as hysteria because they interpret the symptoms literally; the symptoms, however, usually allow the ill person to escape the stressful situation that caused the trauma. The accepted treatment is to have the ill person relive the suppressed event, either through the talking cure (psychotherapy) or for more severe instances through hypnosis. Unlike those afflicted with psychosis, the hysteric does not lose the sense of reality; the imagination is thus central to defining hysteria as different from the purely literal (physical pain) and the purely psychical (psychotic pain).

2. Mrs. Sarah Stickney Ellis was a prodigious writer of conduct books, producing *Daughters of England, Wives of England, Women of England,* and similarly titled books in rapid sequence. Her *The Wives of England: Their Relative Duties, Domestic Influence, and Social Obligations* (London, 1843) codified women's social and domestic role. Although these and other manuals were hugely popular, conduct books were common in Renaissance England and before, and continue to be written today. The conduct book writer, or anyone attracted to the power of this trope, is most often allied with arch-conservativism.

3. On wearing contradictions, see Williams, 196: "When I am fully dressed, my face is hung with contradictions; I try not to wear all my contradictions at the same time. I pick and choose among them; like jewelry, I hunt for this set of expectations that will go best with that obligation."

4. See Easthope (1989) for a full discussion of social phantasy. Also see Easthope (1983).

5. Frug's work is posthumously published as *Postmodern Legal Feminism,* silently edited by Gerald E. Frug. Even prior to this, however, Frug's colleagues responded to her murder and the consequent reactions by publishing her unfinished essay, "A Postmodern Feminist Legal Manifesto (An Unfinished Draft)," along with companion essays by Barbara Johnson, Ruth Colker, and Martha Minow (*Harvard Law Review* 105 [March 1992]: 1045–105).

6. See Bryson, 135–40, for further discussion.

7. At least according to Daniel Schor, senior news analyst for National Public Radio, in a speech to the National Press Club on the role of the media today, April 6, 1992.

Chapter Two

Relational Pedagogy: Rhetoricized Education and Growing Up Female

"For Better or Worse" has been suspended beginning today. The current story line deals with a teen-age character who is homosexual, and it may disturb some readers . . . tell us how you like "Frank & Ernest" or "Galacto Guys." They might just end up in a permanent spot on the comics page.

Ocala Star-Banner, March 30, 1993, 5C

This chapter originated in a concern over the problem of cultural conservation (the political term is "cultural literacy") versus an ethics of culture or what is now called "multiculturalism." The question of whose eyes we get to see through invades our classrooms and our thinking to politicize childhood in ways that seem unprecedented. Or are they? And is the contemporary problem of ethnic diversity and its lack a new one, or a sophisticated version of the earlier—and ongoing—problem of gender diversity and its lack? This chapter traces a brief history of pedagogic politics, reflects on some staple myths of childhood, and looks at dilemmas involved in women's education.

PEDAGOGY, HISTORY, AND GENDER

Human beings are fabricators. To learn, they have to be able to make, to verbalize, to equate. But certain restraints turn fabrication into a hierarchy of permissible, gendered, unacceptable gradations. What children and adults attempt and succeed or fail at depends on parental/familial support or competition, peer emulation or dissonance, teacherly example and expectations, and beliefs about the self.

Pedagogy has historically concerned itself with these concepts, and even though girls were primarily educated in the home, thinkers interested in pedagogy thought about the education of girls. How they thought about it, what they perceived to be its salient points and goals, has important implications for how girls experience school today. Generally, the tradition of pedagogy has been the transmission of male knowledge to the new generation of men, and is homosocial in this sense. Richard Hurd's *Letters on Chivalry and Romance* (1762), Edmund Burke's *Reflections on the Revolution in France* (1790), Friedrich Schiller's *On the Aesthetic Education of Man* (1795) are all texts concerned with education and, more specifically, political education. They are also all written in the form of letters to a young man, and the master-pupil relation they romanticize and glorify resounds in texts such as *Zen and the Art of Motorcycle Maintenance*, *Karate Kid*, and *Star Wars*. It took Jean-Jacques Rousseau to codify the mentor/pupil, man/boy relation as a realistic fiction that narrates the reeducation of the self in *Emile* (1762); the fiction consists of projecting onto the body of the boy the mentor's prior selfhood so that all his teachings can reinstate his sense of self as redeemable, teachable, revisable. Given such a tradition, it is important that Mary Wollstonecraft's *On the Education of Daughters* (1787) partakes of a different, contestatory tradition of women speaking to women. However, her focus is in answer to Rousseau's plan for educating boys at home, and while she argues for the importance of educating daughters at home, she does not provide a blueprint for schooling away from home. Like Rousseau's work, Wollstonecraft's is more concerned with behavior, morals and purity, and with preventing the contamination of society from spoiling the child, than it is with subject matter.

But finally, Wollstonecraft's book, unlike her more mature manifesto *The Vindication of the Rights of Women* (1792), is a conduct book for women. Although Wollstonecraft had not fully worked out her thoughts on the importance of real education for daughters, she does draw on her experience in the school she ran for girls in Newington Green when she was twenty-five. Like many other conduct books written by both men and women, it is written to ensure that women will behave properly and society will run smoothly. Since Wollstonecraft herself was a woman dangerously out of place, outspoken and improper, it is curious that she would begin her writing career with such a book. And she does take the conduct genre seriously, touching on feminine modes of behavior at which daughters should be proficient in the late eighteenth century. But the conduct book trope, in which the writer attempts rhetorically to uphold society by creating proper women who will stay in their place, falls apart in Wollstonecraft's educative hands. Her most important message, which peeps through the rhetoric of conduct lessons, is that children should not experience deprivation through lazy parenting, severe morality, or restriction of learning experiences.

Wollstonecraft's work was soon lost, however, in the more widespread substitution of conduct books for girls' educational texts, replicating society's substitution of women's behavior for a masculinizing education. Nancy Armstrong notes that the force of conduct books is educational only in a political sense:

In formulating what we now know as the middle-class household, conduct books displayed a new form of semiotic behavior. Such behavior—namely, the contracts ... [that are] tropes of self-production—shifted the entire struggle for political power from the level of physical force to the level of language. (98)

Conduct books employ rhetorical usages to paint a world in chaos unless appropriate manners are adhered to; what they teach is not educational in the sense of subject matter, yet it is much of what girls even today learn from their social environment both in and out of school.

In the sense that education means an intellectual grappling with information and concepts rather than social manners and mores, education for every child began with the state's need for thinking subjects. Yet popular education as it was established in the thirteenth and fourteenth centuries in Great Britain was not a success, and even with the church's intervention in popular education in the sixteenth and seventeenth centuries literacy was not widespread. Although Protestantism is based on book reading, the Bible was available to all readers only for a short period: "In 1543 the Reformed Parliament forbade it to all women (except those of high birth), artificers, journeymen, servingmen, husbandmen, and laborers" (Altick, 25). By 1836 things seem hardly to have changed: "of 2,000 thirteen- and fourteen-year-old children in Manchester Sunday schools, 53 per cent could not read" (Altick, 168).

For middle-class families, however, both boys and girls were required to be literate; the girls, it was reasoned, needed to read in order to run their own household one day, and in order to educate the sons they would bear. Pedagogy for girls in the eighteenth and early nineteenth centuries depended heavily on advice from conduct books, and from the essays on female conduct available in periodicals such as the *Spectator* and *Tatler*. Boys' pedagogy was equally benighted: in more elite British schools for boys, such as Eton, classical subjects were taught according to school charters developed under Queen Elizabeth I until 1840; only then were more modern subjects introduced. Girls sent to day schools or boarding schools in the nineteenth century learned reading and writing, languages and arts; just enough to get them married or to sustain them as governesses if they were poor. Carol Dyhouse reports that girls growing up in late Victorian homes in England were still primarily educated at home, while their brothers were sent to boarding schools. Many women later remembered their early adolescence with bitterness, recalling how their "education" even in a middle-class family consisted of hard domestic labor while their brothers were permitted or encouraged to read during hours spent at home (see 3–78). When U.S. seminaries and colleges during the same period began granting degrees to women students, they were momentarily perplexed by the illogic of offering a "bachelor" or a "master of arts" to a woman, and resolved the difficulty by granting degrees for a "Mistress of Arts," or a "Maid of Arts," and a "Vestal of Philosophy" (Baron, 7).

Long before women could become "maidens" and "vestals," men earned legitimate degrees, but only if they had completed the classical education of privileged boys that Walter Ong argues produced a formalized puberty rite and ritual language: "learning Latin . . . involved the isolation from the family, the achievement of identity in a totally male group (the social), the learning of a body of relatively abstract tribal lore inaccessible to those outside of the group" (Armstrong, 28). A classical education provided an initiation into privileged manhood, separating the elite from those who did not have the opportunity to attend grammar schools: men from marginalized classes, and women as a whole. Women who intruded on this sacred space and learned something of the classics on their own— bluestockings and other women intellectuals—were regarded as major threats to the privileged community. Yet for the most part it was men who founded women's colleges. During the late nineteenth century, turmoil erupted over whether women should be admitted to colleges at all, and if so, whether to separate institutions or coeducational tracks. Radcliffe College, for instance, was begun as "The Society for the Collegiate Instruction of Women" by President Charles W. Eliot, who actively sought reform for primary and secondary education, but was nevertheless a strong opponent of coeducation for women. Eliot selected tutors for his women students from the male faculty of Harvard: his plan was to offer young women an opportunity to fully engage their minds and aspirations, yet to do so in order to develop "the capacities and powers which will fit them to make family life and social life more intelligent, more enjoyable, happier, and more productive."[1] Higher education for women remained circumscribed by the moral views of administrators like Eliot, who as cultural presences also extended their views beyond college students to the nation at large.

Le Baron Russell Briggs, following Eliot's lead, seems to have quite rejected the views of older faculty at Harvard such as those of Professor Edward Clarke. Clarke's *Sex in Education* (1873), for instance, argues against educating women on biological grounds; overdeveloped minds would ruin young women's physical health and retard their reproductive ability. Briggs believed, however, that women benefit from an education planned specifically for their social dependency and emotionalism. He began his teaching career at Harvard as assistant to Adams Sherman Hill teaching freshman writing (an innovative approach to education for the late nineteenth century) and was promoted to Boylston Professor of Rhetoric, then dean of Harvard University, and finally president of Radcliffe College. His

To College Girls, and Other Essays (1911) will offer a backdrop for the discussion of pedagogical thinking throughout the rest of this chapter, because even though it strongly favors education for girls, Briggs's book is a clear example of the conduct-book mode. *To College Girls* is a selection of essays taken from his book *Girls and Education*, published the same year. It contains "To the Girl who would Cultivate Herself," "To Schoolgirls at Graduation," "To College Girls," and is intended for both the entering woman college student and the young woman who will not attend college. Of the second group, essentially differentiated by class from the first, Briggs assumes that these girls have not been cultivated by the end of their high-school years: "No girl can learn too early that there is a vast difference between feeling too big for a place and being too big for it, and that feeling too big for one's work and surroundings seldom if ever results in culture. Rather it breeds discontent, vanity, idleness, and not infrequently vice."

Briggs agrees with the conduct-book tradition that girls are frail, given to idleness and to sensationalist pleasures. Yet girls should not desire to be teachers unless they truly have the intelligence and ability required; mere diligence will not be enough. Briggs illustrates this point from his experience at Harvard with educating young men for the ministry:

The minister's work, as every efficient minister knows, needs men that are filled with manly life, men of wisdom, of instinctive—not professional—sympathy, men of fearless leadership, men of power; and no other profession has suffered so much from the artificial infusion of weaklings. The teacher's profession suffers similarly, though less.

Ministers and teachers suffer from the threat of effeminacy, weakness, loss of manliness. The cause and the cure are not long in coming, and Briggs is most concerned to provide instruction in order to stem the drain of manly strength from the nation's elite. This requires that women are trained to embody the proper spirit and energy for a virile nation:

By reading fifteen minutes a day, it is said, a person may become cultivated. Most girls read more than that; but most girls are not cultivated. What do most girls read? . . . we read the fiction of the day whether in magazines or novels; and we get it no longer at our own cost from such circulating libraries as filled the empty head of Lydia Languish, but from free public libraries.

For the academician, the crime becomes wasting precious time on trash novels, sentimental romances that offer ordinary girls magical escapes from their workaday lives. The antidote for girls who must read fiction is Austen and Scott, among others. Briggs does not view their novels as sentimental romances even though Scott is rich in the sentimental mode and both Austen and Scott focus their works on the love plot. What he sees in these cultivating novels is a moral core enticingly covered over with the sugar of romantic love: "Again, no healthy-minded girl comes face to face with the courageous womanliness of Elizabeth Bennet, rising through sweetness and good sense above a mother of humiliating vulgarity, or the delicate conscience of Fanny Price, undervitalized but charming in her sensitive devotion, without learning much." The emphasis on morality reveals conduct-book thinking, as does the dictation of authors and novels from which to derive cultivation without any accompanying explanation as to how one chooses on one's own between pulp and moral romance.

That Briggs's discussion of *Pride and Prejudice* ignores its sharpness and its romance elements is yet another indication that his rhetorical intent obstructs the logic of his argument. Similarly, his choice of *Mansfield Park* belies his earlier dismissal of "whimpering" sentimental novels and "debased fiction," since this novel is Austen's one sustained attempt at sentimental plot. Of Scott, Briggs comments that "no girl with a touch of the romantic, such as every girl should have, can fail to be the happier and the more cultivated for knowing early and always the perennial king of English romance, the author of 'Quentin Durward' and 'Ivanhoe.' " That is, girls are to leave off reading pulp novels about love affairs and elopements, and to read instead novels of chivalry and romance. Even more than Austen, Scott provides heroines that model exemplary femininity and " womanliness."

In the end, the girl who cultivates herself by learning to read classic novels will overcome certain limitations through the strength of character she will have gained from her reading: "She may be a teacher of stubborn and stupid little children; she may write dull business letters at the dictate of vulgar men . . . but when the minutes come that are her own, she steps instantly into . . . a life the breath of which inspires her daily work, however mean, with a kind of glory." Clearly Briggs believes this glory cannot be had from the unlikely denouements promised by pulp novelists to the Lydia Languishes of the female world. But he also believes it important to the smooth running of society that even shopgirls and office workers be properly imaginative about their own love lives and their futures.

In the end the concern for women's education focuses on conduct and on the rhetoric used to endorse this conduct. Briggs substitutes giving reasons for reading Austen with urging young women to take Austen herself, the lady novelist educated at home, for a model. In contrast, Briggs used Austen's novels to test young men on his "Harvard Admission Examination in English," which he published in 1888.[2] If girls must learn from Austen by modeling themselves on her, college boys must be able to critically analyze and interpret her novels in order to be prepared for the work ahead of them.

Conduct books or advice books, like Briggs's, were deeply invested in controlling and even displacing girls' and women's intellectual interests by refocusing their sexual interest. Briggs warns young women against using their "personal charm" to manipulate young men, for instance. While conduct books were at their height in the middle to late nineteenth century, medical interest in children's sexuality was also experiencing an upsurge. Medical observations such as Démétrius Zambaco's "Onanism and Nervous Disorders in Two Little Girls" (1881) were common: "The 19th [September]. Third cauterisation of little Y . . . who sobs and vociferates . . . but X . . . more and more drops all pretense of modesty."[3] The relationship recorded here between two participants involves resistance and interpendence, surveillance and cunning, illness and medicine, morality and learning. It is a relationship based on a desire not entirely dissimilar from Briggs's to control young females' behavior through a discipline that forces them to comprehend themselves as naturally deviant, immoral, sick. The elder child, X, is learning quite effectively to act the part required of her, including hysteria, guilt, rebellion, illness, and masochism. As a medical text of the late nineteenth century the case history reads as one of many such embarrassing texts best lost in the archives, but as a literary text we have something different.

After Scott and Austen, the Victorian age began imposing the serious and intentional surveillance and control of sexuality of society. It was no longer acceptable to be sexually different or even to be interested in sex beyond reproductive functions. Michel Foucault, Elaine Showalter, Peter Gay, Eve Kosofsky Sedgwick, and others have begun to pry out what lies hidden beneath the aesthetic fabric of Victorian socialization processes, particularly in the publicly private space of medicine. Freud becomes a particularly important producer of texts which show how women came to be perceived during the early modern period. But Freud only essayed the mind; other medical experts essayed the body and made remarkable progress in marking the private territory as observable, pryable, controllable. Constraint devices, regimens, genital surgery, and clitoral cauterization (which had to be performed repeatedly because it never "worked") were the legitimized scientific intervention in children's sexual self-discovery. This control, concomitant with the categorization and taxonomies of sexual orientations, of which only one was considered nondeviant, lessened when the new (hetero) sexuality was in place.[4]

Sexuality is closely allied to romance and imagined stories of love, especially for women. Even within the strict surveillance and control of the nineteenth century, women so consumed romantic tales that men feared for the degradation of the society that had so recently been shored up. Perhaps what was most worrisome was the active nature of such reading. Recent analyses of stories of romantic love dispel the conception of the woman reader as a passive receptacle, a dupe of the commercial publishing industry. Women, in fact, use romance plots to imaginatively reconstrue their own social worlds and domestic space both for their own better mental health, and for imagining how to improve the relations in which they find themselves. Austen's novels can actually be read in both these ways: as conduct books, as in Briggs's model for female behavior, and as the material for utopian possibility. Chapter three will further explore why one reading often dominates over the other, but here Austen is most helpful in thinking about girls' changing relationships to the world, and the images they themselves construe for understanding that world and their place in it.

ADOLESCENCE AND THE LOOKING-GLASS WORLD

Literature directed toward girls and young women that has stood the test of time has had to be, like Austen's works, multiply encoded. These works can escape even their authors' intentions, and can bypass what conduct-book pedagogues find in them, to provide their readers with alternative stories of how to be in the world. What these stories describe about social being is not always liberatory, however, as one of the most influential of these stories, *Alice in Wonderland*, reveals.

Although *Alice* resembles a story similarly influential for boys, *Peter Pan*, in that it is about the fantasy of imprisonment, the boys' story is about flight and bodilessness while the girls' is about going underground and encountering the effects of bodiness. Both stories employ a structural constraint typical of the romance or quest genre, "the motif of the double prison, in which a journey of apparent liberation from captivity leads only to a more implacable arrest." As Nina Auerbach notes about the paradox of self-discovery plots, the outward freedom toward which the protagonist struggles becomes instead "a deeply ironic snare" (6). The ironic freedom of running away from imprisonment only to run into a larger prison is that the protagonist's original disgruntlement at social constraints necessarily dissolves into a desire to return to that bondage rather than further endure the arbitrary illogic of the fantasy prison. This snare describes the plot difficulties of the Alice stories and of *Peter Pan*, but is more true for the girls—Alice and Wendy—than for Wendy's brothers or for Peter himself. That is, although in adult literature the self-discovery or quest plot is a masculine one that celebrates the warrior hero, in children's literature it becomes a metaphor for a young girl's journey through childhood itself. The myths that feed our imaginations in childhood, in other words, teach through the conduct-book trope that while boys can experience self-as-hero by rebelliously inhabiting the larger prison, girls experience escape fantasies as rebellious behavior that must be punished. These tropes are self-fulfilling in a society that believes girls must learn to accept and condone the social prison of their womanhood. The older a girl gets, the more entangled she becomes in her doubled, even tripled prisons that lead "only to a more implacable arrest" of passivity or compliance or, like Alice, of going underground.

Seventeen, a well-established magazine for teen-aged girls, mirrors the subject matter of women's fashion magazines while contemporizing the Alice story. It does so by playing with the tease of sexuality implied by the conduct-book trope. In a recent issue (March 1993) the magazine's cover portrays a beautiful woman who is ambiguously adult but certainly no child, her sexuality "innocent" but clear. She is draped in Victorian-style lace, silk, and pearls but her gown is strapless and lowcut; over her head is the caption "Young, lonely, and out on the street—one prostitute's story." Other cover captions read: "Prom Passion," "What do boys *really* think?," "Who's in *control,* you or him?," "*Help,* I'm a flirt." The messages are clear and clearly imprisoning: sex is important, teen-age prostitution is romantic, the prom is necessary and sexual, girls are sexually out of control ("Help, I'm a flirt"). All of this in an age of AIDS; the articles inside are not about condoms but about "Nondiscriminatory, equal opportunity grunge-style dressing for the changing times—and your discriminating tastes." What can girls know about their world when the magazines directed at them turn everything to fashion, a subject that requires constant updating, turns everything to artifice, and nearly always ends in failure? And how can girls understand the double bind of "equal opportunity" dressing which is merely dressing like boys, and which is a sure way to fail in the attempt to catch a boy's eye ("What do boys really think?")? Such magazines are simply modern-day conduct books, designed to form girls' thinking into a pattern of self-doubt, consumerism, superficiality, and obsessions with their body image. At the same time, the pattern is set in place that girls should orient their sexuality toward boys' expectations and needs.

The double bind seems to define adolescent girls as they learn to cope with their changing bodies and moods, society's changing demands on them, and the growing difficulty of finding their place in a shifting terrain. Girls respond to social and educational messages that their identity lies in their body in ways that are not true for boys. Suddenly they must discover who they are just as their bodies begin to take on new characteristics. And they learn that their selves are emphatically their bodies, while boys learn that their bodies are performative vehicles for the selves they are urged to become.

One aspect of how girls manifest the changes they experience is in the way they construe their world not as prisons but as walls or borders. Borders define the private from the public and demarcate girls as belonging to the private, the secret, the silent. Walls operate to produce inclusion and exclusion, cliques and margins; or they produce a barrier between just two people, whether friends or parent and child. Cliques allow girls to mirror the exclusion they will come to experience more fully as women; they simultaneously give girls a sense of power over that exclusion in allowing them to manipulate the walls of the group within their own peers.[5] Yet just like the walls girls can experience between themselves and other family members or friends, exclusionary cliques provide a look at the future of women in our culture. In *Making Connections*, Carol Gilligan views adolescence as a time of relational crisis when girls find themselves blocked off from someone they had been close to or whose support they had taken for granted.[6] It is also when an emotional phenomenon occurs for girls which Gilligan describes as "going underground":

> [A]dolescence is a critical time in girls' lives—a time when girls are in danger of losing their voices and thus losing connection with others, and also a time when girls, gaining voice and knowledge, are in danger of knowing the unseen and speaking the unspoken and thus losing connection with what is commonly taken to be "reality." . . . eleven- and twelve-year-old girls observe where and when women speak and when they are silent. (25)

The registers of silence are implicated in our social relations so that a well-socialized woman understands her own silence and when it is called for. Although Gilligan calls adolescent girls "registers of women's speech," I mean to evoke here social registers of meaning-filled silence. Thus the adept woman has not only internalized social conduct books which are now available in the form of magazines and television, and in the rhetoric of newspapers and other media. She has also overcome the difficult journey between doubled prisons of body and silence which she underwent as an adolescent.

COLLEGE AND DILEMMAS OF SELF

Once children grow up, as Lewis Carroll knew about Alice Liddell, they lose the ability to change the rules of the game because they become invested in those very rules. And they become invested in other rules as well. When women enter college, whether straight from high school or after having explored what lies beyond school walls for a number of years, they must still confront issues of voice and exit, silence and influence, active and passive participation, inclusion and exclusion. Freshman writing classes seem particularly strong magnets for these issues to come to the forefront. In thinking about voice and freshman writing, the teacher part of me invariably turns from notions about voice to states of being, or rather, becoming. While I still rely on theories of empowering student voices such as those underlying Peter Elbow's *Writing with Power*, at some point I began to question his assumption that there is a Voice, that class and race do not intervene in verbalization (except for second-language interference), and that gender can be dealt with by using the feminine pronoun all or part of the time for the posited, universalized, and monologic Student.

The problem with positing a student who is all classes, all races, both genders, and any sexuality, is that "writing with power" is not equally liberating for real students with real variables. For instance, if a student's social class and cultural background predisposes her to see growth and learning only in a tightly regulated classroom, with a highly organized and prescriptive writing teacher leading students on the path to knowledge, then Elbow's "empowerment" seems to that student like fiddling with tuition dollars. If she prefers constriction to freedom because her sense of the feminine is structured in response to boundaries and not through them, then she is not asking for learning that is more passive and more silent so much as for learning that is model-oriented and private. She does not want voice or change or political participation, and in this she is at variance with adolescent needs and desires: she wants, and has come to admire, conduct books.

Teachers of writing and thinking often urge a "voice"-based rather than "model"-based pedagogy on students because voice leads to active learning when it engages the student passionately. "Voice" implies instant contact, lack of protective distance, and an inroad to an unmasked persona. This humanist tradition employs the paradoxical notion that voice is both the revealer of the sincere self, and yet somehow univocal and undifferentiated because we are all emanations of that natural man with his natural voice, the man who needs no mask. The theory of empowering voice is what James Berlin would categorize as situated within the rhetoric of expressionism. Berlin defines expressionism as resting on the assumption of the unified self, a self we know is no longer possible to imagine in a world fractured into too many molecules. But it is possible to reconstrue Berlin's category from an impossibility into a feminism, or at least feminism's dictum that the personal is the political. Thus, to insist on a feminist pedagogy is to insist on voicing, on obstructing silence, and on immolating conduct books.

College students are often once again ready for gender-stereotyped roles after the experimentation, submersion, or resistance of adolescence. They do not want to learn about nontraditional ways of thinking, and they are particularly uninterested in liberatory pedagogies, politics, or epistemologies. Feminism becomes a bad word, learning about minor women writers and thinkers is a waste, and the most important thing is to gain acceptance within the new academic community. This reactionism, I am convinced, is part of the entering students' need to orient themselves within a new environment where the challenges to intellect, confidence, self-image, and endurance are too great for much chance-taking. It is only once students have begun to feel comfortable with college subject matter that they can explore their new world confidently enough to question verities and inequities.

Thus when we confront freshman writing classes with our own pedagogical agendas, we must be prepared for a seemingly irrational resistance. And these social dynamics can influence the confidence and resistances of students of nondominant ethnicities even more deeply. One student I had several years ago illustrates the difficulties freshmen face: Minnie is a young working-class woman from Puerto Rico living with her divorced mother. When she took freshman writing with me, she sat through class each day as sullen as the last; her questions were demanding and angry in class, her student conferences confrontational. After the semester was over she filed a complaint, not over her grade but against me, saying that she was inadequately aided in class, that I had ignored her, that she had not learned what she needed to have learned in the course. The main text used in the course, Peter Elbow's *Writing with Power*, did not speak to her disenfranchisement it seems, and neither did Paolo Freire's *Pedagogy of the Oppressed*. Minnie wanted enfranchisement not on her own turf, or in the community of her peers, but within the establishment itself. Her response to both Elbow's and Freire's pedagogies was the same: anger, confrontation, attack. These were her forms of self-empowerment when frustration and helplessness displaced what she conceived of as actual learning experiences.[7]

Minnie's complaints rested on three main points: she was given no model essays to emulate; she was not given directive commentary on papers so she could "correct" and "revise" them; she was given no formulas to follow for each particular essay genre. In other words, she was denied constraint, she was asked to think on her own, and she was given the opportunity to give and receive peer feedback without an intruding master voice. And in still other words, she was asked to tear down the walls she had built up around herself in order to purposely deter communication and relation.

What Minnie's attack revealed was, first, that the notion of self-revelation through the search for voice made for an insupportable vulnerability. Also threatening to her was the sheer immediacy of voice, a loss of distance caused by the various writing exercises we had employed. It is threatening to lose the protective buttressing that comes from overwriting, and controlled construction of a voice that is not revelatory of class traits, minority-identified communities, or gender. Minnie's anger stemmed from not being taught how to further buttress the walls she had already built around her "difference" and differences. When she paid to learn a mode of conventionalized discourse, she had instead been asked to read herself into the historical present—not to further distance herself, but to become self-consciously present, and to acknowledge the differences she sought to submerge. In one essay assignment, her difference was forced on her most painfully and unwittingly: additionally marked as the victim of a crime only women suffer, rape, Minnie could see no reason to discuss or argue the issues of abortion rights, a topic the class had chosen for the paper. It was only after the course was over that I learned what she had suffered; when I asked her why she had not come to me privately and asked for a different assignment at the very least, she replied that a student's responsibility was to do the assignments, but that I should never have made an assignment that allowed free choice for the group as a whole. That is, the group should not decide for the individual; only the institution may do that. In hindsight I see that she had been doubly violated in having to confront a painful self-identity, and in not finding a corporate or univocal "voice" in which to hide—or rather, in which to help her succeed in taking on a new self. I see that she wanted armor and safety, masking and the loss of personal voice, and all with the concomitant adoption of a new public or institutionalized voice.

I made the mistake during the semester of not confronting Minnie's anger more directly, trusting to the group work and individual conferences to find some way into that anger. The course ended without any inroads or answers, but an answer finally did come when Minnie arranged for an interview between the Writing Director and me. Minnie's manner was corporate-like during the interview, and I learned for the first time that she intended to become a business major. She enumerated her complaints in a strong and confident voice I barely recognized: I wondered, who had power here, who needed to own their language and communicate effectively? She knew how to make the system work for her at least in the corporate sense. It is how, after all, to get what you paid for. But Minnie still cannot write competently; her anger and her distrust of intellectual exploration are blocking agents which I could not defuse. What have dislocation, family break-up, a rape, and the need to work nearly full-time to pay tuition bills contributed to this woman's need for constraint and modeling, or desire for conduct books?

This student made it clear that notions of multiple voices and visions, notions of gender politics and student empowerment, did not touch her need for the proper style, the proper accent, the Doolittle makeover that she had signed up for. It was not that Minnie did or did not wish to embrace her race and her class; it was that she wished to define them otherwise. That is, to define herself as American, middle-class, conservative, genderless: the student, the worker, the citizen.

Graduate students are at the other end of the line from freshmen, and presumably have already experienced educative liberation as well as learned how to be comfortable with the academic institution. In a cultural history of women's education, as well as the personal history of a woman's education, the graduate student represents the achievable apex. Yet she is still employing and fighting the "Alice" myth, embracing or questioning conduct-book determinations, suffering a loss or excess of voice in the public spaces of her field. Part of their final phase of formal education is to learn to use resistance and voice to work through a new set of options and traps for their coming into being. This is a necessary phase for women professionals in particular—women who wish to reject Alice-life and enter the public sphere—because the phenomenon of resistance *with* competency is the hallmark of a self-sufficiency, of a self that truly is working its way into a mature being.

Women graduate students often position themselves by holding on to their ideas and passively resisting their professors' attempts to influence the direction their idea is taking; my own students even resist looking at books I suggest and find their own instead. This level of resistance differs from Minnie's passive aggression because the accession to individual voice is already a given. It is more related to the frustration with parental figures that historically attempt to dismiss one's ideas or to translate them into those of the authority figure. Guidance is read as appropriation; the mentor as intruder and usurper. Women seem to struggle with this issue more painfully than men during this formative process, perhaps because Peter Pan's battles with Hook role-model a confident relational strategy whereas Alice's verbal jousts with the fragile men of her fantasy world reveal her to be the monster. The crucible for women, even more than men students, comes with the realization that professional training makes entering that profession possible; at that crystallizing moment we find ourselves acti- vated as thinking and speaking subjects whose words are taken seriously. To be heard, to be accorded attention, can be frightening, especially if one is used to being unheard or misinterpreted. Rather than risk losing the newly found voice, a student without a strong identity of self in language will often hoard ideas and words because these are often the only posses- sions worth having when one is beginning the lengthy process of dues-pay- ing. And they will resist professors' suggestions about changing those ideas, seeing such changes as appropriative rather than helpful.

Before women students experience the crystallizing moment in which they realize themselves as professional, they experience an intellectual double bind between inclusion and exclusion, sharing and resisting, voice and silence. Not surprisingly, their writing often exhibits the tensions of these problems, often as either a writer's block, or defensive writing that circles rather than addresses the assigned problem. When women are socially invested in relational networks, in the labor of care and sustaining contact, these stresses carry over into formalized communication. This phenomenon, in which women communicate well orally and informally but experience difficulty in the stylized rules of formal writing, can be thought of in terms of the differences between female and male social fantasies: Alice debates well but loses the world while Peter understands the combative nature of Hook's "good form." Another way to understand the same phenomenon is to insist that men and women actually speak different languages, with male language dominantly the public spaces of our culture while female language inhabits more personal and informal space. This is an argument French feminism finds congenial, as do recent American studies such as Dennis Baron's *Gender and Grammar* (1988)[8] and Deborah Tannen's popularized *You Just Don't Understand* (1990). However, given the investment of women as wives and daughters in the tangled relations of dysfunctional families, it is also possible to see in graduate student writing and voice problems the playing out of emotional or family dysfunction as defensive strategies.[9]

Viewed in this context, it makes sense that women graduate students, when required to produce sophisticated argumentation, should express their concerns with voice, silence, walls, and underground tunnels through their writing. Thus these women often "bury" their thesis in the middle or end of their essays; they give too much authority to the voices of scholars and theorists quoted to support their own quieted voice; they produce maze-like sentences in order to avoid being attacked for their ideas. They set up walls at every turn at the same time that they resist accepting professors' ideas. This contradiction—of insisting on proceeding alone while refusing to let anyone listen—characterizes in detail the dysfunctional family member. By playing out the drama of the family on the body of her writing, the graduate student shows what an excellent student she has been all along: she accepts the family's symptom as hers, and she expresses it semiotically on a text/body that will be seen but not understood, diagnosed and judged to be failing but not *heard*. More than the family's victim/caretaker, she reveals herself to be the symptom of the culture at large, the hysteric whose "disease" not only makes her unfit to take on a responsible position in that society unless she is "cured," but whose "body" of writing reveals the fault lines of that society.

Students experience critical stages in their inculcation into rhetorical usage during their college education. In the freshman writing class, writing is treated as a personal and group activity in which students come into a critical awareness of themselves as rhetorical producers and language manipulators. This takes place within an institutionalized expectation that such skills be acquired. The student must undertake learning rhetoric as an issue of rhetorical power—effect on others—versus empowerment—effect on self. Yet this lesson is more problematic and traumatic than teachers of language theory often anticipate. The problem of public and private, group and individual, is a particularly sensitive one for women simply because they are socialized to feel responsible for the well-being of the group and to feel guilty if they are protective of themselves as private individuals. Studies conducted with women graduate students, for instance, show that they tend to speak in class more to support other students' statements, to reduce conflict, or to provide personal experience as examples for the discussion.[10] And group/individual, public/private brings in the dilemma of rape, the logical extreme of the abortion question as well as the question of intrusion and transgression (Hook's pedophilia). Rape is a rhetorical as well as bodily issue. This is so because rape is forced intrusion, and the response to it is resistance. Resistance is also the refusal to speak and the refusal to write, and resistance to writing is hysteria, the inability to write.

Hysteria or resistance becomes a feminine aesthetic put on girls and then women in order to provoke walls and silence, underground tunnels and places to hide what is really being thought and felt. Adolescent girls learn that their sexuality must be buried underground in order for them to survive in a world defined and determined by male sexuality—hysteria as tunneling. Women graduate students learn that they must fight burial and begin to speak out for themselves with the rhetorical strategies that best offer them a way out from hysteria and silence—strategies that they often must work out for themselves.

HYSTERICIZING PEDAGOGY

Speaking out, talking back, finding a voice: all of these terms bespeak a pedagogy of action, of bringing the student into an awareness of her or his ability to think and speak cogently across the social boundaries that work to silence or passify. This pedagogy of enactment politically opposes the approach represented by conduct-book thinking, a reactionary pedagogy aimed at endorsing privilege against (rather than for) the group.

Although the literature on a pedagogy of enactment is enormous—the response to Paolo Freire's *Pedagogy of the Oppressed* alone is enough to fill a library shelf—this section is more concerned with recent books representing the opposite pedagogy by academics who may not seem or even think of themselves as antithetical to a thinker like Freire. E. D. Hirsch is mainly concerned with the national problem of cultural continuity, Dinesh D'Souza is disturbed by the educational institution of coerced liberal politics, and Camille Paglia sees an unnatural agenda in the insistence of academic feminists that masculinist culture should not be celebrated as such. Their lectures and books appeal to the public interest because they offer conservative answers under the guise of liberal or even radical ones. More importantly, their appeal is in the easy implementation of their solutions which are simply reaffirmations of what has gone before. What Hirsch proposes for curriculum change sounds little different from the reading program suggested by Dean Briggs at the beginning of the century to improve the morality of young women. D'Souza's alarmist critique similarly aims to bring education and academia back to its pre-sixties incarnation, while Paglia attempts to do the same for our understanding of sexuality. All of these propose that only the dominant culture and a historical record of sameness rather than variation needs to be taught.

Against these voices, bell hooks's pedagogy of enactment offers a tough argument; her appeal is that she in no way resembles the bleeding-heart liberal these reactionaries inveigh against. Although this section is more concerned to reveal the conduct-book rhetoric operative in reactionary pedagogies and critiques of academe, hooks offers a looking glass in which to measure their proposals.

In *Talking Back: Thinking Feminist, Thinking Black* (1989) bell hooks discusses such strategies for women who seek to educate themselves back out of silence. Although hooks specifically addresses women oppressed on several fronts—gender, race, sexual orientation, class—the same themes recur of silence, tunneling, and coming to voice. Her notion of "talking back" is thus all the more powerful; it is not "taking back" the language as French feminists propose, but finding again the value in one's own voice:

> Once again, the idea of finding one's voice or having a voice assumes a primacy in talk, discourse, writing, and action. . . . Speaking becomes both a way to engage in active self-transformation and a rite of passage where one moves from being object to being subject. Only as subjects can we speak. (12)

And write. Graduate students who write themselves into tangles simultaneously understand the value of collaborative speech in the classroom, understand the work that diffuse and independent minds can do together. What they need to discover in the process of finding their own voice, the passage from object (of others' conduct books) to subject (of one's own writing), is that they can also speak with others in order to support themselves. Women students who organize informal discussion groups out of class in order to debate course material or to work on each others' writing and ideas, learn to express themselves with clarity to their supportive readers. Where a one-on-one relation between student and professor hints of judgment and status to a woman student still wrapped in the complexities of family psychology and judgmental relations, group work between peers takes down walls and builds connection. Deborah Tannen writes that hierarchy or status assertion tends to structure men's interchanges, while connection structures women's (*You Just Don't Understand*, 23–73). And in institutions where masculine thought historically prevails, such as academia, these differences can be codified into success and failure strategies.

Bell hooks suggests that revising these strategies into different growth narratives begins with the teacher's role in the classroom. "How do we as feminist teachers use power in a way that is not coercive, dominating? . . . we must acknowledge that our role as teacher is a position of power over others. We can use that power in ways that diminish or in ways that enrich" (*Talking Back*, 52). One such method of enrichment is what hooks calls "oppositional thinking": this is a confrontational pedagogy that comes from a thoughtful position of values which are other than the norm. Teachers who assume this position do not look for their students' unthoughtful affirmation of them; they are in the classroom to stimulate different thinking, to oppose normative thought, to make thinking uneasy. The purpose is to create a space in which students can "come to voice" not in safety but in risk. But because this risk is equally and openly shared—connective rather than hierarchical or status-oriented—it is a risk connected to passage, and a deterrent to silence. Hooks's pedagogy opposes feminist theories that advocate safe spaces in order for women to speak out because those spaces do not exist in the social reality of the adult world. Traditional pedagogy has "educated" female children into the safety of silence through unsafe classroom space; teen-aged girls grow up learning that safe silence leads to the unsafe, stifling silence of adulthood. It is not fair to continue to educate girls out of the risky spaces that boys and men grow comfortable in, yet this is what reactionary pedagogues argue for.

Tannen also writes that "[t]hroughout history, women have been punished for talking too much. . . . Women were strapped to ducking stools and held underwater until they nearly drowned, put into the stocks with signs pinned to them, gagged, and silenced by a cleft stick applied to their tongues" (*You Just Don't Understand*, 75). They were also sentenced to wear bestial masks that served to hold down their tongues at the same time; talking out of turn also got women burned and hanged for witchcraft. Talking back, or reasserting voice and self, is a dangerous journey, full of misprisions and misrepresentations by those who serve conservative interests. Women are still thought to talk too much, Tannen reports. "Yet study after study finds that it is men who talk more—at meetings, in mixed-group discussions, and in classrooms where girls or young women sit next to boys or young men." Even in faculty meetings, researchers find that when women speak, their "longest turns were still shorter than the men's shortest turns" (75). Such studies are interesting not because they point out myths, but because they discover blindsides. The blindside here is that the important fact—that women talk at all—is hyperbolically mythified into the "fact" that women talk more than men. Because blindsides are easier to believe than verities, they can outlast and cover over the reality at hand. Blindsides are what conduct books teach; children's education should begin again with verities.

Yet, although our cultural assumption is that our being is the result of self-determination, language itself determines us, relentlessly forcing us into roles and stances. If we do not respond bodily ("trust your gut"), then we stabilize our self-representations, and we accrete borders of increasingly rigid do's-and-don'ts. Girls are taught to assume the role of negotiator, healer, web weaver. Those who accept the role of femininity choose their verbs and pronouns with exceeding care as they seek to reproduce, through their manipulation of language, the ideology of community. Boys are taught that language is a truth instrument rather than a caretaking vehicle; those who accept the masculine role learn that there is no need to protect the reproduction of culture because the community is stable. Paradoxically, boys are also taught that in a man's world they must first engage a necessary subservience called "paying your dues," a ritual game involving the caretaking of superiors. Girls, then, tend to evolve a relationship with reality through a syntax of attentive caretaking, while boys tend to verbalize reality as a single truth while refusing to see the caretaking they must perform as either attentiveness or caretaking. Instead, they learn to transform experience which is both real and truthful into mythified game-playing, enacting rituals which will help them succeed in a man's world. Girls, too, learn to ritualize, not only in interpersonal relations where gender expectations demand role-playing and even role achievement, but also in the realm of appearances, where makeup, costume, unnatural hair, posing, and chat allow one to create one or more personae which engage the realities and fictions of career and marital success. For the majority of our boys and girls, then, gender-specific rituals and roles are more formative, and more important to future success, than the pursuit of actual drives and desires.

Children imbibe the valuing of fiction over fact in the home, in the classroom, and at play. All three are sites of learning through the deployment of language, but the classroom is most strongly language-oriented. The role of the teacher in the classroom is not simply that of imposing the cultural strategy of gendering on students; academia itself works to disenfranchise the feminine through rhetorical strategy, which means that regardless of intentions, language itself is at risk in the very place where it is thought to be most stable. Whether women teachers seek to encourage liberatory discourse or to endorse sanctioned behaviors, they are themselves at odds with talk itself. By repeating old speech, women teachers absorb the authority of those they bespeak; by thinking for themselves, and therefore entering into intellectualism, they are doubly dis-endorsed as was their ancestor Mary Wollstonecraft, the intellectual whom Horace Walpole called a "hyena in petticoats" because she wrote philosophical tracts on gender rights (to Hannah Moore, 24 January 1795). The hyena is bestial, degraded by its insensible laugh and its scavenger appetite; in petticoats it is not even dangerous, only absurd. Walpole's other-ing epithet serves to disenfranchise, but more importantly, it designates this denial as a doubled state. Women who talk back are re-embodied and then denatured (made bestial or unnatural), and women who speak out can have no respect. Intellectuals like Camille Paglia, on the other hand, gain power for themselves by bespeaking hegemonic views on women thinkers—that is, writing books that use the conduct-book trope in order to place themselves in the role of (male) pedagogue who seeks to correct (female) wrongful behavior. Paglia's academic credentials provide her with the skills to interpret and evaluate women's behavior as if it were a literary text, while her chosen trope of conduct book pushes her to enact the controlling and political behavior she accuses other women academics of engaging in. Her claim, that feminist thinkers are to blame for their effeminizing taint in an erstwhile strong national masculine culture, deflects attention from Paglia's own masculinist grab for power and media attention. In a recent interview Paglia explains her views, saying "I was inspired by the prewar feminism of Amelia Earhart and Katharine Hepburn. Those very individualistic superwomen of that era . . . bold, independent, not someone who blames other people. . . . Self-reliance—that's my feminism" (Denison, 8). What she ignores about this feminine strength, the iconic strength of the pioneer woman whose back-breaking labor allowed men to build this country, is that Earhart and Hepburn are women from privileged backgrounds whose individual free-dom remained individual while whole classes of women were unaffected by such gains. Indeed, Hepburn spent her career making films about the taming of the shrew, her independent assertions always gainsaid by the film's end. Paglia sees no difficulty here, explaining the endurance of sexism as a positive good, as the endurance of sex itself: "Guess what? Maybe sex cannot be controlled by a grievance committee. How about that? . . . There's something else that's bigger than us, like nature and sexuality. Nature and sexuality are the dog. We are just the tail that's being wagged." The blatantly clichéd metaphor hides Paglia's blindsiding gesture by which she disguises her love of cultural elitism with the potent image of an inarguable Nature. Claiming the incontrovertible reveals Paglia's self-description as a radical bisexual feminist to be again a blindside, a way to tell someone else how to be while claiming the authority and fame for oneself.

Dinesh D'Souza's conduct-book treatise, *Illiberal Education: The Politics of Race and Sex on Campus*, similarly evinces blindsiding and conservative thought. D'Souza begins by assuming that the humanities in academia are effeminate, reminding him of T. S. Eliot's Prufrock: Ivy League campuses are "intellectual and social enclaves, by design somewhat aloof from the pressures of the 'real world,' " and thus all the more inclined to appear like landscapes of "lawns" across which "the scholars come and go, talking of Proust and Michelangelo" (1). This esoteric reference to social decadence and the feminization of society's elite is the first principle of D'Souza's thesis. But his right-wing attack is not after all on issues of race and sex—as his subtitle proclaims—but on educators' attempts to influence the "real world" by implementing political correctness in the classroom. While the first principle of political correctness is presumably race and class, for D'Souza and Paglia the more significant ground is how p.c. manifests the hypocrisy of reactionary "liberals." That is, the reactionary hysteria that informs both Paglia's and D'Souza's work is authorized by their own self-positioning regarding legitimate culture and hegemonic forms; those upholding political correctness, on the other hand, appear to these critics to wave the wand of cultural tolerance while cutting down their opponents with a nondemocratic and intolerant sword. Liberalism in its present guise, D'Souza argues, is really illiberalism.

D'Souza's book provides an example of multiple forms of rhetoric at work. *Illiberal Education* is first of all hysterical, taking facts out of context, coloring them with the taint of effeminacy, and using them to drive fear into the reader. It is second of all the conduct-book trope, focusing not on pedagogical imperatives but on how political correctness forces certain behaviors on professors, restricting their intellectual freedom in the classroom. D'Souza argues ferociously for professors' freedom to teach normative ideologies. Notably, his is also a book that blindsides in that it avoids discussing the realities and concerns that produced the notion of political correctness, and talks only of what he takes to be egregious cases where liberalism has gone awry. His very first sentence—"There are few places as serene and opulent as an American university campus"—speaks to his own privileged education at Dartmouth (a notorious seat of illiberal conservatism among its student body), and to his miscomprehension of the realities of most American college campuses today. With Reagan's budgetary cuts to student loans and tax increases on student stipends and low-income citizens, and with the loss of funds to more and more schools thereafter, few American students have experienced the "opulence" (read "decadence" and "privilege") that D'Souza decries.

Whereas D'Souza focuses on the hystericized moments of higher education, E. D. Hirsch's *Cultural Literacy* is concerned with programming elementary and secondary education in order to eliminate the possibility for hystericization to occur. *Cultural Literacy* is one of the initial tracts in this conduct-book war over who will control the cultural hegemony in the near future. In it he argues that primary and secondary schools need to reinstate necessary knowledge, or "cultural literacy." Hirsch's thesis resembles D'Souza's hysteria in that he views the "illiteracy" he finds currently in school curricula to be result of politically correct pedagogy. Especially deplorable, he finds, is teachers' relativist attitudes that replace an evaluative judgment used to ascertain which subjects to teach or to teach in depth, and which to skip over. And teachers criminally substitute abstract skills teaching at early ages instead of content subjects. It is the lack of content knowledge that continues to disadvantage oppressed students, Hirsch claims, because without that knowledge they will never enter mainstream culture:

Young children enjoy absorbing formulaic knowledge. Even if they did not, our society would still find it essential to teach them all sorts of traditions and facts. Critical thinking and basic skills . . . do not enable children to create out of their own imaginations the essential names and concepts that have arisen by historical accident. (28)

One might ask how children can learn concepts formulaically, but the clearer purpose here is that Hirsch wants children to absorb unquestioningly mainstream ideology by what is almost rote learning. This, in his view, is more liberal and liberating than the liberality of a multicultural curriculum.

The arguments one should mount against Hirsch's thesis are that he assumes mainstream cultural content will have meaning to students from different ethnic backgrounds, that he assumes their backgrounds are not "American," and so on. But it is more interesting in terms of Paglia and D'Souza (both of whom have absorbed mainstream ideology more fully than they can admit) to look at what this content is that Hirsch finds so productive of our culture. First, there are lists. One list, which Hirsch cuts off after the "H" entries, contains the names of twenty-one Americans of historical or literary importance. Two of the list are women, one is a black man, and all the rest are white men; all have done extraordinary things. Yet, as Hirsch notes later, even textbooks of earlier decades included names in lists like these that have been cut out: Martha Crabtree, Betsy Ross, Sarah Smith, and Janet Blair. We might also ask if women like Margaret Fuller, Harriet Tubman, Phyllis Wheatley, or even Martha Washington are included in the full list, and if they are why we are not told. But as Hirsch notes, "Such choices are no more inevitable than the spelling of *monk* instead of *munk*" (84). If Hirsch's argument really is against relative values and for the necessity for a particular cultural literacy, how is it possible that the all-important list that will save our country is so arbitrary, and so recently so?

Apparently the argument is not that we teach children a certain body of cultural knowledge, but that we agree to a body of knowledge that will constitute American culture, which we must then transmit to our students as future citizens. It is the single voice of agreed-upon cultural values and mores that Hirsch and Paglia and D'Souza urge. But they do so through rhetorical tropes that make readers believe they are thinking independently against the agents of illiberal politics. The conduct-book trope assumes an authoritative position defined by normative cultural views, assumes that its author has a privileged position as both the embodiment and conveyor of this knowledge, and assumes that if the addressees of the book do not consume this knowledge urgently and fully, the fate of the present culture will suffer.

The conduct-book trope acts, then, to define a target group and separate it from the author. The author embodies sameness, or normative culture, while the targeted addressees embody difference from the norm. The trope's urgency is aimed at the different who must be made to conform, and even more so at the casual reader who in reading must now become part of this cultural offensive. This kind of Cold War tactic—of defining the enemy and then hystericizing them—cannot constructively address the difficulties our children face or that our nation faces. Such reactionary one-sidedness, for instance, compels Hirsch to include among his cultural literacy items "Peter Pan," "Humpty Dumpty," and "Tweedledee and Tweedledum." Although neither Wendy nor Alice make it on the list, the fragile egghead does, as do the boy who excites pedophiles and the brothers who joust over a spoilt rattle. Why are the girls excluded but not their fragile male companions? The "arbitrariness" of Hirsch's cultural mission begins to look less arbitrary and more masculinst—and more the same.

Those who hold to sameness understand the world only in its relation to them; all others are "othered," "different." What conduct-book tropists refuse to see is that sameness is relative to who is measuring. Hirsch can include as necessary to our cultural heritage effeminate characters with "dangerously" homosexual traits because they take part in his picture of sameness. Yet parents who hysterically fight against allowing their school curriculum to teach about homosexuality as an alternative cultural practice reject these curriculums for teaching that homosexuality is "normal." Through associative thinking, normal becomes normative, and their child is suddenly in danger of becoming homosexual because he is taught that it is the norm. On reading *Peter Pan* or "Humpty Dumpty," this will not occur because these stories are of nonnormative yet safely fictional worlds where everything, including sexuality, is upside down and inhabitable. When such worlds are taught as real and yet safe and inhabitable, "alternative" suddenly becomes a terrible word. The illogic that drives this train of thought stems from sameness-thinking: I can only understand the world in terms of me; therefore if you are like me I understand you, and if you are not like me you threaten my existence.

However, the purpose of multicultural studies in the schools is to teach difference rather than sameness. This is not to say that "I remain the same but I see you as different"; this would keep us in the sameness tautology. Instead, difference means that not only are you different from the sameness that is me, but I am also a difference. In difference-thinking, there is no center from which those not alike are marginalized. For this reason alone it presents a formidable threat to those who currently occupy a cultural center, or to those who aspire to do so. Teaching about homosexuality in the schools is meant to teach tolerance for others by stressing the view that there are several acceptable forms of adult relations that together make up our heterogeneous society. But sameness-thinking is the cognitive practice of the privileged, those who wish society to be defined by the shape of their lives alone. To restrict the reality of society to a social phantasy has been the practice of our culture for the last two centuries at least. But to continue to do so in the face of increasing nondominant populations is anachronistic. It also deprives our children of a way to understand their world, while robbing those who are not centered of a legitimate voice.

Against such (Captain Hook) piracy and loss of voice we can pit bell hooks's theory of pedagogy: teachers who do not consciously work out their own system of values do not notice such discrepancies over what children should know. Without knowing what we think ourselves, we cannot position ourselves ideologically against those who do speak out. If we do not read carefully and recognize the tropes that disfigure social realities in order to scare us into regressive change, then we will be afraid.

Education, hooks tell us, should "engage us fully in a liberatory praxis" (*Talking Back*, 35), and that means having the pedagogical and intellectual tools to free ourselves first.

"Freeing ourselves," however, can itself be a contentious phrase: who is "us"? We women, who are we? How we define ourselves—by race, religion, ethnicity and heritage, class, education, profession, region and nationality, even age—we cannot speak for "us" except in the largest of senses. One of these senses—the sense of "women" and "us" as defined against the terms "men" and "I"—provides the basis for the following chapter. I use the word "against" precisely because politically women have been defined as lack, as not-men, as the negative of a positive. Even our written and visual literature, which embodies the cultural imaginary, narrates the tale of I versus you, men versus not-men. How men and women authors fictionalize and illustrate this tale—the great narrative of Western literature—provides inroads as to how we conceptualize ourselves within the disparate discourses of I and you. How a given author visualizes this tale depends on their own relation to male or female discourse, but is always constrained by their own culturally defined experience as a man or a woman, as well as by their individual regard for the story underlying all of our (his)stories.

NOTES

1. Charles W. Eliot, "The Higher Education of Woman," *Harper's Bazaar* (1908): 167. See his *Education for Efficiency and the New Definition of the Cultivated Man* and *Charles W. Eliot and Popular Education*, ed. Edward A. Krug.

2. Reprinted in *Twenty Years of School and College English* (1896), courtesy of John Brereton, manuscript forthcoming, Oxford University Press.

3. Quoted in Eve Sedgwick, 829. Sedgwick takes her quotations from Catherine Duncan's translation of Zambaco in "Polysexuality," *Semiotext(e)* 4 (1981):22–36.

4. Sedgwick collects these classifications as sadomasochistic, pederastic, pedophilic, necrophilic, autoerotic, zoophiles, zooerasts, auto-monosexualists, gynecomasts, among others (826).

5. Curiously, Gilligan discusses the phenomenon of clique formation among teen-aged girls as more threatening to adults than harmful to the girls themselves: "women teachers may find it especially unsettling to witness some of girls' experiments in inclusion and exclusion—the tortuous clique formations through which girls may discover how it feels to be left out and what it means to be taken in, and which also may provide a kind of dumbshow or dark mirroring of the adult world that girls are seeing" (*Making Connections*, 11–12).

6. "Teaching Shakespeare's Sister: Notes from the Underground of Female Adolescence," in Gilligan, *Making Connections*, 6–29.

7. For a fascinating study of working-class women's relation to hegemonic power and its promise, see Steedman. My thanks to Jennifer FitzGerald, Queen's University-Belfast, for recommending this book.

8. Baron's study of gendered language points out that earlier language experts were concerned with preventing what they saw as a feminization of English:

The not always subtle anti-feminism of the major English etymologists and lexicographers is only one aspect of the sexism that underlies commentaries on the English language. In our examination of the general notions of maleness and femaleness in language we find, for example, that the feminine gender in Indo-European languages [was] often perceived to derive from the masculine and that it [was] a mark of praise to call a language like English a masculine tongue, while French and Italian [were] condemned—by English commentators—as feminine, or even effeminate. (6)

9. This explanation is grounded in family-systems therapy as interpreted by Professor Aaron Lipton. (Personal communication.)

10. See Kramarae and Treichler.

Chapter Three

Romancing the Heroine, Reading the Self: Same Difference

Again, no healthy-minded girl comes face to face with the courageous womanliness of Elizabeth Bennet, rising through sweetness and good sense above a mother of humiliating vulgarity, or the delicate conscience of Fanny Price, undervitalized but charming. . . . without discovering that a style with no ornament, a style which marches straight on, is, in the right hands, a wonderfully effective style, and that a book to be interesting need not leave the beaten track of everyday life.

Le Baron Russell Briggs, 16

In chapter two, the novels of Jane Austen became a kind of test case for analyzing the pedagogical use of conduct-book morality. This chapter offers a similar but more grounding function by treating rhetorical usage and ideological persuasion in the arena of literature, television, and film, beginning with Austen's work. We begin here because Austen's novels have been so influential in Western women's formulation of their social identities for nearly two hundred years and across national boundaries. Indeed, Austen is an artistic master: a painter of modern character, social identities, and complexities within the moral field of the social community. She also becomes a crucible of rhetorical analysis because her authorial skill allows her an ambivalence at the narrative level that both invites and rejects conflicting interpretations of her intent. One focus of this chapter is to examine how Austen achieves this resistant style, and what her own ideological reasons might be for doing so. One of her earliest completed novels, *Northanger Abbey*, and her last, *Persuasion*, were both published in 1818. These two novels, and the productive space between them in which Austen because a public figure as author, in some sense continue each other and become one story—the story of a girl who must learn to accept social pressures, but who manages to carve out a space for herself in the marital domesticity she will finally assume. The space allotted women today is in many ways little changed, but the psychological integrity Austen claims for her heroines continues to appear in contemporary women authors' and film makers' depictions of female strength. These portrayals offer an alternative rhetoric to the insistence of conduct-book ideologues on women's subservient nature.

The romance is the genre that Austen uses to tease her reader within the bounds of this story, and that most secures her use of ambivalence into a clear and unambiguous morality.[1] Literary romance takes form as either the sentimental romance (or romantic love) or the romance quest (a male genre in which the woman has a secondary place, but which portrays her as the idealized quest object and is thus seductively pleasing to the female reader). Romance as sentimental love has long been important to women's imaginations because it offers a seductively escapist version of the world; however, what it demands in return for its gift of fantasy is a self-pacification of the reader. The romance genre in all its forms exploits emotional heightening to bring the reader-heroine identification to life; by engaging the emotions of romantic love, fear, and curiosity, the sentimental romance works on the imagination like a dream, at once making the fantasy hyper-real and the reader over-passive. Yet Austen's novels cannot be considered conventional romances; those who, like Dean Briggs in the epigraph above, are determined to read romance into Austen must read her novels *as* romance, an act requiring a distinct ideological skewing of the narrative which Austen's ambiguity allows.

It is within this ambiguity and our parsing of it that Austen's novels provide a ground for this chapter. Romantic love is, and continues to be, deeply ingrained in our society as a pleasurable way for women to remain pacified within a rich fantasy life that both negates their access to, and negates their need for, an engaging and active public-sphere life. Austen uses sentimental romance to tease her reader into activity, but in the hands of the wrong reader this becomes a flawed strategy that turns her novels *into* romance and toward the desire to be rescued by the perfect hero. This literalization of affective desire prevails among the commercialization of women's social identity: women's magazines, glamorized women news anchors, the glorification of film and tv actors, the cosmetic and fashion industries, soft porn. Certainly the socializing passivity that sentiment reinforces means that romance is an important formulation of the literalization trope.

Romance is also integrally related to another genre form, the detective story; the relation exists through a shared inheritance from the gothic. In the gothic novel, an active heroine who is boldly curious about her world and its anomalies ventures beyond her proper bounds and enters a psychologically aberrant world that is usually manifested as a ruined and secret-ridden castle. Although this heroine is engaged in active detection, the genre is designed to punish feminine curiosity and so the heroine is quickly immured in the castle and must wait passively to be rescued by the novel's hero. Austen herself scoffs at this punishment genre, not because its heroines are pacified so much as because they are unrealistically, even ill-manneredly, active. The better use Austen sees for feminine detection is in aiding her heroine to cope with and rise above the everyday. It is detecting as an active engagement of the intellect that allows Elizabeth Bennet to sustain the "humiliating vulgarity" of her mother and sisters, and not what Dean Briggs in the epigraph above ascribes to her "womanliness." As she does for sentimental romance, Austen uses detection without falling prey to its gothic morality. Although derived from a blend of the gothic and romance, the detective genre can become a vehicle for the liberated twentieth-century heroine, but only if she retains a close resemblance to Austen's actively engaged heroines and refuses both the hero's and the villain's advances until she has won her case.

The romance (both as love story and as quest) is a variant of the literalization trope in which the fantasy becomes hyper-real, or more important to us than everyday life; similarly, detection is an inversion of the conspiratorial trope. Detection unravels the conspiratorial thinking into which the detective must enter in order to uncover the secreted enemy. The disjunction between the literary ways in which men and women express their different relations with their readers is marked by the use and interpretation of romance and detection, literalization and conspiracy, within a larger field of fantasy and realism. The sequence of literature, television, and film texts discussed below reveals a pattern that moves us from Austen's play with romance, to Morrison's blend of romance with detection, to detection, to parody of romance, rejection of romance, hysteria as gothic, hysteria as conspiracy, and romance unveiled. This tropology is neither historical nor genre specific, but merely provides a way to see the tropes at work in a less isolated, and so less hidden, way than we normally experience them.

Literature and film are important to the overall analysis of this book because, like every other arena analyzed in *Eminent Rhetoric*, we take the high art of literature and serious film to be a safety haven from the onslaught on our loyalties and desires that typifies most of our commercialized culture. To the extent that it discernibly is not, we must revise what we consider to be its political engagement. To the extent that it reveals itself to be politically engaged, we must consider the tropes most relevant to both women's *and* men's subcultures: romance as literalization and hysteria as conspiratorial thinking. Between the two poles of serious novel and film I have situated the popular culture forms of detective novel, television sitcom, and instructional show. Despite their status as "high" or "low" culture, all these forms are connected by romance and detection—alternately depicted as hysteria and conspiracy—and all revolve around cultural myths about women. First we will analyze in depth two of Austen's novels, both published the same year, for the ways in which critics interpret and overinterpret her texts for their own tropological ends. Against Austen I place a contemporary writer of Austen-like stature, Toni Morrison. Following this analysis are brief readings of several contemporary texts that are themselves rich in tropes, or that provoke tropic critical responses to their self-rhetoric. The last portion of the chapter examines Oliver Stone's *JFK* (1991), a film that sets out to reify 1960s American culture and ideology as surely as Morrison's novels do Afro-American culture. And as a counter for *JFK*'s use of hystericization and conspiratorial thinking to capture a cultural expression, as well as a return to Austen's cultural vision, we end with Patricia Rozema's *I've Heard the Mermaids Singing* (1987). This is a film that plays out an alternative interpretation of the literalization trope, one that I argue succeeds in the sense Austen's novels point to. Rozema's text uses literalization as a positive and actualizing agent of self-realization within a comprehensive understanding of the negativity of romance literalization. Against Stone, Rozema can be seen to realize the full potential of Austen's ambiguity, and thus provide us with a model for reinterpreting our own coming to self.

AUSTEN, HYSTERIA, AND ROMANCE

In chapter two we saw how Le Baron Russell Briggs, dean of Harvard University and president of Radcliffe, considered Jane Austen to present her women readers with an admirable model of a "style with no ornament, a style which marches straight on." Briggs's conduct-book agenda tropes its reversal of meaning and performative intent in the arena of rhetoric itself here by saying in effect that plain style is natural while rhetorical use is artificial; therefore, in the equation of nature/woman and culture/man, women are inherently unfit for rhetorical use.[2] The literalization trope which underlies and supports his conduct-book rhetoric ironically encourages women to read themselves into the romance Austen seems to offer as a moralizing act. Briggs views the romantic love of second-rate novels as wasteful because readers identify with heroines such as the odious "Lydia Lavish," while his literalizing ploy allows him to perceive Austen's discourse as rhetorical and nonromantic. For him, her discerning lack of rhetorical embellishment and sentimental adjectives proves she is nonromantic—a judgment Austen would agree with herself—but Briggs does not realize that he continues to use romance as the lure for getting women to read about Lizzie Bennet instead of Lydia Lavish. Because women also inherently adore ornament and thus inflated speech, excessive emotion, and other signs of hysterical wallowing, Briggs insists that they must develop the moral fiber—as Jane Austen has done—to resist indulging their desire. That his cure is to read the correct books is not surprising; that the correct books are books of literature and not moral sermons is. But the unusual designation of a literary work as unfigured and without rhetorical ornament—and thus as a moral work—is less the result of Briggs's inclusive pedagogy and more the result of Austen's skill at incorporating counter-tropes into texts that offer several levels of meaning which can each be taken as the only level if one so chooses.

Austen structures her novels on the play between teacher-lover and student-heroine, in which each learns from the other and so grows more equitable. This hero-heroine relation, to Austen's mind, demands a proper way of talking, and an authorial need to configure delicate relations while contending with readerly desire. Against the "charming" quality of her books—the readerly assessment and critical belittlement of her women's novels—Austen pits charm as a counter-trope, a dispeller of the hysteria typical of gothic novels and a dispeller of hystericization and other male-imposed tropes. Many of the very women or girls who read her novels were, like Austen's heroines, engaged in sentimental or "romantic friendships" with one another; these friends often exchanged locks of hair, fashioned them into charms or relics, and then pinned them on as symbols of their affection. The charms signified a strong bond that was to endure despite the marriages to come, and although they do not literally figure in Austen's plots, they are literalized as rhetorical devices that ward off ill-reading.

Quite often Austen's charms have to do with the mother or her absence. In *Persuasion*, for instance, the narrative begins with a book of family pedigrees, a literalizing metaphor that reveals the early death of Anne's mother: the book "loses" the textual body of the mother. It is the loss of this sensible mother as much as the appearance of the family book that initiates the plot, since without her mother's support Anne feels she cannot go against her family's wishes regarding her unmoneyed suitor. Once she has lost her lover, Anne also loses much of her will to live, and both losses can be traced back to the loss of the mother. Although Anne herself has no close "romantic" girlfriend, her mother's closest friend, Lady Russell, acts as her confidant and mentor in her mother's stead and it is she more than anyone who had convinced Anne to give up Captain Wentworth as a suitor. Lady Russell was Lady Elliot's "one very intimate friend, a sensible, deserving woman, who had been brought, by strong attachment to herself, to settle close by her, in the village of Kellynch" (11); she is thus the bearer of the charm of female friendship, a charm Austen uses to ward off the spell of the (male) book. Yet, although best friend to the mother, Lady Russell seems to have enacted the romantic charm on the daughter, using her influence with Anne to stave off men and to keep her within a female world of friendships and obligations. The irony of Lady Russell's protection of Anne from a man of inferior background and fortune is the loss of his superior spirit and abilities: the charm, as a gendered trope, has failed as sadly as the masculinist tropes.

Thus the mother's charm keeps the daughter between women, precisely the outcome critics of women's sentimental friendships were afraid of. Against this women's realm Austen positions the fraternity of the British navy; a network of naval friends enters the novel when Anne's family is displaced from their ancestral home by financial embarrassment, a loss of home clearly associated with the loss of the mother and her domestic economy. New homes and new friendships lead to a reversal of charm against trope which reunites suitor with heroine. The reversal takes the book of family that records the mother's death and turns it into a love letter that turns Wentworth's dead love into life again. Charmed and impassioned by a conversation between Anne and his fellow officer, Wentworth dares not speak up but writes by letter, " 'I can listen no longer in silence. I must speak to you by such means as are within my reach. You pierce my soul . . .' " (223). In the conversation he has overheard, his friend tells Anne the precise reasons she is in need of charms and counter-tropes:

But let me observe that all histories are against you, all stories, prose and verse. If I had such a memory as Benwick, I could bring you fifty quotations in a moment on my side of the argument, and I do not think I ever opened a book in my life which had not something to say upon woman's inconstancy. Songs and proverbs, all talk of woman's fickleness. But perhaps you will say, these were all written by men.

Anne's reply makes clear how well she understands what she is up against rhetorically:

Perhaps I shall.—Yes, yes, if you please, no reference to examples in books. Men have had every advantage of us in telling their own story. Education has been theirs in so much higher a degree; the pen has been in their hands. I will not allow books to prove any thing. (220–21)

The one-sided tales of men's histories reveal women as shallow, inconstant, unloving, and veritably *absent* from men's lives. If Anne is to avoid her mother's fate—and she is nearly invisible in her father's eyes even now—she must recover a way of telling her part of the story. Disallowing "reference to examples in books" and insisting on the morality of her own story in her own words, Anne also refuses to diminish men's stories: "God forbid that I should undervalue the warm and faithful feelings of any of my fellow-creatures. I should deserve utter contempt if I dared to suppose that true attachment and constancy were known only by woman" (221–22). Anne's declaration is necessary both to reverse her conversant's hystericization of women, and to transform the book's deadening charm against women into the letter's life-giving charm, the kiss of life.

Anne's heartfelt plea is against being misread. Yet ill-reading, the very act Austen seeks to avoid, finds its foothold in the absence of passion in her texts, or rather a different passion which is affective, heroic, and aesthetic rather than sexual. Her narrators seem to shield sexuality with another layer of charm as if they were interfering chaperons who won't let the lovers get on. The charm both hides and enables detection, and thus D. H. Lawrence can write of Austen, "Already this old maid typifies 'personality' instead of character, the sharp knowing apartness instead of knowing in togetherness, and she is, to my feeling, thoroughly unpleasant, English in the bad, mean, snobbish sense" (Dowling, 7), while Anthony Trollope writes, "I cannot but notice Miss Austen's timidity in dealing with the most *touching* scenes which come in her way. . . . This is a cowardice which robs the reader of much of the *charm* which he has promised himself" (9; emphasis added). For Trollope, Austen's charms are read as charming or as determinant devices rather than as structural and meaningful. Henry James says of Austen that she "was instinctive and charming" (Dowling, 6). Austen's difficulty lies in using the fairy touch or magic amulet of charm that renders romance charming to disguise the rhetorical battle of wits she is fighting. Austen's love stories become readable as sentimental romance themselves by those invested in hystericizing them away from the crystallizing moment of novel realism.

It is perhaps Austen's tropological countering that accounts for her ongoing popularity in the late twentieth century. Her importance for us, others would argue, is in the conflict between twentieth-century readers' admiration for her construction of the love relation, and her production of that relation through narratives of reading and writing a new relation into being. Indeed, Nancy Armstrong sees Austen's creation of a new community as based on a liberal linguistic economy, a "fundamental currency of language" that synthesizes regional, class, and profession marked speech into a shared linguistic ethic. Wealth and status become a semiotic code that can be properly read from inside the new community. To get inside, heroines must learn to read and communicate appropriately; Austen's novels are all predicated on the moment of miscommunication which must then be undone as a progression toward a new stability of language (Armstrong, 137–38). As pertinent as this argument is, its complexity prevents a full rehearsal here; instead, the discussion that follows examines the political side of this linguistic economy as contractual relations in order to show how Austen's worldview can be reconstrued from the hysteria of romance into a more energizing narrative.[3] Contractual reading plays out the implications of detection rather than romance while it makes room for a new marital discourse.

Laurie Langbauer examines the political uses of romance in the development of the novel and notes, "Women supposedly dream of romance—or so Freud tells us," and then draws up the system of oppositions in the nineteenth-century literary imagination in which romance is posed as the novel's other, its prior self, its naive origin, and a seductive genre that induces daydream instead of action, delusion instead of motivation.[4] "In this economy, woman is a scapegoat too, a counter given value by the system in which it circulates. Like romance, she is constructed in opposition to a standard—man—and (circularly) seems to uphold that standard by deviating from it" (3). But Langbauer's claim that romance is not an oppositional form but "a counter within a grammar of meanings" (17) must undergird our reading of Austen, for both *Northanger Abbey* and *Persuasion* employ a romanticization of romance that supplies a grammar of different values: romance as heroine-ism, as the conversion of space, as a process of reading, as a family affair.

Most importantly, the opposition of romance to novel must be understood politically, as the argument between a focus on the individual, and on the social.[5] The romance hero and his woman reader are held to be self- or ego-centered, concerned only with inner emotion and excitement. The novel hero or heroine is held to be socially invested and selfless, liberal in the radical sense of communally responsible. This difference develops because the romance's love dyad which structures the hero's confrontation with evil in order to find himself in his beloved's love is self-consuming at the expense of community. That this love might give rise to new generations is beyond the scope of the romance until Austen, among others, takes it up; it is here that Austen in particular sees her novels as socially responsible and a correction of romance, a point she vigorously argues in *Northanger Abbey*. The Austen novel is always about the production of a new kind of family resulting from the mutual self-corrections her heroine and hero engage each other in, in order to begin to reproduce a new society without the violence of romance war. Ideal domesticity offers a reform of the state.[6] Austen does not argue for a feminist utopia, a revolutionary equality, a Romantic soul-sharing, or a bourgeois economy of the family. Instead, she argues for a discursive community, that is, a family that talks to each other without resistance because it is without appropriation. Once the hero learns to value the body/mind/spirit of the heroine as virginal, that is, intact and nontransgressible, then he becomes appropriately spousal. Once the heroine understands she will not be transgressed, she learns to dehystericize or disarm herself; it is then that she can enter into gendered relations with a realizable equity.

What the heroine needs in romance in order to withstand or escape it is the charm that dispels the man's story—history as quest romance, history as the pacification and conquest of women. The charm or counter-trope—particularly if we think in terms of Clément and Cixous's witchery—provides a resistance against the fantasy of romantic love and the quest romance, and thus a resistance against hystericization. Hystericization exploits the bodily virtue that conduct-book tropes demand of women, by turning the despair caused by virtuous silence into hysterical illness. Resistant witchery becomes witchcraft, charm becomes hysteria, and equity turns into "shrillness."

Romance and then nineteenth-century society both claim that women should be the embodiment of virtue rather than the social system of manners that Austen can still argue for. Virtue is that which organizes and subordinates personal interests to that of the group both morally and politically; for a society to believe that one sex can incorporate this selflessness into their person is to silence that group to the larger community, and this is the basis for Victorian repression of sexual self-discovery in social life as well as the popularity of the social work novel with its female heroes. But Austen still inhabits a world where both sexes must engage virtue in the sense of responsibility to others, and must do so through a propriety of manners. Her discourse, therefore, is the contractual discourse of domestic economy. In this sense, resistance is no longer the only real psychological recourse of the heroine, and it can be differentiated from resistance as manners. In an early parody, Austen laughs at the mimicking of true virtue in order to appear sensible (as in sensibility) rather than sensible (as in thoughtful):

One fatal swoon has cost me my Life. . . . Beware of swoons Dear Laura. . . . A frenzy fit is not one quarter so pernicious; it is an exercise to the Body and if not too violent, is I dare say conducive to Health in its consequences—Run mad as often as you chuse; but do not faint—.

That is, hysteria is a useful device, but not to be confused with the loss of sense. Austen's novels play out this distinction between sense and sensibility, thoughtful self-containment and hysteria, until in Anne Elliot we have a woman who learns from deferring her own pleasure to others' judgment to understand the difference before the hero has to teach it to her.

But Anne has had to suffer too much for her education, a sign that Austen's counter-trope of charm maintains her within a tropological rhetoric that too easily plays against her. Such maintenance is a safety precaution against the attacks she fears, but it cannot protect her against undiscerning readers looking for romance. But Austen has not merely cast a rhetorical net around her characters; like all masters she creates a narrative universe that operates on a variety of levels, many of which imitate and comment upon the layering of social realities her readers experience firsthand. At the level of contractual relations Austen offers an alternative to charm that is less palatable to her masculinist critics but more real to her characters.

THE SOCIAL CONTRACT

The social contract is the meta-trope society devises for itself in order to sanction and legislate political relations between the individual and his leader. The social contract changes with historical and social changes, but it is always a story we tell ourselves about why we give our individual power over to an elected or appointed statesman. Because this story explains all our social relations—political, communal, professional, familial, sexual—we tell it repeatedly. The individual contracts with another individual or body, giving allegiance in exchange for something. This is an allegory, a story which is also a trope, a generalization that explains all the particulars.

Allegory is what Austen begins to work toward in *Northanger Abbey* (an ideal society predicated on a new family unit of mutual regard and understanding), and what she realizes in *Persuasion* (love as trust). Trust is the one allegorical move always demanded from women as an implied element of a social contract, and it is always the assumed condition for sentimental romance as an appositive to sympathy. In *Northanger Abbey*, Isabella's manipulations of Catherine instanced the advantage taken of such trust, but like her parents Catherine will remain unsuspecting of the dishonest heart because trust is not an issue; her trust for Henry is presumed while his is gained through catechistic questioning of her impulses. Anne, on the other hand, has learned that trusting trusted advisers loses her heart, and that learning to incur trust from a man requires not only a trustworthy heart, but constant vigilance and careful reading.

Catherine is in some sense Anne Elliot's younger self, because what she cannot do despite her delight in novel reading is read correctly. She believes the gentry's aspirations to be grounded in her romance notions of the generosity of feudal lords, and so she says of General Tilney, "—Your father is so very liberal! He told me the other day, that he only valued money as it allowed him to promote the happiness of his children" (165), and the facial expressions of both Henry and Eleanor do not tell her that this is not how they read their father. Catherine, in fact, does read well, but only in the literal register. The metaphorical escapes her to such an extent that the abbey can become the place of gothic horror because it literally reproduces the architecture of gothic romance. When Henry disabuses her of this ("Does our education prepare us for such atrocities? Do our laws connive at them? Could they be perpetuated without being known, in a country like this . . . ?," [159]), she is mortified but not wrong. What the French Revolution accomplished openly men have wrought in the privacy of their homes; more women die from spouse abuse than the law admits, yet in her already-given trust Catherine cannot doubt Henry's truth. Her suspicion of conspiracy in the home and Henry's disabusement is Austen's joking subtext to Henry's paternalism: *Northanger Abbey* was composed during the Pitt government, whose use of a spy network to quell subversives at the homefront turns in Austen's hands into neighbors spying on the home.

Anne Elliot agrees with Henry, however, advising a young man to desist from using romances as a guide to human behavior and to life. But her reasoning is not that literature is superficial, but that it is partial: "Men have had every advantage of us in telling their own story." Her response is to the witticism that "I do not think I ever opened a book in my life which had not something to say upon woman's inconstancy." Inconstancy, as the breaking of trust, and therefore of consent and contract, is the charge male writers put on women because consent is woman's condition. Carole Pateman's formulation of the paradigmatic case for this is explicit: "Women are held to lack the capacities required by individuals who can give consent, yet, in sexual relations where consent is fundamental, women are held always to consent and their explicit refusals are reinterpreted as consent" (191). Catherine Morland's friend Isabella represents this inconstancy as both feminine and verbal, a construction Catherine in her naïveté does not accept about women's constituent natures. When Catherine receives no letters from her brother's fiance, she recollects that "Isabella had promised and promised again; and when she promised a thing she was so scrupulous in performing it" (162). Yet Isabella herself does not accept Catherine's characterization of the promising act; instead she assumes that when she breaks her promise to James, she is under no obligation to respect the break and thus she can ask to be readmitted to the promissarial contract as if the inconstancy of her promise were natural, incontestable, expected. Despite any evidence to support her own reading, Catherine believes the promise to literally promise or oblige, and she thus trusts Isabella as a friend who is therefore trustworthy.

If women's trust elevates promise into the realm of contract *because* consent is presumed, then for women the contractual act is troped as mirror refraction, as improper mirror stages in which the reflection preexists the woman looking in. In part, refraction occurs because of a differential obligation. In promise-making, each party is *not* equal to the other, as the assumption of promise by John Thorpe over Catherine makes clear. The party with more social standing, whether by class, gender, wealth, or education, leverages the promise as well as the more firm contract. In *Northanger Abbey*, contracting ensues as dance. It is at their third dance together at the Bath pumproom that Henry compares the "country dance" to a marriage contract:

We have entered a contract of mutual agreeableness for the space of an evening, and all our agreeableness belongs solely to each other for that time. . . . I consider a country-dance as an emblem of marriage. Fidelity and complaisance are the principal duties of both. (56)

However, this contract came about because he asked for the dance and under the rules of the dance room, she could not have politely refused. Since dances were held as much for couples to meet as for entertainment, a woman could not refuse or pick her partners: the dance was the man's prerogative. Henry acknowledges the differential of the obligation involved in dance by remarking, "—You will allow, that in both [dance and marriage], man has the advantage of choice, woman only the power of refusal" (57). This moment is the key to his analogy, for he makes room for resistance as a social gesture, refusal, which is not allowed in the sexual contract, except by psychological resistance which is always construed as illness. Catherine can legitimately refuse John Thorpe without resisting because he assumed her promise but did not in fact contract; therefore she is under no legal obligation to him in a liberal state despite his presumptions.

If the contract can run in the opposite direction, as Austen arranges by rechoreographing the dance so that Catherine signals desire and Henry responds—at first only because she desired him—then the social contract is in danger, because it is predicated on a monodirectional power relation from the state to the individual. If Catherine can ask Henry to dance, or even dally in the dance with other women's husbands, then society is in chaos, as the dallying Isabella portends. Catherine can only signal choice through her expressive eyes, which sparkle when Henry asks her for the dance. The narrator comments that her eyes virtually speak when Catherine wishes to congratulate her brother "but knew not what to say": they shine out "the eight parts of speech . . . most expressively." Alternatively, they fade into ill "looks" when she is sent home by General Tilney. The choreography of the dance includes engagement, resistance, refusal, and promise as couples split and each woman temporarily gains a new partner—a temporary courtship before she regains her own partner in another pass.

But resisting is all the woman can *do* because it is all she *can* do, must do, since it is already scripted or contracted. The marital contract is modeled on the social contract, as Henry observes: the woman (citizen) consents to hand over the legal, political, and economic responsibility for her well-being to the man in exchange for his protection and ability to provide. *Northanger Abbey* translates the negotiation of this contract into its figurative social dance of manners and virtues which replicates that of the marriage market in a competitive economy; refusal ups the stakes and therefore is vital to the consuming fashion of dance. An alternate trope for this is the game of cards that Isabella finds such enjoyment in with Catherine's brother, a game called "commerce" (67).

Henry, too, understands the inversions and replications of the country dance as a game; in explaining dance as marriage to the female ingenue, Henry flirts with her naïveté and literality through a commerce of words. Comparing the contracts of both social practices reduces both to games, and in the process marriage becomes a verbalization that promises, a *mot juste* in place of the thing itself. Against Henry's gaming, Austen metamorphoses his game card into the structure of the narrative so that the entire novel becomes a playful dance around the marriage plot. What began as words at play used to forestall employment turns out to have been plotting all along to make the words real. In this sense the narrator must also contract with Catherine and Henry so that they will consent to a marriage of "true" love; for Austen, though, true love is not simply fated love, but persuaded love, prejudiced love, sensible love, until finally chosen love.

DETECTION AND BLACK ROMANCE

In African-American literature, devices like romance and detective must be reconceived. Romantic love is an artificially produced notion of sexual relations dating back to the twelfth century in its Western manifestation; it promises ideal love, eternal devotion, and sublime emotions. Although Austen differentiates herself from sentimental authors with her skeptical attitude toward romantic love, she also depends on its allure in her portrayals of her hero-lovers. African-American authors like Ralph Ellison, Alice Walker, and Toni Morrison cannot write about romantic love because that is not the notion of sexual relations ideologically prevalent in black culture. The love they depict is a mixture of female strength and male transience, sexual joy and a comprehension of its fleeting sublimity. If romantic love is an end in itself in the literature of white culture, the literature of black culture uses love to discover identity. In one sense this turns the use that black authors make of love into a device very close to the medieval romance quest. The quest is the journey a hero takes in order to discover his own inner identity; he may or may not engage in romantic love in the process since it is not necessary in achieving the end result, although it can be an aid in self-discovery. His quest, however, is that of the transcendent individual whose self-discovery is idealized and particularized. Black literature follows this use of romance as quest rather than as romantic love, but it does so with a more exaggerated sense of how the hero's love relations rediscovers the community's identity at large.

African-American literary romance, or what we might call the "black romance," plays out in the relations between people rather than in the relations between ideals.[7] At its most potent, black romance can be between women, as in Alice Walker's *The Color Purple* (1982). Here, the love affair between Celie and Shug, the identity questor and the woman who teaches her to know and love herself, transcends the man they share. Their sublimation of his exploitative attitudes into a love between themselves spreads outward and allows the hateful way the community views and treats itself to heal into a positive cultural history.

The same theme occurs in Toni Morrison's *Sula* (1973). When two women, or in *Sula* two girls, who have been fractured by social conditions find each other, they become complete in each other even though they are not lovers. Their mutual detection allows them to proceed with both discovering and inventing their own identities: " 'I'm me. I'm not their daughter. I'm not Nel. I'm me. Me.' Each time she said the word *me* there was a gathering in her like power, like joy, like fear . . . her new found me-ness" (28–29). Their need for self-invention is driven by Sula's mother's love for male children alone, and Nel's conformist mother's programmatic "dr[iving of] her daughter's imagination underground" (18). Nonetheless, these identities are mutually supportive but not identical: "She [Sula] had clung to Nel as the closet thing to both an other and a self, only to discover that she and Nel were not one and the same thing" (119). The process of invention is fraught with impediments and it is only toward the end of their lives that Sula and Nel realize that they were only complete identities when they were together. Alone, they only existed in relation to others: Nel to her husband ("The two of them together would make one Jude" [83]) and then her children; Sula as one who "never competed, she simply helped others define themselves" (95). Yet these two questors *are* rent by sharing one man between them, unlike the women lovers in *The Color Purple*, and in becoming divided from each other they become lost to themselves. Karla Holloway writes that

Because there is an essential link between the natural, physical world and the spiritual world in African ontogeny, when women carry knowledge, it can be manifested in things from either world. The rocks, trees, grasses all hold magical powers. As little girls, Nel and Sula experiment with this awareness of body/self and world while playing in the dirt and are brought to the trembling, excited agitation that presages awareness of their womanly power. (69)

Obviously Sula continues to live out this womanly power, but we should think about the terrible consequences of Nel's mother pushing her daughter's inherent creativity and curiosity underground. The interment or death of her spiritual self condemns Nel to a passivity in which she loses her ties to the actively seeking Sula. One becomes a wanderer, ungrounded once she loses Nel to marriage, while the other loses her invented self in making herself into the grounding home for her husband's ego.

Morrison suggests that when strong women in search of their identities—and thus of their cultural history—are not allowed the freedom to do so, they become empty wives, like Nel, or witches. Sula tells her male-loving grandmother that she does not want to have babies simply to "settle" her: "I don't want to make somebody else. I want to make myself" (92). Her grandmother's condemnation ("Selfish. Ain't no woman got no business floatin' around without no man") is repeated in the community's conviction that the manless Sula who sleeps with everyone's man, even white men, is a witch. Morrison reaches the same conclusion as Clément and Cixous when she writes that a witch is a woman artist bereft of tools.

In a way, her [Sula's] strangeness, her naïveté, her craving for the other half of her equation was the consequence of an idle imagination. Had she paints, or clay, or knew the discipline of the dance, or strings; had she anything to engage her tremendous curiosity and her gift for metaphor, she might have exchanged the restlessness and preoccupation with whim for an activity that provided her with all she yearned for. And like any artist with no art form, she became dangerous. (121)

But the black community tolerates its witches, with Sula only one of several in their midst, for witches complete the entirety of human life. As if Sula's part in the social template is an untold necessity, people respond to the bad harvest that follows Sula's death by converging to perform a *danse macabre* to the river's edge where several die. It is as though they had followed Sula there and not the mad Death figure that led them but did not die. Later Nel wonders if it had ever been a community, or just a place without a significance or a history; its wholeness registered only when it had Sula to scapegoat, for she completed them as artist, dissident, witch. And Sula does reconstruct ancient lineages through her elemental associations with death through fire and water, her ungovernable energy, and her childhood fascination with earth that she shares with Nel.

The community compellingly resurrected in the novel becomes a mythic bit in the history she would lay down. As Barbara Smith notes, Morrison "remembers and recreates our lives so extremely well" that she "constantly achieves what critic Stephen Henderson calls the 'macon' image: *a massive concentration of Black experiential energy.*" The narrator's rich lyricism provides a history and a cultural remembrance into which Nel can retrace the links that couple herself to her female complement: " 'O Lord, Sula,' she cried, 'girl, girl, girlgirlgirl.' " The cry itself makes the bond whole again, a "finding" that is also true of Morrison's authorial act: "Morrison articulates and merges the linguistic, creative, and mythic traditions within the novels of Black women that have recognized, asserted, and celebrated the powerfulness of voicing: she has given language the stature it deserves in terms of its connection to a generative force" (25).

Romantic detection is different in these women's novels from the detection in a novel like Ellison's now canonical *Invisible Man*. Whereas Ellison's hero falls into a detective mode, his quest ends in romantic disillusion rather than relational love and healing. The *Invisible Man* diverges from *The Color Purple* and *Sula* in its resolution, its community, and its hero even more fractured rather than healed. The healing Walker and Morrison seek, in contrast, is larger than that of the narrative community. This is the true romance, in a sense, because while Ellison wants to record the pain of fracture and erasure of identity, Morrison and Walker are writing into myth a cultural history with which to plug the void of lost or unrecorded stories. They take as literal the notion propounded by Clément and Cixous that women need to write themselves into myth and their stories into history. *The Color Purple*, for instance, produces a vernacular mythology, a folk bible that takes on Milton and his design to "explain the ways of God to man." And in *Sula*, Morrison paints a landscape of a forgotten neighborhood,

> where on quiet days people in valley houses could hear singing sometimes, banjos sometimes, and, if a valley man happened to have business up in those hills—collecting rent or insurance payments—he might see a dark woman in a flowered dress doing a bit of cakewalk, a bit of black bottom, a bit of "messing around" to the lively notes of a mouth organ. (4)

Recuperating these long-gone communities, as Walker writes in *In Search of Our Mothers' Gardens*, is more than an act of archeological remembrance. It is a reconstitution of self *as* community, self allegorizing community, women finding themselves and their families through each other, women "remember[ing] the days when we were two throats and one eye and we had no price" (*Sula*, 147): "I don't recall the exact moment I set out to explore the works of black women, mainly those in the past" (*Mothers' Gardens*, 9).

Gerda Lerner points out in her recent *The Creation of Feminist Consciousness* that all women in Western culture suffer from a loss of history because under patriarchy women's experience has no cultural or political significance; women thus live in a continuous present, "ignorant of their history." Walker discovers in her mother's garden ways in which to remember or reconstruct women's history when it is not recorded; Lerner demonstrates how hard that recuperation is even when written records are left. Part of women's subordination is their sublation to history, both Walker and Lerner argue. But Lerner views the reconstitution of women's history *through* history as the repeated reinvention of a feminist consciousness that does not know its prior incarnations. Walker, on the other hand, believes that the continuity of women's experience was known in the sense of communal experience, woman to woman, and that it is this that we need to retrace *as* history. Morrison also believes that a woman's great handicap is her need to invent herself, as both Sula and Nel must do, and that on a larger level this self-invention must take place as a cultural one. She takes on this historicizing task most explicitly in her two latest novels, *Beloved* and *Jazz*. However, her restorative project is closer to what Clément and Cixous argue for than to Lerner or Walker in that her novels weave a mythos out of the fragmented bits of past consciousness; this mythos is not a historical restoration but a substitution for (white male) history itself.

Morrison's novels reveal that it is not just women at large who have lost their history, as Lerner argues, but the entire black community. In Morrison's worldview, communal history as myth brings the woman back to herself: if she were further fragmented by being cut out of her whole experience and pasted into a framework of the female only, the resultant myth would heal no one. It is the whole that must be brought back, with women portrayed in all of their potent power and abilities as well as their weaknesses, and portrayed in relation to their men. This is the black romance, its mythos made possible only through the detective work of the recuperative imagination. And on a smaller level, it is equally dependent on the detective work of the self-inventing black woman who must learn to love herself.

In African-American women's novels the black romance is made possible through detection, and as stated above, detection derives from the quest, which is the true romance formulation. But romance implies narrative and a departure from history; it can take in romantic love and pacification of the heroine. When we switch the orders of importance to make detection the primary device and romance the underlying form, and when the author is determined to keep the heroine active against the forces that attempt to pacify her, we have the feminist detective novel. This genre is a form of romance narrative that exploits the dark terrors of the gothic while undermining its patriarchal strength. In this regard, the feminist detective novel bears a close resemblance to Austen's novels while replicating Morrison's heroines' need to invent an active and powerful self.

Sara Paretsky is one of several contemporary feminist detective novelists who are enjoying a growing popularity. Paretsky's novels feature a smart, hard-talking woman detective who is at the same time courageous, sensitive, and deeply moral. These traits mark her heroine, V. I. Warshawski, as having deep affinities to Austen's Elizabeth Bennet and Morrison's Sula; these characters are also similar in their self-confidence and independence, their intolerance for hysterics, and their sense of social responsibility. Their closest character trait is their perceptive wit. Book reviewers tend to praise Paretsky's novels according to how close her heroine comes to the grittiness of a Philip Marlowe; in focusing on the tough independence and street-smart cynicism of Warshawski, they ignore the close relation between Marlowe or Sam Spade and literary heroes of the Romantic period, such as Austen's Mr. Darcy. Darcy is of higher class than Marlowe or Spade, but he is also a good detective, locating Elizabeth's eloped sister where she has been hidden away in London; and Marlowe is secretly a gentleman, although he tries to hide it as much as Darcy hides his ability to detect. Marlowe is simply romantic, and like Darcy, is a gentleman parading as a Byronic hero.[8] In the formula Edgar Allan Poe lays down for the detective archetype, the solver of criminal puzzles is a fallen aristocrat who maintains his idleness by attentively "reading" the superficial clues available to him. His detached superiority, the hallmark of a Byronic hero, is supported by the apparent passivity of his detection, even though mentally he has to first project himself into the mind of another before he can accurately read the clues.[9] Although Spade is a man of action, he does maintain a passivity of emotion and response that shows his superior affinities. But Paretsky's heroine is less a spinoff of Hammett's Spade or Chandler's Marlowe than she is directly descended from Austen's spirited Elizabeth, and in this the reviewers are off the mark. She is a captivating heroine not because of a hard-boiled stubbornness, but because she is actively alive and assertively independent in a dispirited and corrupt world. Elizabeth Bennet's world is dispiriting and patriarchally corrupt as well, since women can have no profession and men's estates are entailed to male heirs only (as Elizabeth's father has had to do to his estate). Warshawski and Elizabeth attract us not because they see the bleak world as bleak—as both Darcy and Spade do, in fact—but because they refuse to see the world as bleak even though they look at it straight on in the attempt to do away with self-deception. So, while Spade's tone is the cynicism typical of the Georgian dandy or Byronic hero, Warshawski cheers herself with an inelegant repartee that nevertheless reminds us of Elizabeth's exchanges with the haughty Caroline Bingley:

"I just don't understand Montgomery, though. I've worked with him before. He's not an easy guy—not much looseness there—but I've never seen him as nasty as he was to you this afternoon."
  "Must be my charm," I said lightly. "It hits some men that way." (65)

TELEVISION, WOMEN'S PLACE, AND GOTHIC HYSTERIA

It is television even more than novels like Paretsky's that has succeeded to the cultural importance nineteenth-century novels held for their audiences. Both offer escapist pleasure to the bored or tired individual in need of imaginative stimulus, and both rely on sentimental romance and detection to maintain that imaginative interest; at the same time they often also invoke an element of fantasy as a seductive draw for the reader. Romance and fantasy seduce through pacification while detection and realism offer a kind of hyper-reality that stimulates and awakens the viewer's impulses. Pooling both these directives into one tv show produces the situation comedy or sitcom. *Murphy Brown*, which has gained notoriety from Dan Quayle's attacks on it, has a place in this chapter on its own merit as a narrative about the romance of journalism, the detective work that entails, its spirited and witty heroine, and that heroine's willingness—like Elizabeth's and Warshawski's—to remain independently single.

Murphy Brown is also a vehicle for combining the pacifying *and* activating effects of fantasy and detection. There are two possible outcomes produced in the combination: either an alternation of active and passive, or a cancellation of each by the other. In the later case, which is the outcome typical of most sitcoms, the result can either produce a self-conscious artifice that unwittingly approaches farce, or it can produce a parodic commentary on reality. The show *Murphy Brown* achieves the later effect of parodic commentary, making Dan Quayle's literalization of it doubly ironic since literalization is most effective and most easily so with the fantasy genre. That it is parody rather than detection is obvious from the invisibility of any actual detective work by reporters for their stories, or in any real import being put on their work other than for comedic underscores. That it parodies reality is apparent in its occasional borrowings from the romantic love mode, as in Murphy's sentimental singing of "A Natural Woman" when her son is born, a song chosen to appease the shows' critics and to undermine her professional personality with a clue of her "real" longings for femininity. When the show later portrays Murphy as incapable of grasping the purpose of nursery songs (she sings to the baby of Watergate instead), her character is again on track but the slip reveals the show's ties to sentimental romance. Nonetheless, Murphy's position as a highly rated journalist and her character as an outspoken and self-reliant professional attest to the nonromantic detection she is supposed to do and thus ally her with Austen's energizing and self-determining heroines. In fact, Murphy already knows who she is, her worth, and her potential worth: she is already the product of detection as identity quest, the "me" that Austen's and Morrison's heroines seek.

At the same time, her professional identity overwhelms and undercuts her personal life to the same degree that Warshawski's does; in this the two female heroes are distinctly differentiated form Austen's heroines whose domestic lives overwhelm and obviate the possibility of any overtly public life. These female heroes' similarity lies in how each character uses the same personality traits to position herself powerfully in relation to her world, traits that flirt with romance and detection and thus situate them seductively between action and passivity. This is the very quality by which the romantic or Byronic hero seduces us, but by transposing this seduction onto the female character, Austen and her heirs have recovered the spirited heroine from the simple fate of marrying well, and given her instead a mind and heart we actively want to live for ourselves. Flirtatious seduction is a dangerous device, however, with which to ward off the wrong reader/viewer and entice the desired one. In the wrong hands, such as Dean Briggs's and other conduct-book writers', flirtation can be reconstrued by literalizing the author and characters. Briggs literalizes Austen by holding her up as a proper feminine model for women readers; Dan Quayle literalizes Candice Bergen's rendition of Murphy Brown by attacking her as an improper feminine model for women viewers. The only authority either man possesses for his tropological argument about femininity itself, which is neither literature nor politics, is their dismissal of flirtation as a politically effective device *in the realm of the real*. It is only by turning women's literature into the literal that these men can dismiss it as either natural (Austen's style) or unnatural (Murphy's "style").

Literalization turns women's texts into female bodies, and female bodies do indeed fall into the realm of pedagogy and politics, of the behavioral and the governable. What our rhetorical analysis reveals is that the text that interactively engages women readers threatens the hegemonically illiberal mind, which reacts either by quashing or revising the text. It is not surprising to read Briggs's declaration that "[t]he feminine mind, with its quick intuitions and unsteady logic, may keep the intuitions and gain a firmness" when "improved into a judicious solidity" by education. Indeed, the educative male is doubly repaid since the "emotional mind has its charm, especially if its emotions are favorable to ourselves" ("To College Girls," 89).

Murphy Brown's emotions, however, are defiantly not those "favorable to ourselves." Although Dan Quayle insists that what scandalizes him about the character "Murphy Brown" is her single motherhood as "just another lifestyle choice," it is probably more accurate to say that he is scandalized by what Morrison's Nel calls "me-ness": the valuing of female self over male other. Murphy's me-ness consists of her sense of self-worth, comically exaggerated and parodied but not undercut in the show. As a professional, she sees no difference between herself and a man because her professionalism (for her) transcends gender difference. She does not cross-dress, smoke cigars, or talk dirty because she is not switching genders; she crosses gender lines, and does so in a way that frightens literalists like Quayle. Gender transgression breaks conduct-book thinking and forces tropes like literalization to be put into place as a way to stop the fractures. Literalization is the dark underside of comic exaggeration, making the transgression visible but also falsely highlighted so that it looks eerily inhuman, horribly selfish, or insanely mad.

Another, and a seemingly very different kind of, television show, *The Frugal Gourmet*, has provoked the same response for similarly transgressive behavior. This show is an instructional series that derives its popularity from an exploitation of hysteria through an abrupt energy and fragmented sentences, and an exploitation of Seattle pop through cuisine as multiculturalism. Although cooking shows are traditionally oriented toward women viewers, Chef Jeff Smith's acculturation of the socially feminine traits of hysteria and tolerance produces in one woman critic a socially masculine response whereby she calls literalization into play in order to read Smith's tongue-in-cheek hysteria as hystericization and his tolerance as hypocritical intolerance.

What so scandalizes Barbara Harrison, writing for *Harper's Magazine*, is Smith's appropriation of women's place, feminine affects, and female morality: he is an emotional cross-dresser who, unlike Murphy Brown, transgresses for profitable appeal rather than the expression of me-ness. Harrison's strategy is both to fully hystericize Smith and at the same time to portray his television show as a hypocritical attempt at romancing the gullible woman. This twofold attack is more sophisticated than Quayle's simple literalization because it accuses Smith of being both self-conscious in his deceitful appropriation of the place belonging properly to Julia Child, and of being unconsciously taken over by this cross-dressing which he can no longer control. Harrison's simultaneous use of literalization and hystericization reveals Smith to be a fool and a conman, treacherous and childishly self-deceived at the same time.

Jeff Smith is invested neither in sentimental romance nor in detection; it is the critic Harrison who accuses Smith of romancing the female viewer, and who uses detection as a critical genre for rereading the symbolism of Smith's self-presentation into a larger "p.c." conspiracy. Harrison begins her trial with a personal memory which effectively feminizes Smith through appositive thinking. In her article "P.C. on the Grill: The Frugal Gourmet, lambasted and skewered," Harrison writes:

In junior high school I knew a girl who, upon drinking her first pint of Southern Comfort, pressed her fingers to her pursed lips, applied them to her cheeks, and: *I Love (kiss, kiss) Myself.* . . . Nowadays you don't have to get drunk to do that. . . . If you're terribly, terribly sincere and muzzily user-friendly, and have intellectual pretensions and the gift of over-simplified gab, you get to go on PBS with your message of Self- and Universal Love, joining the ranks of Loving Leo Buscaglia, Sam-the-Man Keen, and dreadful John Bradshaw, tutor to those . . . who need to talk to and (kiss, kiss) love their neglected Inner Child, also their Inner Toddler. (42)

The virulence of this opening passage responds to the feminizing threat of sentimentalism, self-help groups, and shows promoting political correctness. But Harrison's proof against Smith is the "me-ness" she finds in a drunken centeredness: Smith's self-presentation is like drunken self-love, addictive self-centeredness, hysterical selfishness. Harrison has presumably read her Ann Douglas (*The Feminization of American Culture*), and understands the seduction of sentimentalism as hypocritical in its modern self-conscious instance.[10] The very invocation of a virulent feminization reminds us that, as Douglas argues and Dean Briggs attests, many believed a degenerate morality was spread in nineteenth-century America by effeminate ministers. Smith, the ex-minister, hysterically energetic and driven, puts on a show with devastating implications for American culture according to Harrison. What is true of its spiritual leaders must inevitably infect the entire nation.

Hysteria infects when it becomes a bodily mode of speaking when the tongue is blocked from saying what is deeply true. That which is not said is usually an illicit desire, which Harrison determines in Smith's case to be an effeminacy overlying more serious and abhorrent urges. Harrison's essay attempts to cure or dispel Smith's witchery by using the readerly contract to command our acceptance of her interpretation of Smith's performance as literal. Rhetorically, she employs talk in the same hysterical way she herself accuses Gloria Steinem, Oprah Winfrey, and Jeff Smith of doing. Making frequent use of textual marks such as exclamation points, one-sentence paragraphs, italics, parentheses, capitalizations, and scare marks, Harrison whisks at dizzying speed through her tirade: "And if you do—always provided that you eschew 'elitism' and forbear making distinctions or (God forbid!) judgments—you might even get to talk to the Muppets! Imagine! The bliss of pitching speech and making nice to inanimate fuzzy things!"

Harrison's own frenzy is not contained in emphatics, and she elaborates her meaning by shaping her response to what so repels her about Jeff Smith—his preaching PC-ism while he cooks—through the hysterical body which produces the text:

> To be frugal, " . . . means that you use everything and are careful with your time as well as with your food products" . . . an unexceptional culinary goal, except that he cooks so many dishes on any one frenetic TV show—more loaves of bread than you might reasonably expect to have time to prepare in a month, pasta enough to have fed the entire Italian resistance, if somewhat incoherently—you want to send out for a purgative. (42)

The venom in this passage is literally that, for Harrison has literalized Smith's entertainment as a nurturance she finds poisonous. She not only imagines actually cooking the dishes Smith provides as spectacle—which is the way most viewers understand the intent—but eating them as well. Her vocabulary reflects the understandable effect of her taste-treat: she becomes voracious, bulimic, incoherent, in need of purging. Her visual experience literalizes into a comprehensively sensual act of eating and what she eats makes her bodily sick, hysterical. At the end of her lengthy essay she seems cured but empty: "How starved we are." The talking cure, with its hysterical hostility aimed directly at the physician, presumably surmounts the impasse, but not until Smith has been viciously dissected and dismissed atom by atom:

> He wears a dangling talisman, a three-hundred-year-old jade fish, around his neck. . . . He has an awful lot of facial hair (a grizzly beard that joins forces with a full mustache, some of which must surely find its way into the cock-a-leekie) and a kind of halo of wiry Bride-of Frankenstein hair on his underpopulated head. A toothy grin. Hard eyes behind thick glasses. He twitches his eyebrows at lobsters, slaps and tickles tongues (not his own, which would be a mercy), caresses lamb livers, fondles kidneys; he addresses internal organs with the anthropomorphic infatuation of a Jeffrey Dahmer. (43)

The telling points here will recur shortly in a different text: the feminizing traits which insinuate that play can also be gaiety, gayness, the hypocritical halo-cum-monstrous hair, the gender of that monstrosity which is unnatural, insincere, artificed, an underpopulation which metonymically implies loss of brain cells as well as hair, miraculous eyebrows, intolerable touching, cannibalism.[11]

Cannibalism is the greatest crime, the illicit primal act that the Catholic mass reenacts transubstantially. Smith's greatest crime is the anecdote he the Methodist minister tells of Christian ritual. After his ordination, Smith's mentor told him, "Always remember that no priest should ever raise the chalice and pronounce the presence of the healing blood of the Lamb without being able to turn to the congregation and state the vintage, and state it proudly." Smith's tag, "He was right, of course," is followed by the "appall[ed]" Harrison's "He was wrong, of course." The cannibalism which sits behind this telling of an anecdote, the Jeffrey Dahmerism, reveals itself as the unsayable something that gagged Harrison so that she could only make meaning of her hysterical disgust (or "appallingly bad taste") by virtue of hystericized discourse. The conflict is over religion, the aversion a protestation of the Protestant reading of the miracle of the body of Christ: it is symbolically rendered into blood but physically unchanged, a metaphorizing of the Catholic sacrament in which one literally drinks the blood of Christ. Harrison reads Smith's mannered preachiness as yet another perversion of Christian belief: political correctness as religion. By a series of apposite phrases, Smith becomes shamanized, bestialized, feminized, perverted. Egregiously, Smith preaches a theology Harrison cannot accept ("This is the kind of theologian he is: Theology means that you admit you are dependent on something outside yourself") because theology is a discipline not a belief. The loose acquaintance of words on a "show" which features cooking, tasting, touching, slapping, fondling, reduces Harrison to vitriol.

Harrison sees her interpretive act as crucial for ferreting out hypocrisy in the postmodern, multicultural world of "intellectual" popular culture, a culture the highly educated yet pragmatic Smith represents. However, when Harrison takes for herself the literalization and conspiratorial thinking that are normally read *into* and *onto* art and popular entertainment forms, she hystericizes herself even more than does Oliver Stone in his hystericizing tactics in *JFK*. However, her obsession with eating, literalized as ritual eating or cannibalism—the most bodily of acts—is better compared to Peter Greenaway's *The Cook, The Thief, His Wife and Her Lover* (1991).

Greenaway's film is literally about cooking and eating, proper food preparation and improper consumption. But its larger significance is allegorical: *The Cook* is a gothic film that does not pretend to be anything but allegory, its metaphors literalizing social criticism into concrete details so visually awful as to evoke Dante's *Inferno*. The metonymies Dante uses between acts of vice and acts of the body become part of the Thief's world order. Every act of violence the Thief perpetrates exudes from his own inner corruption, and every act is aimed at forcing others into a social contract with him that signs over their legal and social rights to him. When he stabs a woman in the cheek with his fork for having told him of his wife's adultery, the woman becomes disposable like food; when his gang strips and beats a restaurateur and forces dung into his mouth for refusing to make a contract, the Thief tells this man that his food is excrement. The

Thief demands that each person "sign" his verbal contract at the same time that he marks each signer as disposable either through humiliation, disfigurement, or murder.

The Thief's tyranny mocks civilized society, yet he spends his time acquiring culture and buying beauty: tyrants know that cultural capital—high culture, the fine arts, sophistication —becomes as important as actual money in order to keep subjects under their bond. But this tyrant believes he is enriched by the cultural capital he takes into his mouth or counts as a bodily possession. Objects and people are literalizable as the significance or lack of value that he sees in them. Similarly, he cannot differentiate acts that he sees as variations of the same essential behavior: sex from bodily function from eating. His world is entirely metonymous, and its imagistic connectedness enrages and disgusts as much as it pleases and empowers him.

The allegory *The Cook, The Thief, His Wife and Her Lover* tells is a gothic one because its courageous heroine, the Wife, is tangibly losing a battle with her dangerously infantile thief-husband over her dignity and strength of character. Childish, the Thief is also the patriarchal gothic villain, the powerful man who enforces the illogic of gothic fantasy. As patriarch, the Thief turns the Cook's restaurant into his private castle into which he spreads his personal contagion. This gothic is a fantastic story in which the romance that takes place between the Wife and the Lover, both educated connoisseurs, acts out a moral rescue of culture against tyranny and debasement. In this sense it ironically responds to Harrison's reading of *The Frugal Gourmet*. But it is also the Wife's dreamed-of rescue with a lover-hero bold enough to take on the Thief. That her rescue fails and the Lover is killed turns the gothic into reality: ideal love is not as strong as evil, cultural capital is not the same as power. Her revenge on her villain husband is to realize his metonymic literalities by having the Cook prepare the Lover's body for a ritual feast in which the Thief is the only diner and his dinner one bite of the Lover's body. That he refuses to eat the bite she specifies—of the penis—reveals his own phallic loss and his sick infertility at the same time.

While it is characteristic of the gothic that the confrontation between the villain and lover should be formally over the heroine but actually about a phallic struggle, it is not characteristic that the heroine should realize the penis as life but the phallus as death. Peter Greenaway's disturbing vision uses literalization to deromanticize both the gothic and detection; his visual metaphors are literally gut-wrenching, disgusting in such a pure rendering of socialized illness that we are activated. The heroine's strength reaches us because unlike any other strong character, including the sage Cook, she withstands the Thief and his illness and cures the world of his taint. The illness is clearly, unmysteriously phallic in this film and not hysterical; the disorder involves no gender transgressions or effeminacies, but simply the sexual perversions born of power and lust. Greenaway's answer to phallic madness is the woman's strength of mind and knowledge of self. The cannibalism that so tortures Harrison's imagination becomes the antidote to evil. In this Greenaway resembles Austen, who also finds the heroine's strength to be the curative for disordered relations.

CONSPIRACY PLOTS AND THE DEATH OF THE SUBJECT

Both Harrison's and Greenaway's readings of contemporary society incur a paranoia in response to the postmodern world. Oliver Stone's *JFK* (1991), another postmodern work, is perhaps more deeply paranoid, finding the locus for its fear in a complex conspiracy theory. Anxiety propels reading into paranoid misreading, and into conspiracy theories of national proportion. These texts assume something of the national character in the present age, writing into history a cultural identity. This identity clearly writes out of history woman's place on the scene: *JFK* renders the heroic quest of one man whose detection will avenge his president and alienate his wife. His wife, and any woman, is unnecessary to the script because gender crosses over into other forms: homosexuals, hysteria, conspiracy. The salvaged national character is clearly defined as straight-white-male in order to reduce the conflicting and too-numerous stories being told: Stone discovers that under liberalism, persuasion can compel the individual beyond consent into blindness because "no" is the only restrictor on non-verbalized contracting. If resistance defines the individual as not effeminized, then hysteria as a structure in the masculine turn of mind can be disavowed and doubly reconfigured as feminine: the hysterical hero is thus reconfirmed as being undeniably masculine in an increasingly domesticized, feminized, and nonheroic world. Oliver Stone finds the Hollywood epic the ideal ground for a reification of hysteria as the only thing left once the subject has been murdered.

JFK inverts fact and fiction, manufacturing footage to simulate period newsreel clips, and presenting the clips as "real." This manufacture of the real creates a differential reality in which it is possible to believe that the CIA conspiracy factualized in the film by docudrama technique is a more realistic portrayal of the presidential assassination than any other explanation provided. Hysteria allows the literary to transcend its nature and become the literal truth. The heavy tomes of the Warren Commission, with all their concrete detail, explain nothing but the conspicuous absence of an intolerable, conspiratorial presence. Stone's vision, to decode the top secret message hidden in the CIA archives, parlays conspiracy theory onto screen memory, and as he clearly hopes, into history.

Stone's hysteria turns Kennedy the man into "JFK," a docu-figure too idealized to interrogate. He becomes body and then symbol in a perfect metonymy of body royal and body politic. And like Louis XVI, beheaded precisely because his person embodied the symbolic source of his power, JFK is also beheaded as a mob-like crowd watches. The film's fascination with this moment of being headless makes us feel that we, too, are not in our right mind. Stone's hystericized text inscribes on the body the unsavable: the possibility that kings can die by the hands of those sworn to protect the state.

Stone is an epical director, locating historical cruxes in military and consumer warfare and revealing the deep paranoia of those moments. Each crux represents a historical moment when the national character is in crisis and our culture at stake. In *Platoon*, *Wall Street*, and *The Doors*, Stone psychodramatizes how character warps in the crush of historical forces, how man makes war on man and thus on himself. Stone violently misreads apocalytic texts to show the darkness of the psyche in a hystericized, fragmented, disoriented present tense. His project differs from Morrison's enculturating texts because he seeks to redramatize a history already fully encoded, and he does so in order to further silence alternative stories rather than to empower them. Stone's revision is that the Kennedy assassination crystallizes a historical crux in which heterosexual and homosexual cultures vie for power; by killing the one true man, the conspirators effactually feminize the nation.

JFK uses family values and "an abstinent hero" against feminizing and effeminate agents in order to produce an "image of the son . . . [as] the true son" (Grundmann, 21). Garrison, "the emotionally stable, interrogating patriarch whose fertility and potency are paralleled with that of Kennedy," is the avenging son of Kennedy in a way the president's young namesake cannot be (20–21). The question of the true son, of legitimacy, becomes entangled with the question of the true or truthful self in a fatherless state, and both problems are "resolved" and made history through oppositions with homosexuality.

The gay threat that *JFK* reveals is that of the murderous self as the false son. Homosexuality threatens heterosexuality as a problem of fathering and generation: homosexuality blocks the genealogy because it literally cannot father. Viewed from the perspective of the state, homosexuality blocks the "natural order" and the reproduction of the state. Viewed from the place of heterosexuality, homosexuality is an internal otherness, a self that is not self, a maleness that acts out as not-maleness, an other that is not enough other for safety. Homosexuality becomes the site of hysteria in *JFK*, the body on which to displace fears about being "the true son," and about the integrity of the state. When Willie O'Keefe explains to Garrison, "You don't know what the world is like because you ain't never been fucked in the ass," he produces a homosexual perspective that unravels the film's straight fears of submission and inversion. O'Keefe's message cannot be integrated with Garrison's true mission despite its truth-revealing perspective because of the nature of the speaker. For Roy Grundmann and Cynthia

Lucia, Stone's homophobe story produces O'Keefe as perversion, "making him a cryptofascist, a KKK wannabe" (21). They also criticize Stone's projection of hysteria onto gayness, writing that "*JFK*'s dichotomous imagery places homosexuals on trial, associating them with artifice and deception and pitting them against 'the real' " (20). Because this description is so obviously also the stereotyped treatment of women as scapegoats in literature, the male focus of the film becomes clear: war is a man's story, conspiracy domesticizes war, domestication feminizes war. War's homosexualization aids presidential murder, the film implies, and provokes the death of the Father by transgressing his laws. The prosecuting hero, whose own nuclear family provides the film's normalizing backdrop, represents generative history as ongoing despite the hysterical blockage to history-making that homosexual conspiracy represents. Garrison's insistence that the murder was a coup d'état produces a way to read the history of the clandestine state as a deliberate undermining of "the very notion of constituency-based, representative democracy" (Sharrett, 11). Conspiracy theory sorts out blindsiding proclamations from facts that do not fit, in order to produce a theory that does. It allows a way to reintegrate the shattered body and restore it to its predestined mythic power.

To emphasize the importance of such a quest, the film obsessively returns to the body which has been perverted, castrated, and fetishized. Such obsessive seeing signals that while the viewer's attention is directed one way, something else is not being regarded. Hysteria is the turning away of the disgusted subject from an untellable want: pleasure as a driving force is never far from disgust, whose excess produces an unspeakable regression caused by improper love.[12] Thus Stone's film, which synecdochally speaks *JFK* for JFK, ideal ego for man, film for history, turns its face/gaze from the mutilated head of the ideal's corpse to explain what has gone awry in 1990s politics. Like Quayle and Harrison, Stone's answer is an effeminizing something, and the displacement of a conspiratorial "politically correct" for the presidential "true."

What the film *JFK* turns to in its disgust is the conspiracy within conspiracy that plots homosocial, homoerotic, and homosexual with the pressure to save the national face in the Cuban crisis. By using disaffected and disreputable "Ferries" to carry out a fake assassination, disposable nonmen would throw suspicion on Cuba and protect the insider conspirators at the same time. The masterplot folds in on itself, crumples like the president's body. Their mutual death expresses Stone's conviction that evil walks the streets in real time, our time. What is it we have not seen, what has been manipulated so that we see something other than the thing itself? This question revises romantic fantasy into postmodern hallucination.

Hallucination, the hallmark of hysteria, raises questions of identity, of who has the right to speak and to speak for, of who has primacy and who dissents from that ordering. William Connolly argues that within the constitution of identity, social forces pressure us to organize our dispositions into "entrenched" or normalizing contingencies—those dispositions which become the grounds of our identification through accidents of birth, history, region, race, and which therefore become "natural" and necessary to our self-making—and the dispositions which sediment out of the normalizing process and which are then "purged" (Connolly, 158–97). Entrenched contingencies allow us to impose a "reflective genealogy" on our family tree so that what we consolidate in our sense of self and of nation a normative history (this is how it's always been) that represses alternative formations as unnatural, perverted, threatening, other. By the very nature of individual contingency, however, several contending disposition clusters organize themselves as natural and inherent; at any given time in cultural history, a set of identities contend for hegemonic control, each claiming to be the only real identity (e.g., male-white-hetero-Protestant-Republican). To claim the real means imposing a rightness, a righteousness, on the disposition cluster supported as the one true identity; this is only achievable by claiming at the same time an ethical purity in this cultural identity choice. Connolly sees this part of the process as generating the purging of difference:

> it calls upon you to purge any such dispositions lingering in yourself and to support the treatment or punishment of others who manifest them more robustly. This demand grounds your sexual ethic in the self-idealization of a contingent, relational identity that takes itself to be natural and independent. (177)

But the constitution of such a self as primary necessarily produces a state politically constituted on the same normative model. The liberal state constitutes the social order as masculine and writes its history to corroborate that claim; the individual identity situates itself within that claim as an "objective" and "rational" proof of its literal existence; "rationality is measured by point-of-viewlessness, what counts as reason is that which corresponds to the way things are" (162). This statement accurately describes Dan Quayle's authority as cultural critic. In the repression of dispositions too different from the normative constellation of the ideal individual, differential identity becomes a distinctly gendered affair.

Where contemporary critics derive their hysterical pronouncements of disintegration of cultural and personal identity is in the double act of installing ethical purity and purging difference: what is not the same as me threatens me when it returns as the repressed. Because the postmodern aesthetic is devoted to exploring the nature of alienation and to identifying the repressed (devoted, that is, to dissent), it threatens the normative identity or disposition cluster and thus incurs a hysteria that will effect the purge. We can see the process of purge in this chapter from Austen and Freud to Harrison and Stone, and the deep impact of ethicization on dissenting disposition clusters. But what has not yet been clarified is the relation of hysteria to the nature of political correctness. Why are both formulations of political correctness not coterminous? Connolly's theory of identity constitution allows for a way to see contending policies of ethicization as both normalizing and purging even while mutually exclusive. Jeff Smith's "Frugal Gourmet" is an oxymoron that sets off his embrace and condemnation of social attitudes and norms with which he catechizes the viewer; it finds it counterpart in Barbara Harrison's alternate set of correct social attitudes and norms with which she condemns Smith. Both "shows" are, as Connolly might say, a "closure of identities in response to the fragility of things . . . an intensification and territorial extension of pressures for normalization" (172). Both correct incorrect personal polity, but both would/do see the other as dissent, perversion, illness.

THE ME-NESS IN POST-POSTFEMINISM

No author discussed so far answers illness and dissent as well as does Austen, yet she writes of class snobbery, perverse characters, manipulation, and hysterics. What holds her world together is the authorial belief that self and other can dissolve difference through marital synthesis, producing a new, healthier world order. Stone's paranoid world demands to be answered by a modern Austen who cannot be misread by her charm. The Austen bill requires a taste of romance, a heroine coming to know herself, and a mutual regard that undercuts the purging normalization of being "correct." Patricia Rozema's *I've Heard the Mermaids Singing* (1987) offers something like a talking cure for Stone's and Harrison's hysterical malaise. The protagonist, a self-described "gal on the go," tells her story to a videocamera she has brought home without permission from the workplace. Seated in front of the autonomous camera eye, Polly confesses her life and hopes to the unediting tape. Rozema's film continually plays with this difference in authority and medium: When is she narrating and when has she departed into daydreams? When is it film we are watching and when the confessional video? Can she see us as we watch her—and if not, then why does she play with us as if she could?

The games are suggestive but not titillating, her daydreams and narrative wondrous and wondering but not suspicious or conspiratorial. In fact, the film does contain a literal, plotted conspiracy in which lesbian lovers attempt to deceive the art world, but the conspiracy is not paranoid, only the way out of an infelicity. The lovers become, in their conspiracy, mermaids, sirens whose seductive talk and creative genius compel Polly's love, attention, and curiosity. But the dream is unhealthy and in fact the lovers only mirror the mermaid figure, and ultimately drown in the conspiracy they have created. The real mermaids for Polly are voices and emanations derived form the Wagner she plays at night which impel her into dreams and their self-completing adventure. It is Polly herself who is finally the natural (if not great) artist, Baudelaire's post-albatross who is gracefully aflight in imagination but clumsy on land.

The making of art as a self-affirming activity independent of desire marks the divide between art and life in the narrative. Polly learns to admire, emulate, and desire the Curator in the art gallery, the place of spectatorship and exhibition. The Curator, Gabrielle, reproduces herself in this publicly private space as both worldly and archly otherworld-like. Gabrielle and her lover Mary meet in this space where Polly can watch them and we can watch her watch, but the Curator remains a public figure, entering the private only through Polly's dreams about her. In Polly's one attempt to introduce Gabrielle to her own private world by showing her previously unshared photographs, the Curator's unfeeling dismissal of the "anonymous" works mutilates Polly's self-respect. This places her where the private must collapse in on itself, as in Catherine Morland's humiliation at Henry's debunking critique of her imaginings in Austen's *Northanger Abbey*. But like Catherine, the castrating act only pulls Polly closer to Gabrielle as she seeks to find what is lacking—a better art than what she had.

Where *JFK* makes a practice of its turning away, this film becomes an incessant turning *to*; because the desire Polly experiences lacks vocabulary and authority, she must watch and learn from those who clearly seem to know. There is disgust but no turning aside—the gaze is frank, admiring, unresistant, and unfrenzied. This is a film of acceptance, and of the wondering self: the feminist Romantic artist and her self-discovery. The contrast is with the cultural elite, the Curator and her art world: they are wordy, spouting jargon that ensnares Polly with its incomprehensibility. Their language is hystericized because the unsayable—the desire to be the great genius, the original artist—reveals the elite as mundane, pathetic, pitiable. But if the Curator is disgusted with her inability to make art, she is not disgusting. Polly's only participation in anger or rebuttal at anything other than her own lack comes when she realizes how the Curator's superficial values have hurt her. What she had tried to edge in on, befriend, even haltingly emulate, was an insincerity that betrayed her for no reason. Despite this, the lover, Mary, understands Polly as the Curator never will because she is the unemulatable great artist of the story whose work the narrative can only represent symbolically as light.

The most obvious aspects of the film seem ripe for derision: the conventions of Romantic artist, the conceited art connoisseur, the superficial and hypocritical elite. The ironic contrasts involved might place *I've Heard the Mermaids Singing* in line with those fighting the entitlement and elitism of the politically correct. The right things are set up for mockery, the formula—despite innovative camera and narrative techniques—is comfortingly old, the right people get punished, and although the three main characters are single women, no one gets pregnant. But the Right would not be comforted by this dehystericizing film because it is a narrative about the love of women, the bonds they sketch out between them through different imaginary levels of loss and gain, mermaids singing. The mermaids are not Wagner's after all, but these three women—Polly, the Curator, and Mary—who sing each other into relation and into health *despite* the losses each of the three suffers. The film sings against postfeminism by recuperating Romanticism's destabilizing questions of individual relations without comforting the viewer with a marriage settlement. Polly's romance was to effect change in others while confirming the importance of her art to her self; where her art represents moments of freedom in relation (a child jumping high, electric wires stretched across a cityscape), the film refuses to resolve that dance into mirrors or refractions. Post-postfeminist, it opens up the dance to asymmetries and exploration not subservient to the hystericizing function of social control exhibited in reactionary postfeminism and propagated in Hollywood's fantasies produced for women's consumption.

What hystericized the other texts discussed here is precisely what cures in Rozema's film: millennium angst over the fate of the national character in the twenty-first century. This tremendous millennium-dread causes outrageous social panic when the calendar turned one thousand into two, and historians have long predicted that we are only slightly less available to end-of-the-world thinking than our ancestors were. Conspiracy is only one way to trope this fear; weakened nation through feminizing agents is another. *Mermaids* bulwarks us against this reading by playing with the different levels of consciousness and affection as alternatives to the mundane world. Such a Romantic reading of disaffected life willingly revives the romance Austen tried to write out of her texts, because the war of domesticization is best fought on Stone's dark ground of intrigue and patricide. Romance is not bad in itself, Polly might tell the videocam: mermaids are half women and half fish, but it is men's lore that makes them monstrous. In truth, their doubleness means they are at home in two different elements, that they are each their own otherness, and that each is an artist-poet. This mutual regard is presented in the film's conclusion by a combined narrative/fantasy scene in which the videocam turns off and we are left to an illumination that refigures the unrepresentable brilliance of Mary's paintings. The Curator and Mary come for their first visit to Polly's home and enter her space; suddenly she is legitimized as self-identificatory in their eyes because she is no longer defined by their space and their norms. The photographs on her "gallery" walls engage them, but Polly diverts them from these images through a door to an imagined natural exterior of lush greenery and sun where they are dazzled into wonderment. Her directive to engage this otherness in wonderment literalizes Polly's artistic role as producer, narrator, and director of her own home movie into the scriptor and director of her own story. And as in Austen, the end is left to our imaginations, but with enough information about the re-clustering of entrenched and floating dispositions to spell out for ourselves, enspell ourselves in a new generation, a generation of anti-hysterics.

Austen is, by critical consensus, a conservative writer, but she is also a revisionist of the liberal social contract; her narratives plot to protect the heroines she will contract to that order by reordering the naturalized contingencies to which they are subjected. Dan Quayle's hysterical mis-reading of family values locates the metonymy of literal/literary as a way to blindside contingency clusters as either inherent and natural or dissent-ing and perverted. Harrison's hystericized critic is the most blatant escala-tion of Quayle's rhetorical politics. Her loathing of Jeff Smith produces a reversed mirroring in which she projects what she believes she has purged from herself as unethical—hysteria, monstrosity, perversion, effeminiza-tion, fragmentation—onto another in "an uncritical imperative of moral purity and an overly developed enthusiasm for normalization" (Connolly, 177).

Stone is the most blatant expression of millennium thinking and con-spiratorial frenzy, of self-identity in crisis because the angst of millennium is the fear of the end of history—a fear that represses as the desultory boredom of progressive destination (we have arrived) and reexpresses as anxious nostalgia (if only we could go back). But for Stone it is a hysterical fear that when the truth of history can no longer be retrieved, then history itself has ceased altogether. With such fear comes the need to reconfigure even more strongly the homeostasis of the entrenched identity, but because he who was the "true man" has been shot in the head, beheaded, Stone sees a society left in splinters. With the death of the nation's father, the screen is filled with alternative narratives told by aberrant identities. Aberrant nar-ratives are not history; they are postmodern in the sense of posthistorical, postreal. And the characters who represent these contending identities reveal their ahistorical nature, their ineffectual bid to take part in the historical contract, in the way Stone invests them with excesses of libidinal energy. They are not permitted to contain "me-ness" in the way that the heroines of this chapter do: Catherine and Anne, Sula and Nel, Murphy, the Wife, V. I. Warshawski, Polly.

Me-ness dispels masculinist history just as surely as masculinist history includes women only as bodily tropes: feminized men, hystericized plots. Stone depicts the contingent dispositions that have settled out of his ideal identity which "*might still be lingering in . . . [the] self*," as infectious, as self-hystericizing. They must be "punished" in others " who manifest them *more robustly*" (Connolly, 177; emphasis added). James Snead shows that white American culture represents itself as metaphorically whole, accruing to itself by means of "collection" all cultural aberration (245): this is the melting pot as still white, male, and single-classed. Against collection African culture, for instance, represents itself literarily as "contagion," a metonymic force that invades the bodily whole of white culture; but because "contagion represents the existence of recoverable *affinities* between disparate races of people," it is a "benevolent contagion." The metonymy Snead deciphers applies to "other" literatures as well, other stories beyond that of Western history. But to hystericists anxious to preserve the bodily integrity of masculinist history, this contagion is anything but benevolent since "[p]erhaps the most important aspect of cultural contagion is that by the time one is aware of it, it has *already happened*" (245).

A contagionist herself, Rozema dissects Stonean phobias by a return to the Romantic moment via Wagner's mermaids, the Romantic lamia whose siren song seduces and terrifies so many of the early nineteenth-century male poets but which only inspires Polly to exuberance. They speak to her because she has not completely closed her identity cluster; dispositions are added and subtracted as she gains acquaintance with the world, but they are contingent rather than part of a formulated ideal ego. In an interview, Rozema explains that the film's title is a reference not to the Wagnerian soundtrack but to T. S. Eliot's "The Love Song of J. Alfred Prufrock," with Polly the inept and socially embarrassed Prufrock, the outsider who can never get "in." But Polly remodels Prufrock, since he is hindered by his insight that what is beautiful and unknowable is beyond him: "I've heard the mermaids singing each to each . . . I do not think they will sing to me." Her sight allows her to imagine what the mermaids put into song, and if what she sees is at times unrepresentable, uncapturable, she is still willing to envision it.

As an openly contingent character, Polly's vision becomes doubly important as a way of configuring her being-in-the-world in terms of her art. Thus her sight is also contingent when she creates a naive space for herself in the world as observer, artist, spectator, commentator, recorder. Her unsedimented artistry establishes itself as unfixed photos, her seeing and her sight-seeing as the true art of living. Polly sees correctly in a fundamentally feminist way which is not mannered, not heroic, and not hysterical— but open to what Connolly calls "incorrigible elements of difference, incompleteness and contingency within them" (173). Her watching reflects the incorrigibility of resistant dispositions, and as she opens herself more and more to Gabrielle and Mary Joseph—figures whose latent religious iconicity suggests a doubling and tripling of roles and gender inversions for the bedazzled heroine—Polly opens herself up like a camera eye. She begins the film in direct consultation and confession with the audience, but as she tracks the Curator through the narrative in an obsessive desire to see more of her ("watching her through windows, through cracks in doors, reflected in mirrors—always framed and at a distance, always slightly altered from 'reality' "), she opens herself up to imaginatively trying on different sexual relations without foreclosure. Polly's experimentation with watching as an art form as well as a formulation of the self recirculates the problematic of private and public in the war of domesticization that so embattles *JFK*. In Rozema's film, the domicile is the space of fabrication, both of art and of artist dreamer, but the workplace and street is the place of sexual fabrication and relation. "Family values" becomes a constellation of individual identity values in this film as adult women work through an Austen-like dance of relation and commitment which is not in relation to men. Rozema had originally scripted the Curator as male, but rewrote the character as female in order to reconstitute the authority figure as free of any "anti-masculine-authority statement" (Jaehne, 23). In shifting genders, the authorial curator of Polly's fixation is strangely marginal and ineffective, strangely unauthoritative in her world. The dance reduces and raises all participants to an equity unlooked for in Austen because unimaginable in her economy—but nonetheless predicted by her implementing of mutual regard.

The compelling aspect of *Mermaids* is its resistance to its Hollywood counterparts, "mass-produced fantasies for women" (White, 41). Mimi White characterizes recent women-centered films as romance at play, narratives which employ a new-age "both/and logic" in which heroines are both adventurous and romantically fulfilled. These delusional films, according to White, sustain "a constitutive undecideability" of the both/and which promises everything but is unrealizable because still sentimental or quest romance (*Romancing the Stone, American Dreamer, Thief of Hearts*). *I've Heard the Mermaids Singing* refuses the inevitable reducibility of female autonomy to a male-female binary, a Freudian thralldom, and so escapes the either/or constraint, but this does not free Polly of romance—nor does she want to be freed. Rozema's and Austen's achievement is not to destroy romance, but to disenchant or dispel it in favor of the heroine. Elizabeth Cowie explains that romance functions by staging desire as a "setting . . . in which we can find our places(s)" (White, 49). Narrative conventions work to organize story elements so that desire gets normalized, directed into either/or, both/and. When the characters are clearly targeted for specific places in the setting, films spell out romance in sexual terms. But when characters are free to try out different roles and positions of sexual difference, and to transgress normative assignments of place, then romance can become a way to free up subjectivity from received expectations in the liberal state. Liberalism itself may sit in that space of trying on roles without preconceived commitments to sexual and social difference, and always threatened by a sedimentation of fixity and assigned place.

The difference between being manipulated by words and our ability to use words to conceive ourselves lies in a mutual exchange in which the speakers learn from each other and grow together. This may seem simplistic except that it is difficult to achieve, a rare event in which two people agree that no one individual will lead another or master that other or talk over that over. They agree to listen attentively, to account the words of another as important, and to respond with considered words. This is what Austen and Rozema devote their texts to illustrating; this is what Harrison and Stone elide as they slip into single-perspective narratives where words have no weight. It is in the fast-paced world of hysteria that words bounce off meaning without effect, or that words cease altogether. Hysteria is necessarily the great fear of patriarchy because it can devastate the lawful order, which itself runs on a ritualized use of words. To conceive hysteria as feminine seems the cruelest joke of all, but it effectively stops women from taking a voice in the patriarchal proceedings—a step that would be necessary for the equal exchange of considered words. No wonder Austen used charms to ward off the terrible silence of hystericization, or that Rozema gives her artist, Polly, so many camera eyes to look through.

Camera eyes play a crucial role in chapter four, because in looking at the media as an arena of politically invested language use, we are also concerned with an institution in which looking becomes doubled and fictitious even as it is supposed to report the factual and true. Yet the speed with which the media can interact with all parts of the world and then with the viewer or reader is so great that the interaction possible can result in a noninteraction. The speed turns to hysteria, the information becomes hystericized, and the viewer becomes pacified and silenced.

NOTES

1. For an authoritative delineation of romance, see Frye.

2. Sherry Ortner's early article "Is Female to Male as Nature is to Culture?" draws on the basic formulation given by Simone de Beauvoir in *The Second Sex*: within patriarchal society, women are viewed as natural and outside of culture, while men are viewed as culture-makers; women are immanent while men are transcendent.

3. The quest romance is equally hystericizing to the sentimental romance; Robert Browning realizes this truth in his poem "Childe Roland to the Dark Tower Came."

4. Langbauer, 1. The reference is to Freud, "Creative Writers and Daydreaming," 9: 141–67 in *The Standard Edition*, trans. James Strachey, 24 vols. (1953–74).

5. On definitions of romance, see Clara Reeve's early *The Progress of Romance through Times, Countries, and Manners*, 2 vols. (1785); Richard Hurd, "Letters on Chivalry and Romance" (1762), ed. Hoyt Trowbride (Los Angeles: William Andrews Clark Memorial Library, 1963); Sir Walter Scott, "An Essay on Romance," in *The Miscellaneous Prose Works*, vol. vi (1827), and Frye.

6. For the argument on Austen's relation to the state as a liberal rather than conservative tradition, see Evans.

7. I use the term *black romance* to signify the project I take Afro-American women authors to be collectively engaged in. "Romance" in conjunction with writing on racial difference, as in Abdul R. JanMohamed's use of it, usually describes the project of *white* authors such as Joseph Conrad in *Heart of Darkness*. JanMohamed notes that "[r]acial romances . . . pit civilized societies against the

barbaric aberrations of an Other, and they always end with the elimination of the threat posed by the Other and the legitimation of the values of the good, civilized society." See "The Economy of Manichean Allegory: The Function of Racial Difference in Colonialist Literature," in Gates, 15–48. See also JanMohamed.

8. The Byronic hero is an early nineteenth-century literary figure drawn both from Lord Byron's narrative poems and from his own public persona. This dark, brooding man—familiar to us as Emily Brontë's Heathcliff—is characteristically a passionate man with a mysterious past and a guilty secret. He is handsome, aloof, unconcerned with mores and social conventions, and deeply seductive to women. He is closely linked to the Lucifer/Satan figure of Milton's *Paradise Lost*.

9. For an introduction to the underpinnings of classic detection, see Brand.

10. Ann Douglas's infamous execration of early American culture sets out to prove that the bedrock of our social formation was deeply tainted by women's and effeminate ministers' ministerings to the public *for* the public. That is, both groups working in tandem were meddlers in the masculinity of the social community. The relevance of this "feminist" study to Harrison's attack on p.c.-ism is that both writers view their work as restorative to the social homeostasis.

11. Jeffrey Dahmer's criminality—the seduction, murder, and preparation for cannibal "meals" of nonwhite boys in Wisconsin—is ghastly both in its literalization of the Catholic mass, and in the fact that he carried on his perversion of collective religion for more than a decade before his oddity was suspected. The evidence presented at his 1991 trial made jury members sick to their stomachs several times, in an interesting replay of Harrison's bulimic rejection of a different kind of gourmet chef.

12. See Sigmund Freud and Josef Breuer, *Studies on Hysteria*, trans. James Strachey with Anna Freud (New York: Basic Books, 1955). My understanding of this text has been greatly dilated by Monique David-Menard's *Hysteria From Freud to Lacan*, trans. Catherine Porter (Ithaca: Cornell University Press, 1989).

Chapter Four

Media Warfare: Newsmakers and Militaristic Thinking

For language being the great conduit, whereby men convey their discoveries, reasonings, and knowledge, from one to another, he that makes an ill use of it, though he does not corrupt the fountains of knowledge, which are in things themselves, yet he does, as much as in him lies, break or stop the pipes whereby it is distributed to the public use and advantage of mankind.

John Locke, 149

From the romance and detection of literature and film, we turn now to an arena that contains its own romantic seduction, and that depends upon the investigative skills and insights of tough journalists. Although the term "media" broadly refers to the medium of film, broadcasts (television, radio), and other avenues of transmission, the media as discussed in this chapter refer to the news-specific forms of newspapers, news magazines, telejournalism, news commentary shows, pundit shows, and radio news broadcasts. However, the implied references are broader: for instance, when court cases or senate hearings are broadcast, they become part of the media network in that the participants themselves succumb to spectacle through a new awareness of audience and self-presentation.

The media appear here as a broadly defined arena, then, in which language and camera images provide the principal vehicles for the provision of news which is bi-directional in its production and in the ways it encodes a particular cultural identification on the news consumer. Group identification produces identificatory thinking; the media provide a playing field for the enculturation of stereotypical identifications because their main vehicles are rhetoric and visuals used in hard-hitting and fast-hitting modes. As these adjectives suggest, news reportage is like warfare in its aggressive quality, its reliance on stereotypes, and its nose for conspiracy. Not surprisingly, warfare is a major component of news reportage, and so this chapter also includes the uses of rhetorical tropes in military thinking as part of our consideration of how rhetoric produces and channels thought. Militarism becomes important in gender analysis when we query the origins of the blatant prejudice women face in the military: clearly, once women are soldiers they can no longer be the object of rapine; clearly, once women are officers they can no longer be the justification for protectively aggressive behavior. But militarism also opens up less obvious gender queries about metaphorical interpretations of society, such as those in which attempts to reinstate male supremacy can be read by journalists like Susan Faludi as an "undeclared war against American women." Public and private violence against women, the restriction of their rights, and their subordinate social status mark women as victims of socially engendered hostilities. This aggression is received as necessary to a balance of power between the sexes; its harm to women is rhetorically silenced when reported either by referring to women's sexual prowess and insatiable desire, or by interpreting what women said they experienced as a hysterical exaggeration.

Within any facet of warfare, whether military, social, or political, one of the rhetorical ploys necessary to the essential hystericization that keeps such wars in place is appositive thinking. One of the most powerful and little-examined uses of this trope is journalism's own appositive blurring of the media's phrase "newsmaking" with the phrase "policymaking." Once the media decide as a group to focus on one particular story (say, starvation in Somalia) to the exclusion of other equally devastating stories (say, the simultaneous warfare in Bosnia), the tendency is to continue with this single focus until the White House is forced to act. The power of the media to compel political action is itself compelling when we think of journalism's supposed commitment to nonpartisan objectivity. However, even a careless observation of the gender stereotypes portrayed in the news reveals how the making of news also makes us.[1] But because the news enters into the privacy of our lives on a daily and repeated basis, its import goes deeper than just as an efficient vehicle for the deployment of a consensual code by which to depict matters as gendered. One aspect of this code has to do with the competitive nature of journalism which lends itself easily to aggressiveness and militaristic thinking. This chapter is devoted to analyzing the reasons for gendering and aggressive politics in the media, to separating out the rhetorical tropes that allow the media to construct its own nonobjective power base, and to examining the effects of gendered aggression in the media's close ally, the military.

EDITORIALIZING HEADLINES, MAKING NEWS

Although objectivity is supposed to be a prime requirement for journalism, the media nevertheless engage in ongoing attempts to make policy. This trend in media influence and self-presentation fluctuates with the administration in power: the media were strongly critical of Carter's administration and of Dukakis's campaign, and were forced to overhaul their reportage after such blatant opinion mongering. But despite this supposed change, nine days after Bill Clinton's inauguration news headlines described his presidential start as "bumbling," while news services nationwide ran polls to determine public support for Clinton's initiatives for homosexual standing in the military. Not surprisingly, the statistics showed that public support was down several points on average from his poll ratings prior to the inauguration. But rather than accepting this as a typical voter response to any controversial measure, news shows on every channel attempted to interpret this as lack of support for Clinton's programs and as evidence that his administration was off to a rocky start—bumbling, actually, as in David Nyhan's January 31, 1993 editorial, "Clinton's Stumbling, Bumbling Start."

Curiously, Nyhan's political-cum-sexual bigotry ("After the giddiest inaugural since Kennedy's thirty-two years ago, it's been one fiasco after another for Mr. Bill 'Hi-I'm-your-president-where's-the-men's-room?' Clinton") sits on the page spread next to Caryl Rivers's provocative editorial, "Year of the Woman is now Year of the Psychobitch." Nyhan attacks Clinton's masculinity, insinuating that the president's personal style of collaboration, dialogue, and compromise is effeminate, and somehow equivalent to being weak-bladdered, unable to hold it in like a man. The logic here is that a man who makes policy like a woman (listening to others, willing to compromise or to come up with group decisions) must also urinate like a woman, be otherwise ungirded, and act uncomfortably homosocial, uncomfortably gay. But Rivers's editorial precedes Nyhan's and sets a possible path for understanding the vehemence and lack of critical logic in his piece.

"Year of the Psychobitch" begins by exploring the possible reasons for *Spy* magazine's January cover: a photo of a dominatrix in leather straps and studs, with the head of Hillary Rodham Clinton pasted onto its neck. The satirical cover only repeats a cultural obsession in the 1990s with psychotic women figures. Rivers asks if there has ever been such an array of movies about psychotic women killers in film history. That a strong feminist presence in the White House comes at the same time, can only inflame the fantasy fears already being played out on screen. Two facts are illustrative: the paucity of female roles in recent films was so severe that there could be few nominations for the 1992 Oscar for best actress; the first lady's office was resituated in the West instead of the East Wing of the White House, an announcement which "caused what can only be called hysterical reaction in the media." As Rivers points out, "Let's face it, there have been some scary guys who have had the president's ear. . . . But [Hillary] Clinton seems to represent not herself, but some fearful aspect of female power. Would the press be in such an uproar if a male corporate attorney was the president's closest advisor?"

Obviously part of what is at stake here is the sexuality of the nation's "representative man." He who represents all of us to ourselves and to the world, the press implies, should be manly, a man among men with close advisers who are manly men. Rivers comments that the discrepancy between Nixon's advisers and Clinton's may be that "we tend to see men as individuals, but women as members of a group. Charles Manson and Adolf Hitler do not represent all men. But [Hillary] Clinton seems to represent not herself, but . . . female power." If Bill Clinton insists on working collaboratively, he assents to a feminized group identity that confuses the gender-defined boundaries around policy and policymaking. Bush understood the necessity of manliness, and quickly put a stop to the "spirit of collaboration" that was to transform his administration into one of bipartisan coexistence. He simultaneously took great pains to wardrobe himself in endless athletic suits, to stand strong against the bleeding-heart (read feminine) Congress, and to speak strongly about everything whether or not he really had had a chance to make up his mind. The thrust of this media-targeting was the media's attacks on candidate Bush as weak, indecisive, "bumbling." Yet his visible strength as president accomplished little domestically except popular support for his decision to enter the Gulf War, and a record-breaking use of the presidential veto against recalicitrant Democrats. If strength is what the press and the nation want, then Nixon's and Reagan's legacy of conspiratorial strength provides no roadmap to press relations. Caryl Rivers compares conspiracy to straightforward policymaking and sees only perverse success: Nixon's men helped him achieve "disgrace and near impeachment, and Ollie North and crew dreamed up the neat idea of [Iran Contra] . . . it's [Hillary] Clinton—who wants to help kids and reform health care—who gets cast as the psychobitch" (Rivers, 68).

And there is another insidious aspect to all of this. Pundits are obsessed with the horror of conspiratorial pillowtalk and undue influence in the Clinton bedroom, but this was never a concern with the Bush administration. Bush was strong because Barbara Bush appeared so weak, so unable to comprehend the enormity of her husband's job. The Bushes' pillowtalk could not possibly, it seems, have taken in the day's events, controversial decisions, or the CIA. That Mrs. Bush was finally revealed during the campaign for reelection to be forceful, ideological, and politically astute seemed to disturb no one since she had been silent for so long. Their literal pillowtalk continued without worry from the press over undue influence; indeed, Bush's ratings increased as the public perceived Mrs. Bush's influence at work during a critical year for the Republican party. Yet one of the gravest charges against the Clintons is that Hillary Rodham will have undue influence with her husband; the insinuation is that only she will have his ear during the night, and that pillowtalk is notoriously the most influential of all talk. A rumor was discussed on the *Joan Rivers Gossip* show in January 1993 that the Clintons would have separate bedrooms. Although this never circulated in normal media channels, it would prove a fact that makes political pillowtalk as impossible as intimate pillowtalk would be. Such was the case for Jackie and John Kennedy, who slept apart, but there the similarity ends since it was Marilyn Monroe and not Jackie who was the cultural icon with destructive possibilities. The cultural myth of the emasculating woman is that of the woman who wants power as much as she wants sex and always for the wrong (i.e., selfish and male-destroying) reasons. This myth continues to color media depictions of Rodham Clinton.

Spy magazine's naughty depiction of the first lady as a sexually depraved, sadistic purveyor of power games plays out more overtly but not less aggressively recent cultural and media images of women law partners and corporate businesswomen. Diane Keaton in *Baby Boom* proudly referred to herself as "the Tiger Lady of Wall Street," and the women lawyers of *L.A. Law* were no less tigerish when confronting men at the scene of business; but women who do not consider themselves tigers are too often similarly depicted, such as psychiatrist Margaret Bean Bayog and Attorney General nominee Zoe Baird. The tiger in the corporate jungle is admirable when she accrues seven-digit salaries, but her economic success has no place in the power-sensitive arena of national and international policymaking. Ordinary politicians are not bound by this logic, but the president, vice-president, and their spouses are symbols of national integrity, and this iconic status sets their lives above all others as to ethical and moral choices. But in the media's representations, ethical and moral choices are interpreted by ideological indexes; thus it is not ethical for Hillary Clinton to be overtly all of those things Barbara Bush was secretly, because within representation only the representable or visible is judged.

Another way of saying this is that the investigative acumen of our journalists is bound by the ideologies of their editors and publishers, and by the news those men wish to promote. The image of the tiger woman is only an aggressive, man-eating, and self-serving version of the femme fatale, a useful stereotype recently so displayed in Hollywood "psychobitch" movies. Where the tigress is ruthlessly logical, the psychobitch is just ruthless, all the more terrifying for her illogic and her abusive emotionalism. Yet successful businesswomen and their milieu can have nothing in common with the oppressed status of these mythical avengers who act out a sexual "return of the repressed" for the male imaginary. The exploited secretary (*Batman Returns*), spurned mistress (*Fatal Attraction*), nanny (*The Hand that Rocks the Cradle*), nurse (*Misery*), and office worker (*The Temp*) are all haunting figures out of a landscape of masculine privilege; these empty, stereotyped characters arise like Scrooge's ghosts but with terror and death, not morality lessons, to offer. In each case the woman's revenge provides the vehicle for a terrifying crossover and confusion of the boundaries between public and private lives; because it is these boundaries that allow for exploitation, their transgression is frightful and deadly. A movie like *Single White Female* plays on a slightly different fear, where women who lead working lives can be victimized by passive, mysterious, and therefore more feminine women—who are, because of their essential femininity, deadly and psychotic. Psychobitch movies seem, in the media's eyes, to explain the inner workings of women involved in domestic violence, women like Amy Fisher, the Long Island woman who attempted to kill her lover's wife. For the media to blur the distinction between these imagined figures and real women is mere sensationalism; this is not the confusion of literary with literal that Dan Quayle stands convicted of, but an appositive comparison of the two that infers the imaginary and real woman will act the same. But when the media perform the same appositive on real women who have achieved tangible power in their communities and professions, it attempts to control through such blurring how women are perceived when they achieve real positions of power. Rodham Clinton provides a sane face in the midst of screen madness, but the media war being waged on her affects all women taking part in the public sphere.

The media are so visually and narratively invested, so convinced by their own storytelling, that making headlines at times resembles film synopsis leads. For instance, it is equally important to the impressions "cast" by the press that consideration is given to the juxtaposition of articles and op-ed essays. Perhaps the most curious aspect of the page spread discussed above with the Rivers and Nyhan editorials is that the front page of the op-ed section that contains them includes a small article on this press itself. "All the News that's fit to Advertise: Editorial content no longer sacrosanct." John Carroll claims that although the first commandment of journalism is "Thou shalt not mix editorial content and advertising," and although "the independence of the news from its financial underpinnings constitutes the 'silken curtain' or 'Chinese wall' of editorial integrity," nonetheless the media are succumbing to the underwriting:

With newspapers and magazines garnering 50 to 75 percent of their revenues from ad sales, and with the big three television networks losing ground to cheaper, more narrowly targeted cable programming, many news executives are disinclined to go to the mat for editorial purity.

Carroll includes in this increasing mix of advertising and editorializing such recent media concoctions as infomercials, relationship marketing, transactional talk shows, advertorials, and the paid-for box on the *New York Times*'s op-ed page. But corporate America's takeover bid on the media is only part of the problem. Even when a watchdog group like The Center for the Study of Commercialism reports such interference as *USA Today's* use of a front-page banner to promote a new Warner Bros. movie (the unlabeled four-page section, the Center notes, was paid for by Warner Bros.), the real problem lies less in false presentation, as in the sponsor's purchase of journalistic perspective and a hold over information. Perhaps more crucial, however, is journalism's willingness to believe itself capable of becoming the public spokesperson who must battle it out with political spokespersons. Reporters through rhetoric and story presentation, and editorialists through argumentation, believe the impact they have to be legitimately theirs. The end goal of their influence is not newsmaking but policymaking in the sense that their reportage is a clear bid on creating a version of reality that by sheer repetition becomes history. To be able to make history—to make news by making up how news will be received, or obscured and silenced—is a form of force, a way of potently influencing how policy will be made or how a group will be perceived. Susan Faludi reports that through the Reagan-Bush administration women were pejoratively and inaccurately portrayed in the media, women's political groups were consistently misrepresented, and women's struggle for equal rights as a constitutional amendment was powerfully undermined and upended.[2]

In this increasingly militaristic scenario, news reporters literally transform themselves into newsmakers whose polls and insistent, adjective-laden headlines make much ado over certain events while ignoring less interesting news as unworthy of report or of above-the-fold placement. For instance, in NEH Chairperson Lynn Cheney's speech to the National Press Club in October 1992, she (a doctorate in literature from the University of Wisconsin) denounced feminist professors and college teachers for "shoving" their ideology in the faces of students who shouldn't have to take it. This in short, Cheney announced, was precisely the virus rampant in universities that is destroying the intellectual health of American youth and culture. As polemical a statement as this was, the press did not take it up. It did not become a story perhaps because this is the "Year of the Woman," or perhaps because it followed too closely on Pat Robertson's allegations of witchcraft and militant lesbianism underlying the façade of all feminists and thus the feminist wife of (at the time) one of the presidential candidates.

In any case, the difficulty with the blurred boundaries between sponsor and editor, the mass voice of the public and the voice of the mass media, is again a rhetorical one. The news show that presents itself as the public's voice gives over any pretense to journalistic objectivity and caves in to a metonymous self-representation *as* the public *to* both the public and the government. Because the public likes to see itself glamorized in the mirroring faces of news personages and pundits, there is little outcry over the media's proclamations of what American wants or how America perceives its politicians; the identification between viewer or reader and news reporter is too strong and too seductive for easy criticisms. Similarly, when news reporters raise questions at news briefings, they do so as representatives of the public while they perceive the spokesperson answering their questions as not representative, as not metonymous. Rather, he or she is synecdochal, a mere mouth that gives voice to what the president wishes to have said. And if the president or other politician is personally conducting the briefing, he is seen as again not representative, but as individual, and therefore idiosyncratic or inconsistent. In either case, reporters conceive themselves as privileged by virtue of their representativeness to launch "tough" and even unfair questions in "hard-hitting" style at the podium occupier. Such questions necessarily pervert facts or slant statements precisely because they aim to get underneath and behind the prepared statements being dished out, but the implications and insinuations of such rhetorical framing of the questions invariably colors how such briefings get written into the evening news.

On the other hand, the alliance between powerful corporations, interest coalitions, and administrations can produce media cooperation to such an extent that presidential statements are reported without relevant contextual information or discordant facts. Michael Parenti writes that

when Reagan claimed that his administration had advanced the interests of minorities and females more than previous ones, the press dutifully reported his assertions without pointing out that he actually had threatened to veto the Voting Rights Act (and only signed it because it passed both houses by veto-proof majorities), and that he had cut back on minority and female appointments and civil rights enforcement in his administration. (14)

Particularly powerful groups of the Reagan years were those that had helped sweep Reagan into office: the Moral Majority, the Kingston Group, Library Court, the Stanton Group, the National Right to Life Committee, the American Life Lobby. These are all affiliations of the New Right, and as Timothy Phelps and Helen Winternitz point out, their single strongest common denominator is their stand against abortion rights. They also are militantly against women's rights, gay rights, and other radical causes which they consider part of an overall "war of ideology, . . . a war of ideas, and . . . a war about our way of life."[3] But the media's willingness to accept these groups' "way of life" as the truthful one, its willingness to support Reagan's rhetorical strategies for putting false faces on legislation designed to kill that same face, indicates the media's own ideological base.

Ironically, the fear of journalism's corruptibility has receded in this century after two hundred years of the tabloid as a venue for court gossip, political lobbying, and "yellow journalism." During turn-of-the-century Progressivism, as Murray Edelman notes for instance, journalism achieved its heyday as an ideological mover, "for journalists were an intrinsic part of the Progressive movement" which evolved simultaneously with the rise of the mass-circulation newspaper. During the Progressive movement, "journalists achieved a level of power and influence in American life they have not held since, except during the years of the Watergate scandals" (204–5).

Historically journalism comes down to gossip and transcriptions, two diametrically opposed modes of information transmission. Today's journalism strives to combine a strict ethical code with an objective reportage that combines and defuses the fiction and fact provided by gossip and transcription. However, genre rules continue to cross paths with the bias inherent in language use. Gossip is intrinsically the viewpoint of one person, conveyed as if it represents communal consensus; that language used in nonfictional and public ways intrinsically adopts a similarly unified voice and viewpoint as if it were consensual, and works with rather than against the grain of the spectacular or gossip. Thus language works with reportage to reproduce, as it were, "naturally" the omniscient perspective which signals truth rather than one side of a story.

One way in which the media intersect with rhetoric is in their interaction with the happenings of the day to constitute history itself. History, the recording of events from a perspective dictated by political values associated with "enduring" or "fundamental truths," is made by a process which is highly determined by the terms the media themselves use to describe their activities and professional goals. Given the number of women journalists in increasingly high-profile positions, we may take the supposed objectivity of news stories as achievable in the belief that if news staffs are gender-balanced, so too will be their prose. But more determinant are factors that affect history-production in the name of objectivity including editorial decisions as to what news events are given front-page space "above the fold," what language is chosen to convey facts and actions related to those events, and who reports what.

Language works with reportage to reproduce, as it were, "naturally" the omniscient perspective which signals truth rather than one side of a story. Gossip as news about political and sexual court intrigues continues to inform what will make the front pages of both serious and tabloid papers. The appointment of yet another conservative Republican to the Supreme Court is newsworthy because of the imbalance of power hidden behind the racial screen of nominating Clarence Thomas. The accusation that Thomas sexually harassed those working under him was treated by the Senate committee and staff as court intrigue and scandal mongering, gossip on a high order. It is a Court scandal of enormous resonance for the future of women's rights and freedoms to allege that women working closely with the nominee were treated such that a woman's professional body becomes the personal site at which integrity and competence are confused and threatened. Because this chapter focuses on the interplay of news media and language around events of historical importance, the problem arises of talk about events or transient ephemera prescribing what will be determined to be of historical newsworthiness. This in turn leads to an analysis of the historically hidden agenda of newstalk as gossip, gossip as news.[4]

Newsmakers themselves perceive their work as distinguishing between ephermera and chronicle, disdaining the transience of unimportant details for the detailing of important facts and statistics. Such a distinction seems clear from a comparison of *The Inquirer* and *The Washington Post*, but in fact it is a distinction more of the editorial mind than of actual editorial decisions. In addition, how newsmakers view their jobs in the sense of chronicle or history-making is entangled with how they are restricted by publishers and network producers and the pressures of selling their product. As professionals who must represent the happenings of the day to the domestic and nonprofessional public, reporters chase happenings that themselves seem perpetrated by those acting out of or against their professional capacity. Both ends of this vise (market pressures versus relative professionalism) serve to hyperventilate newsworthiness. In its almost hallucinatory, bit-by-bit accretion of facts that seem to find relation only to themselves and not to national or world affairs (the Patty Hearst case, the Pamela Smart trial), stories can appear sensational because they have no history or not wider relevance than the immediate circumference of the facts. This is the case when the news reports what has just happened, barely happened, perhaps happened, which is often corrected and reported in the next days' news. There is not sufficient time for retrospect, wider implication, historical trends, foreshadowing, and even the pundits can only ponder as much as time allows.

In addition to the conflicts of time and space intersections that prevent detailed reporting from being the same as truthful reporting, the media's own interpretation of its intervention in the historical sways the way events are covered or ignored, given front-page or midsection burial, extended to several columns or condensed to a paragraph. The media envisions the world as a swirl of events not always connected and not extendable past a certain duration of interest and attention; attention span itself becomes a matter of control, of politicking, of new details and revelations, and of an editor's patience or impatience. It is almost never a readership's attention span that delimits a story's relevance; a news story is rarely a rational sequence of import and reportage. Instead, it more resembles small vortexes where an info-byte, a partial story, gets chased by every news agency until the dust settles, whether or not it deserved to outpace more tepid happenings. If reporters think of themselves as hunters chasing quarry with the excitement of gossip and leaks, breaks and confessions, the rhetoric they use to describe professional excitement brings to mind the language of seventeenth-century court intrigues combined with that of inquisition and torture. Certainly those who have been hounded in or out of office, on their way to court, or throughout some controversy may have felt so. Those with savvy and experience bank on the media phenomenon to help win popular support, confident that they can control how they will be represented in print or on the airwaves. Ronald Reagan was so comfortable with media attention that he was able to exert this control through his cultivation of the press and his personal charisma. His successful self-representation depended on his ability to embody and personify the values on which American conservative ideals are founded; his successful media presentation depended on the support of conservative network and agency owners and sponsors.

Politicians and public figures who refuse to embody archetypes such as this one discover that the media cannot love such resistance. Reagan understood that to take on the archetype is to embrace a feminization of the self as body, as portrait, as nurturer and protector: the president as parent to the nation. Those who misunderstand this role and embrace instead a militantly masculine persona, as has George Bush, find themselves attacked as the mother-*manquée*, as inadequately archetypal and therefore *effeminate*, hysterical. Those who alternatively embrace the spectacular persona, like Pat Buchanan and Pat Robertson, find themselves playing out the role of the power-hungry mother who seeks to gain by destroying other women, accusing them of witchcraft, lesbianism, desertion of family, and other atrocities. To understand that the presidential position is ultimately a maternal rather than a patriarchal one in the present age—negotiator, protector, provider, and reassurer—is also to understand the deeply conservative nature of a liberal democracy that holds onto values that have long been gendered in ways we still do not recognize, but continue to uphold.

The self-presentation of the president cannot be underrated, since it extends to his entire term, to the legislation he passes, the wars he engages, and the people he appoints to positions of power. The media understand the importance of the president as a symbolic individual, and extend that synecdochally to new reportage in general: the individual, whether known or unknown, focuses the story so that we can be guided in our sympathies and deprecations. Herbert Gans notes that reporters often insist that the news ought to be about individuals rather than social groups or forces.[5] And most news is: Marilyn Monroe, George Bush, Leona Helmsley, Jim Baker, Saddam Hussein, Michael Milken, Magic Johnson, Oliver North, Oliver Stone, . . . as well as individuals whose names lose relevance quickly but whose stories appeal to a taste for the sensational or lurid. Like the presidency, these names tie events to a body, physically focusing responsibility where there might otherwise be any matrix to organize information. Scapegoating is the most common outcome of this need for bodily accountability, and the news machine can find itself less concerned with locating real sources of responsibility once a scapegoat has been named.

Alternatively, depictions of women in the news all too often occur pejoratively in terms of embodied rhetoric, or language that emphasizes their sexual and bodily aspects regardless of propriety or context. Helen Benedict discovered several catalogues of factors that apply to women but not to men who are covered in the media. For instance, women rarely appear in the news (only 11 percent of the people quoted in news stories in 1989 were women), they predominantly appear as victims of a crime (usually sexual), they are predominantly depicted by the media as responsible for the attack in some way, and they are mostly represented as being at home (women workers are extremely underrepresented) (20–23). What these descriptive protocols for writing about women mean is that women are not individuals but always scapegoats or symbolic individuals who stand for anything but themselves. Thus women in themselves cannot be newsworthy but only representative of a larger news item; their names become identifiable as belonging to a kind of story, and so cannot be said to have the same kind of name recognition as a man's name has, particularly if the woman is a crime victim.

Our need for name recognition in order to make sense of an event promotes the particular discourse we know as "news"; as such, women are not considered newsmakers because they are not considered to inhabit the public world in which news occurs. Name recognition, as a male attribute in contradistinction to the female attribute of body, produces news and produces it within protocols that make the story easily assimilable. Editors and reporters do their best to fit stories into easily recognizable patterns, a procedure that allows the press to consent to political rhetoric when occasion requires. Michael Parenti calls this type of new "disinformation," and notes that the media are comfortable with two distinct types of disinformation: "the transformation of falsehood into unconscious 'fact,' " and the unquestioned transmission of official falsehoods, or "face-value transmission." In fact, Parenti notes, "[t]he major media not only go along with official disinformation, they readily launch their own energetic disinformation campaigns to buttress the policies of the national security state. . . . The press will go out of its way to promote an official disinformation story with embellishments all its own" (194). Thus the media put political alliances above their journalistic ethos because they understand themselves to be an agent of politics and big business, and a vehicle of conservative values. The media must then put a higher value on persuasive effects, through tone and word choice, than on cross-researched fact or context or history, to determine how a story should be understood or emotionally responded to. And the force of journalistic "objectivity" is most overturned in a growing sector of the media enterprise which most depends on spectacle and emotionalism: telejournalism.

MAKING SPECTACLES

Telejournalism is an extreme version of the media profession. It divides into subgenres: the evening news, the morning entertainment news, the news analysis show, political pundit roundtables, investigative reporting shows, special focus "editions." Before the news became a round-the-clock venture with its own cable channel, the nightly news pronounced what history had been made each day, and regardless of which broadcast network one watched, virtually the same editorial process produced a visibly similar picture. Such decisions are based on values consciously projected onto the news in order to produce for consumption a sense of homogeneity. Journalism with a single perspective allows the idea that one reporter could discover the facts adequately and tell us an objective story about them, thus reducing conflicting stories and expensive duplication of reporters' salaries.[6] Editorial considerations rely on the reductive perspective to provide an overall homogeneous tone to the messier process of channeling reports and the individuals giving them, along with stories and the newsworthy individuals standing in for them. Editors base homogeneity in a news show on what Gans calls the "enduring values": ethnocentrism, altruistic democracy, responsible capitalism, small-town pastoralism, individualism, and moderatism (42–52). Regardless of how much we change channels, the broadcast and local nightly news shows differ only in the attractiveness or liveliness of the anchors. However, homogeneity for a heterogeneous nation becomes a form of false consciousness, the enforcing of a political vision that can only satisfy one section of the populace. It can also become so patently ideological that news shows begin to turn reportage into spectacle, thus increasing their need for audience "draws" such as beautiful women anchors and expensive technological visual aids.

Morning entertainment news hours exploit the public's fascination with spectacle even more, but produce a less overt tone of a shared populist vision. Instead, the morning shows are arranged to give different views in the time-honored attempt to open up women's simple home-bound lives beyond the kitchen and living room. Political pundit shows, on the other hand, are aimed at specifically male audiences, and develop the spectacle of multiperspectival debate while the moderator carefully funnels insights so as to produce a finally monoperspective assessment of the week's events. Just as the morning shows aimed at women viewers replace the old-fashioned coffee klatch with one's neighbors, the pundit shows aimed at men replace chats at the club over martinis with men of equal or higher stature. Both types of shows maintain these speaker to viewer ratios: coequal for women, hierarchical for men. Also, unlike the morning shows where the "hosts" smooth over discrepancy and point out commonalities among their materials, their guests, their audience, and themselves as the show's "family," pundit shows use a variety of tactics to highlight differences and ensure strong position statements. The pundit show moderator then employs other tactics to dispel the strong statements he has just encouraged, to embarrass a speaker, or to prop up a weak guest. John McLaughlin in particular uses a repertoire of spectacular ploys directly antithetical to the ploys of morning show hosts. During one show McLaughlin asked the only woman panelist, "Eleanor, in the words of Ross Perot, are you trying to show your manhood?" Clift answered, "John, on this show I have to!" (October 4, 1992). Sexual innuendos are only one of McLaughlin's success-ful ploys, charging male debaters with effeminacy or charging the female debater with high testosterone, depending on how their answers have displeased or tickled him. His view remains the counter on which the show runs, but is deployed as if it is the only real view against which the out-of-touch pundits flap their wings. Pundit shows (unlike morning shows) reveal in exaggerated terms the rhetorical positioning characteristic of journalism as a whole. Unfair comparatives are posed, intimations of unnatural gendering are made when an individual steps out of the system of "enduring values," and a single-perspective editorializing controls the process of representation.

Between punditry and the evening news lies a gray area filled by shows such as *The MacNeil/Lehrer Newshour*, a nightly show that turns spectacle to account by "bringing" guest speakers into the studio via large screens so that teleconferencing produces more varied and informed debates on the day's issues. While the morning shows replace one kind of traditional talk in the home, and the pundit shows replace another kind of talk in the public sphere, the *Newshour* seeks to offer a version of the nightly news as it was before entertainment achieved a higher priority than information on news shows. Robert MacNeil and Jim Lehrer formulated a program that would prevent journalistic professionalism from impeding our interaction with other professionals and their specialized knowledge. Of particular impor-tance is the emphatic way in which knowledge is presented without signifi-cant attempts at the synthesis or viewpoint monopoly such is found on shows like *60 Minutes*, *Washington Week in Review*, *The McLaughlin Group*, or the nightly news. The multiperspectival forum of the MacNeil-Lehrer pro-gram, with its anchor team of two men and two women, each a top journalist, attempts an objectivity not possible in the fierce investigative reporting that characterizes *60 Minutes* and its spinoff shows, or in the choreographed opinion debates between professional journalists on the pundit shows. At the same time, *MacNeil/Lehrer* presents in-depth reporting and analysis by guest commentators not possible in nightly news shows. To dispel the power play possible in the televisual medium, MacNeil and Lehrer use different cameras and screens to make obvious the nonunified vision they are pre-senting. In addition, they disregard the conference-room settings of pundit shows or the busyness of active newsrooms that background nightly news anchors, opting instead for nonthematic backgrounds and isolated anchor segments that then change to teleconference discussions. Despite the clear drive toward professionalism and away from spectacle, *MacNeil/Lehrer* can find it difficult to navigate the dynamics inherent in telemedia, particularly when a powerful issue must be analyzed in all its nuanced implications. Because of its professed objectivity, *MacNeil/Lehrer* will focus the discussion which follows of tele-news talk and the Thomas/Hill hearings. Because of the high standing of Robert MacNeil and Jim Lehrer as respected journalists, this show will also provide an opportunity to examine the distinctions between ephemera and historical material.

Before turning to that analysis, however, it is important to note that both stories and the way they are told, portrayed, and debated depend on old habits of the telejournalist industry that promote the idea that one unified and truthful vision of an event is obtainable. Yet Murray Edelman questions whether events make history or people's perception of events make them historically real: "Rather than seeing political news as an account of events to which people react, I treat political developments as creations of the publics concerned with them. Whether events are noticed and what they mean depend upon observers' situations and the language that reflects and interprets those situations." (2). Pundit shows reaffirm this inverted perspective of news production: in assessing recent events, pundit shows make clear that historical veracity is partisan-affiliated and perspectival, and that interpretation and analysis is nonconsensual and not methodologically differentiated from gossip. Not only do events seem to exist historically only if they are debated on news shows, but how these events are showcased and arbitrated determines the extent of their newsworthiness.

This itself is a matter of gender politics, a subtle way to differentiate between what is important and therefore public domain, and what is unimportant because transient and therefore privately entertaining. Matters of import are discussed formally between serious men and a sprinkling of serious women, while forgettable news or gossip is showcased in lively spectacle format between old friends as a matter for home consumption. One is not aware that beyond one's home the whole nation is watching the latter kind of engagement, while the former hardly seems to be taking place in one's living room because it transports the viewer out of the home into a larger debate forum. Yet it is this division into the public and private formulations that asserts an uncomfortable gendering, since home entertainment accrues to the feminine and the nosiness of gossip and tidbits— while public forums focused on serious matters accrue to the masculine and the difficulties of unifying the nation. When the issues discussed cross the boundaries between domestic and national, then sensationalist murder stories like that of Pamela Smart and stories of racial and community outrage perpetrated by murderers like Charles Stuart establish the difference between feminine gossip and masculine news: if the Stuart case is a wrenching landmark, the Smart case is only a disturbing anomaly.

In contrast, when serious news formats specifically take on issues concerning women and women's rights, they de-gender the news by discussing it between men, as matters concerning men, and from male perspectives. To establish news as historical and not ephemeral, news shows must work against the transient nature of the news itself, its susceptibility to new news or to new details about old news. Thus it is necessary to draw the line between feminine ephemera (morning shows, evening news shows, and talk spectacles) and masculine history (serious talk shows, investigative reports, and documentaries). John McLaughlin consistently parodies this boundary line by stagemanaging debates about serious issues in spectacular and gossipy ways, and by consigning women's issues to sexist jokes. When Geraldine Ferraro was announced as Walter Mondale's running partner, for instance, McLaughlin used as his lead-in title, "It's a Girl" (A. Hirsch, 36). The evening news, too, confuses public and private, masculine and feminine by telling bedtime stories about events "out there." Bedtime stories remain safeguards against sleepless nights if they continue to assure that the nation is still precisely the one we (are told to) deeply hope it to be. What we tend to forget about how these bedtime stories get produced is their market value.

Pundit shows, on the other hand, provide bedtime stories that reassuringly make news ridiculous, and at the same time provide mock hostilities that appease viewers' aggressive instincts while simultaneously moderating the talkers' discord so that it concludes as consensus. The enormous market appeal of *The McLaughlin Group*, for instance, is derived from a discontinued segment of the more serious *60 Minutes* "Point/Counterpoint." This debate format showcased two pundits engaged in fragmented debates. James Kilpatrick and Nicholas Von Hoffman "managed to compress their views on controversial issues into the short time span by speaking in vehement bursts that left no room for qualifications, balance, or subtlety," as Alan Hirsch notes in *Talking Heads* (32). "Point/Counterpoint," so commercially successful, became even more so when Shana Alexander replaced Von Hoffman, thus increasing hostilities by introducing gender into the arsenal. Hirsch comments that " 'Point/Counterpoint' had already made its mark on television by demonstrating that viewers enjoy aggression masquerading as political commentary" (32), a fact *The McLaughlin Group* exploits fully both in terms of masquerade and gender wars. If the history of pundit shows is analogous to the history of newspapers in their appeal to consumers' appetite for conspiratorial supposition, slander, and judgments predicated on incomplete disclosure of facts, then telejournalism must also come in for its share of negative telemarketing and gendered roles.

The MacNeil/Lehrer Newshour, in contrast, attempts to avoid both gendered pitfalls of masculinized and feminized news genres. Instead, the *Newshour* has expanded its anchor team to represent more equitably the

U.S. adult population; in addition, the guest speakers are consistently diversified for gender-neutral issues as well as gender-specific issues. The reasons for the *Newshour*'s integrity concerning representation can be traced back to its public television funding, in contrast with network broadcast news shows which arise from a historical relation to the Federal Communications Commission, a regulating body that ensured by the 1950s that broadcast networks would underwrite the political views of whichever Washington administration is in power.[7] Nonetheless, even when such historical pressure is resisted, the genre constraints of telejournalism itself intrude on the MacNeil-Lehrer effort to avoid a single editorial viewpoint and to avoid supporting any governing political ideology. The drive toward unity and consensus is integral to Western culture; traditional Western thought forces us to hold onto stabilized concepts of ourselves, and it is this safety net of identity that the telemedia plays to, encompassing us in its vision of who and what our national community is. Such a vision, of course, ignores the very different peoples that go to make up who "we" are, a problem only slightly ameliorated by the hiring of men and women of different ethnic and racial backgrounds. It also ignores the identity problems arising from journalists' sense of their own professionalism in the face of a populist viewership, and the fracture between those viewers' private and public selves. It is precisely this fracture that seduces us in those news shows that deploy spectacle: the morning shows aimed at women that confuse the "host"'s private and public persona, the nightly news shows that interlace sections of the show with anchor banter. Even *60 Minutes* depends on Andy Rooney's highly personal ruminations and "research" to end the show on a jovial resolution between professional and private lives.

Although the deliberate confusion of public and private in the media is used toward an economic end—higher ratings, increased audience interest or loyalty—there is a professional investment here as well. Audience identification occurs when the telejournalist enters our homes nightly and familiarly; identificatory sympathy allows for the transmission of perspective as well as information. Newscasters are thus able to sway opinion in addition to reporting facts and events. Indeed, the main rhetorical abuse of journalism appears in this persuasive effort, which is the exchange of politicians and movers as "newsmakers" for those journalists and editors who "make up the news," deciding what is "news" and what will be forgotten. Making up the news, which sounds as fictive as it almost is at times, should not be synonymous with the activity of political "newsmakers" who "make" the news—in the sense of *appearing* in the chronicle of events—and who make or make happen events which are newsworthy and which thus appear as events in the chronicle.

News talk shows deliberately play this line between public or professional and the private individual, and also play the line between rhetorical persuasion and rhetorical abuse. These shows are fully aware of their importance as television's op-ed pages, with their ready-made jurisdiction over our opinions and understanding of national and world affairs, and the history of these shows reveals that they are far more ready to form our opinions than to inform our minds. As a medium, television lends a particular viability to this blurring of purpose because the entertainment value of a network television show remains the highest priority, far exceeding the informational value. *The McLaughlin Group* gets its high energy and entertainment value from staging politically polarized pundits in a "discussion" group format which is not roundtable but instead one-on-one with the host. The host is not objective, nor does his choreography of the show even pretend to engage the participants in more than just position statements. Free play is so rare, and the positions so unremittent, that *The McLaughlin Group* resembles ritualistic war hostilities rather than informed debate. Its entertainment value is predicated on the pretense of debate which is already disintegrated into war games before airtime. Certainly McLaughlin's rapid-fire questioning and aggressive rather than incisive dismissals or agreements predetermine the tone of the exchange. But there should be no mistake: the exchange is neither informational nor economic-based; it is the exchange of missile fire. McLaughlin had originally organized a cast of all men and one woman in his pilot show, but Judith Miller and Chuck Stone were immediately replaced with Pat Buchanan and Morton Kondracke. The replacements provided the necessary chemistry and weaponry for Jack Germond and Robert Novak (now on *The Capital Gang*), providing an all-male cabal until Elinor Clift joined the ranks. Her entrance into the scene of ritual warfare was followed by an apprenticeship period in which she gradually learned how to take part, to make herself heard, and to maintain the opinions for which she was hired. Her insertion into the fabric of the show reveals that the show's rigid format disallows individual members' attempts to change it or to resist its militaristic ethos.

MacNeil/Lehrer, on the other hand, assumes a civil, informational, and ethnically balanced format. Of course, because the show mixes up its format—using anchored news, one-on-one interviews, interviews with two opposed spokespersons, refereed roundtables, and editorials—and because it aims to be neutral and information-oriented rather than polemical and opinion-oriented, it cannot be classified under the "pundit" rubric. Nor does it have the same agenda as the pundit shows and television journalism to influence policy, to form and sway opinion, and to entertain over and above informing. Because a show of tough, in-depth journalism like *60 Minutes* also holds at least some of these goals high, *MacNeil/Lehrer* holds an unusual position in television news shows in that it only occasionally comes near the first two goals and almost never near the third. Still, *MacNeil/Lehrer* has lessened the distance between it and talk shows like *The McLaughlin Group* by increasingly incorporating paired-off position spokespeople in its interviews or refereed panel discussions. A large difference here, even so, is that *MacNeil/Lehrer* relies on professional and credentialized position-spokespersons, unlike the pundit shows where a participant's credentials for the position he or she represents are their journalist backgrounds. With the clear differentiation of interviewees as authorities from interviewers as objective journalists, *MacNeil/Lehrer* is able to present information as firsthand and therefore less likely to be opinion-informed. But, as has already been said, the increasing tendency in that show is to pair off polarized position representatives. Thus the interviews are no longer procedurally interviews but have instead tended toward arbitrated statements of unyielding positions. Even professional authorities who are placed in a defensive posture against professionals of ideologically opposed camps will not be able to discuss intelligently or objectively, and will be almost required to give biased views and information.

Pundit shows similarly distribute the debate between opposed camps, but they do so with regular participants who have known positions. As players in a tactical war, pundits can either offer the views expected of them in a show of force against their chosen combatants (as when Mark Shields squares off against Robert Novak on *The Capital Gang*), or they can state the unexpected in order to reveal themselves as occasionally diverting from party line (the staunch conservative Mona Charen, for instance, would not choose this avenue). The second option mixes up the formulaic nature of the pundit show, and it is here that it is most effective, since in a regular news show the viewer is rarely cognizant that nonparty positions have been taken. However, the party position *cum* personality is far more important to the seductive appeal of the pundit show, and Robert Novak—John McLaughlin's choice for a far-right columnist in his original cast—so perfectly personifies his position that he has received volumes of hate mail over the years. Alan Hirsch notes that Novak's character, regardless of the show he is on, is that of the "frigid cold warrior" who "found a communist or fellow traveler under every bed, [and] never recanted his view that Mikhail Gorbachev was a fraud, and derided Ronald Reagan, George Bush, and just about everyone else as too soft on communism" (33). Yet it was not Novak's far-right politics that defined his militaristic position, but his manner, a manner specifically concocted for his role as pundit, since according to Hirsch, Novak "is known among his colleagues as being cordial and urbane" (34).

What place, then, can women participants have in these allegorical war games? Allegory traditionally used typed characters, while warfare usually reserves for women the place of booty, or carnage. Either the woman pundit must become one of the men, as Charen has and as Clift has almost succumbed to becoming, or they must hold a strong line of absolute reason, a broad range of the most recent information, and an unyielding objectivity of emotion and manner as did, until recently, Margaret Warner. Charen and

Warner, who appeared alternately or together on *The Capital Gang*, and now Charen alone, had to position themselves against Novak and Shields, who appear regularly along with host Al Hunt. Charen holds her own against the male majority at the table essentially by ignoring or rejecting the difference between them, a posture in line with her hard-right politics and verbal assaults on political figures under discussion. Warner's strategy, which was to uphold her difference while performing her job better and more intelligently than any of the men, put her at odds with Charen. However, neither can be said to have "won," simply because both women play the game set up by the show's premise; until a cast member succeeds in changing the militaristic thinking that structures the show, the only thing that truly wins in these war games is the show itself.

In searching for ways to characterize the discussants in relation to the show format, it is more instructive to consider one of the men than the women, oddly enough. That man is Mark Shields, who speaks on both *The Capital Gang* and *MacNeil/Lehrer News Hour*. On the first show Shields is a position player, spouting the views expected of him in a somewhat irascible and sputtering manner. He and Novak play ardent foes, with Shields toeing the hard liberal line against Novak's virulence. Shields's characteristic paper throw at the show's end symbolizes his persona's disgust with the lack of intellectual discussion or any real working-out of a problem. This negativity creates a real discrepancy with Shields's personality on *Mac-Neil/Lehrer*; there he presents himself as a commentator of deep sincerity and intellectual engagement. The movement from a position play to a thinker where intellectual exercise is allowed reveals the force of the show's structure on the person; factors such as entertainment priority, political atmosphere, adversarial relations, and intellectual freedom clearly affect how the commentator or pundit will respond. When a woman is put in this situation, she does not share the camaraderie extended to any man regardless of race or ethnicity; her gender puts her outside of the cabal of wise ones, the pundits who can handicap the president, predict electoral races, and sway public opinion. The puzzle is that pundits present themselves as self-determined, independently informed, and in possession of Truth rather than opinion at the same time that they are formatted by the show, as it were.

It is especially true that shows that emphasize their entertainment value, like *The McLaughlin Group*, hold expectations that their participants exhibit particular and unchanging personalities. Audiences respond well to this sit-com type of format in which characters are readily type-recognizable from their first sentences. Yet the notion that those whose job it is to keep informed about the intricacies of political events should maintain a singular character with more or less typecast views is ironic, and underscores the force of this news genre's attempt to be newsmaking. News shows like *MacNeil/Lehrer*, which work hard to remain at the informational rather than entertainment level, dip dangerously into the realm of type-casting when they pair off position representatives and then attempt to "interview" them.

The insufficiencies of this interview strategy were clearest during the last weeks of the 1992 electoral campaign when staunch supporters of each side squared off against each other on *MacNeil-Lehrer* using the party line like a weapon, and without the least intention of discussing an issue at any level above a skirmish of party ideology. In such situations of heady political import, a position speaker who is willing to entertain discursive give-and-take is perceived as lacking in confidence, "weak," and "bumbling." These are the very terms used by pundits and reporters alike to describe President Clinton after his first week in office, terms which reflect Clinton's willingness to appear publicly in positions of negotiation and open-mindedness. "Clinton seeks control after rocky beginning," one paper declared and most papers and talk show casts agreed; the fact that this headline appeared on the front page of the Sunday edition, however, exacerbates the charge and intrudes criticism of collaborative labor into the family space of Sunday morning.[8] Many women responded to Clinton favorably during the electoral campaign because his collaborative approach, his willingness to openly share respon-sibility, and his use of compromise rather than concession, make him in effect the first "feminist" president of the United States. The press's derogation of Clinton's approach, their open declarations that he has failed in his first weeks to take a strong stand and to put his administration in place, reveal that nonmilitary thinking has no place in public leadership. This is devastating news for the private individual, and the lesson is that women's ways of interacting, working, and even stating their opinions are not allowed in the businesses of making policy and making news.

Insinuated into these two male-dominated activities of the public sphere is another form of vested interest or making. Media scholars agree that one of the prime factors of journalism is economics. Reporters or telejournalists must bow to readership, to advertisers, and to owners or producers. The political views of the last two are particularly potent forces pressing on the journalist. They can determine which stories get covered, what perspective the journalist applies, how big or buried the story is, and how rhetorically loaded the reporter's language is. In part this is a local question involving a reporter's own department, editor, and colleagues. But it is also a larger, national question in which each network station and newspaper scrambles for the same few stories and gives them the same slant and rhetorical treatment.

SPECTACLE AS HISTORY

When news shows must engage in a highly concentrated reportage and analysis of an extraordinary event, such as a televised Senate hearing for a

Supreme Court appointment, the factors that draw us in to watching such shows often revolve around the confusion of public and private lives. What we do not consider is the perspectival rhetoric used to comment on a sequence of events that we already have some thoughts about. Law professor Anita Hill's belatedly disclosed accusations about Clarence Thomas's behavior as a superior in the workplace made us question Thomas's ability to perceive the ethical dimensions of Supreme Court power, and those of the power inherent in a permanent and powerful position. It also made us think that we, or at least those of us who experience vulnerability in some form, knew something about what may or may not have gone on in the EEOC hallways and offices. We knew what it was to have our bodies touched by colleagues or bosses, our work questioned or passed over, our careers dependent on the good word of some one person, our peace troubled by dirty jokes or innuendos. Whatever we knew, we thought we could imagine each scenario offered by the different parties in those hearings. Thomas called the proceedings a "high-tech lynching," but these were hearings not a trial, and the Senators who were predominantly legally trained were unskilled questioners. The confusion over genre—the less formal hearing versus the highly formalized trial—was caused in part because nearly all those who took part were lawyers. Timothy Phelps and Helen Winternitz point out that the failure of Anita Hill and her legal team to convince the panel was due to their inability to understand the hearings outside of a trial context and formulation. Thus the Senate panel's investigation was as much rhetoric, bombast, posturing, and political skin-saving, as it was any real attempt to discover how Judge Thomas conducts his business, or who his ardent supporters are (nearly all are coalitions of the New Right under the leadership of Paul Weynitz).[9] Nor did they pursue precisely why the EEOC under Thomas was allowing age-discrimination complaints to lapse until 7,456 discrimination complaints had been allowed to accumulate by the time Congress investigated the EEOC in 1989. In the meantime, equal-pay cases for women were barely being filed at all (Phelps and Winternitz, 119–21).

In the media's coverage of the hearings, a rhetorical ploy that recurrently appeared both in the Senators' questions and the media's narratives of each day's events is one we have encountered earlier, appositive thinking. Apposition, as we have already seen, juxtaposes two names or terms for a single subject. Rhetorically this trope offers the opportunity to confuse by near identification, to say two things that are nearly but not quite conceptually similar and then to offer them as identical. The best single political example of this for women remains that offered by Anita Dunn: "the conventional wisdom [in the Democratic Party] is that you shouldn't run a candidate who's perceived as liberal, as are most Democratic women in the House . . . and 'liberal' [has become] a code word for 'woman' " (quoted in Kaminer). House and home become not synonomous but mutually exclusive as the equation is made between female and liberal, both identified as illegitimate politics in today's political climate. Women, whether political activists or deeply conservative traditionalists, fall foul of this ploy. Anita Hill found herself pitted against the machinery of such rhetoric despite her deep commitment to the Republican party and her deep respect for the man against whom she brought charges. This, of all the emotional and political strategies used by Thomas's defenders and attackers, was the most obvious choice given the all-male, all-white fourteen-member Senate Judiciary Committee in the Thomas hearing.[10] However, when one watches the hearings, the choice was not clearly recognizable because the emotionalism it provokes inevitably obscures reason. Appositive thinking alone would have produced the allegations that Hill was a lonely, sex-starved, hallucinatory career women similar to the Glenn Close character depicted in *Fatal Attraction* and other narratives of psychosis. Senator Orrin Hatch helped to make this clearer when he alleged that one of Hill's harassment charges was similar to (but not identical with) a passage from another psychosis narrative, *The Exorcist*.

It is due to more than the purposeful obfuscations caused by appositive thinking that we could not see from the beginning all the forces that were at work in the Thomas/Hill hearings—including disclosures all too recent or still to come about senatorial misconduct involving Senators Kennedy and Hatch. The difficulty in comprehending the Thomas/Hill deliberation was that multiple codes were at work, while we were directed by commentary to believe only one code was operative and all else was either strategic or naive diversionary ploys to confuse the issue. Meanwhile, the overarching consensual code remained invisible. This code invokes enduring values, assuredly, but also reflects presidential intent in both the committee's and media's language: as Anthony Lewis notes, "[a]ppointments to all the federal courts have been subject to ideological screening of a kind never seen before," and the intensity of this scrutiny produced posturing and counters among senators who struggled to balance ideology with policy, racial politics with careerism. The initial suppression of Hill's information reveals that truth and historical events were less important than the battle between those aiding the president to stack the Supreme Court with strong conservatives, and those opposing that project.

To understand the posturing and rhetorical games played out in the hearing room is to also understand that history can be displaced by fundamental ideologies and fantasies which serve to constrain us as well as to comfort us. Even as we discussed the incomprehensible dilemma of Clarence Thomas when confronted with the charges leveled by Anita Hill, even as we puzzled over all the information, testimonies, ludicrous or believable attestations, we were faced with the visible invisibility of gender dominance, race dominance, and Republican party line as generated by

President Bush.[11] Repeatedly, reporters commented during the hearing that one person was telling the truth in that room and one person was not, and we would not find out which was which until the committee had voted. How were we to see the spectacle for what it was when a technology exclusively directed toward drama, fantasy, and virtual reality but which sells itself as reflecting (rather than refracting) the experience itself, was the medium by which we experienced the event? When Senate hearings were closed sessions, our reception of their documentation occurred through written modes. But the perception that we are experiencing firsthand unedited news events, which we have with cable news coverage or live broadcasts, makes it more historical, less a product of rhetoricized language. Yet there was not one person in that Senate hearing chamber who spoke the "Truth" while the other did not, there was never a possibility that a heterogeneous panel of empowered lawyers could evince this truth, and there isn't a chance that those whose profession has been historically and practically based on the art of rhetoric and persuasion would not use what they do best to manipulate the scenario being enacted. Nor was it possible that the two individuals whose names now metonymically represent the affair did not also use their considerable rhetorical and persuasive powers to influence how the story/stories got told.

Once Nina Totenberg and Timothy Phelps, journalists from National Public Radio and *Newsday* respectively, reported that law professor Anita Hill had made allegations of prior sexual harassment by her then-boss Clarence Thomas, the hearings became a trial of her character as well as Thomas's. For some senators, it became a trial focused solely on her motivations for coming forward, for career, for gender confrontation at the level of a Supreme Court appointment. That the Supreme Court is referred to as "The Brethren," and refers to its members as "brother," points precisely to Hill's stated motivations at the same time that it allows us to understand the fears and nearly incomprehensible misunderstandings of a committee representing an all-but-two male Senate body. The use of "body" is odd in this sense because I base my argument on the notion that language is integrally tried to body, but that in the furthest reaches of language manipulation for social use—that is, the composition and litigation of legal codes—language becomes so distanced from the body that a body substitute must be found, and this substitute is "woman." In the legal arena, where cases are tried on their "landmark" or "casebook" quality, people are often typed in particular ways so as to produce "landmark" decisions which can sway trial proceedings for decades after (and memorialize the name of the decision's writer). The alternative is that people are cased according to a prior "original" or landmark decision; that is, a person's actions are judged according to the similar actions of a prior person, while the person undergoing trial loses identity in relation to the needs of the court to change the course of the legal code. When a second arena intercedes on the first, as when the media take interest in a case, the discourse expectations of the first arena (the court) are disrupted by those of the second (the media) both in the public's reception of reported information, and in the historical reception of the case's importance or eccentricity. Within this system of language intercession, body becomes symbolically represented by women participating in the spectacle. The media themselves often construct a spectacle around the spectacle-event which at times supersedes the event. Even when media commentary is responsible and thoughtful, the screen it puts on the body of the event can confuse and obfuscate issues even further.

However, the October 15, 1991 *MacNeil/Lehrer Newshour* which immediately followed the nomination of Judge Thomas to the Supreme Court devoted its entire format to analyzing the proceedings, and thus promised to finally render the truth from the conflicting and unresolved data and testimonies. This particular edition was divided into four parts, two larger counterpart sections, and two smaller counterparts. None of the groups that interacted during these sections were disinterested and none could be taken as authoritative pronouncements, but all presented themselves in this role. In the first section two white male journalists frequently on the show were interviewed by Jim Lehrer, while the second section consisted of Charlayne Hunter Gault, the show's black woman reporter, interviewing a panel of four lawyers composed of two women, two men, three of whom were black, one white, and two of whom were for Thomas while two supported Hill. The third section involved two top white male politicians, Thomas Foley and George Mitchell, interviewed by Judy Woodruff, while the third section was a self-interview, or editorial, on sexual harassment by a white male editorialist, Roger Rosenblatt.

In each case the people speaking are interpreting events. The commentator in the final section, for example, argues that sexual harassment is not lust but dominance, not desire but frustration. Each speaker argues that in actuality the Thomas hearing was not about this but that. Each performs an interpretive act, with the exception of Thomas-supporter Phyllis Berry Myers, who performs an emotional act of loyalty and support rather than scrutiny. In particular, Mark Shields and Hill-supporter Emma Jordan perform rigorous acts of scrutiny, while their oppositional partners do not, or do not to the same extent. However, the construction of the entire show is itself odd. We begin with commentary by David Gergen and Mark Shields, move to a discussion by lawyers who participated in Hill's testimony and examination, receive the careful statements of bipartisan power, and end with an editorialist who scrutinizes the larger moral picture tellingly, but whose position of power is so obviously privileged that his analysis provides a curiously authoritative endpoint that closes down dialogue. What comes out from this text is the understanding that the larger picture is landmark.

One marker in the show's sequence of commentaries is found in the response to the Thomas/Hill debacle as a woman's tale threatening to interrupt a man's achievement, the marker being woman-as-body. Or its conspicuous absence. Gergen avoids discussing Anita Hill except to say, "When a charge comes out of the shadows as this one did, I don't think it's appropriate just to take it at face value without questioning both the person and charge," but he neglects to mention that initially the charge was buried by the Senate panel. Hunter Gault, on the other hand, begins her interview of the four lawyers by asking each what their emotional response was to the vote. When Emma Jordan, Georgetown University law professor and Hill's lawyers at the hearing, refused to answer this question and instead provided an intellectual response as to what the hearing represented, Hunter Gaulet pushed her for her emotions: "Are you sad, are you happy, do you have an emotional response. . . ?" Only one of the four engaged the question, the former EEOC employee under Thomas, Berry Myers, and her response is interestingly out of place in the debate. But why does Gergen end the first section with an emotional plea to Bush to heal the nation's racial division immediately, a plea which Shields reminds him he has made twice before publicly to deaf ears? And why do all the participants in the show disagree as to the actual issue at stake in the Thomas/Hill debate?

Shields begins the post-spectacle by arguing that "Thomas played the race card," even though Bush claimed that this was not a race appointee, by using the term "hi-tech lynching," which caused the Democrats to lose "their nerve and their edge." Gergen returns with the comment that "[h]ad the women of this country decided that they by a majority felt Anita Hill's story was much more believable, I don't think we would have seen this outcome today. Had the blacks also decided . . . but I think it was the women's decision that they believed Clarence Thomas over Anita Hill." For Shields it is the political use of the race issue, for Gergen it was the inability of women as a body to hang together. Shields furthers his point with:

The Republicans came out and what were the charges at the outset? She [Hill] was a pawn of all these interest groups, she was being duped, she was somebody who didn't know what she was up to. She was an ideologue. . . . Turns out she's for Bork . . . she passes the lie-detector test. . . . At that point they say, "Oh no, she's not a pawn . . . she's obviously delusional." When did Strom Thurmond become Sigmund Freud?

In the face of Shields's rhetorical analysis, Gergen can only respond emotionally in order to bring us back to his contention that the hearing was about race and not gender. By throwing the question of race and divisiveness out to an absent third party, the president who nominated Thomas, Gergen effectively disorients Shields's critical scrutiny for the viewer. To do so displaces political analysis with emotionalism, a strong use of appositive thinking (gender gives over to race, politicking gives over to healing) to bewilder scrutiny. Gergen's plea is a potent reminder that the illogical mark of appositive thinking is to first blame women for their disunity and then to disregard the woman, Anita Hill, as coming from the shadows and as perhaps a shadow herself. It is no surprise that Gergen chooses to answer Shields's logic with the emotionalism and plea for nurturance and healing culturally reserved for women, and it is ironically appropriate that it is his chosen response to the dispassionate and scrupulous testimony of the woman he chooses to disregard.

Although *The MacNeil/Lehrer Newshour* is an extremely creditable news show, scrupulously representing both sides of an issue by inviting speakers to appear who represent opposing positions, clearly key political events impose their own demands on the historical imagination. The choreography of the edition analyzed above and the directiveness of the questioning reveal the hidden agenda affecting the production of this show. Likewise, in the face of Charlayne Hunter Gault's relative inability to elicit emotional response from her panel, David Gergen's uncharacteristically emotional commentary in the prior segment reveals both a conservative fear of women's demands, and a comprehension of the disastrous nature of divisive politics as practiced by the then Bush administration. To what extent is this telling news show, with its interventionist and even corrective analysis, a player in the construction of historical chronicle?

It is perhaps too soon to be able to craft a reply, but interestingly, one of the important documents to appear from the Thomas/Hill hearings does not mention the *MacNeil/Lehrer* coverage at all: Timothy Phelps and Helen Winternitz's *Capital Games: Clarence Thomas, Anita Hill, and the Story of a Supreme Court Nomination* (1992). Indeed, although Phelps does note the accretion of newspaper coverages of the Anita Hill story, he includes only one mention of Nina Totenberg's part in the revelation of Hill's story even though she endured hearing proceedings for her own part in the news leak.[12] Like the *MacNeil/Lehrer* edition, Phelps has a particular story to tell and the 433-page book he wrote with Winternitz about the chronology of events leading up to Thomas's successful nomination poses an interesting counter to the *Newshour*'s rendering of events. Leaving aside such a comparison for a moment, the genre of each account must raise questions in the nature of history-production. *MacNeil/Lehrer* could be considered ephemera, in that debates occurring on the show do not take their place in historical chronicles while Timothy Phelps's account of his investigative reportage of Hill's story is a historical document that will have to be taken into account or purposefully ignored. On the other hand, to what extent does the scrutiny of political thinkers influence the construction of historical recording? This last question is about the incorporation of ephemera in official histories, the sublation of such documents or their supervention. Whereas any debate stage-managed on *The McLaughlin Group* might incite or entertain viewers, no writer of official histories will take seriously such hodgepodge opinion-throwing that, on the whole, as Ronald Reagan once commented, has a "nutritional value . . . somewhere between potato chips and Twinkies" (Hirsch, *Talking Heads*, 38).

It is a dazzling task in itself to sort out what is of lasting historical importance and of standing veracity from what is of fleeting interest amid the flood of facts and news stories. But this is a task impeded by the claims on our attention from the literature itself. It is not clear-cut whether such literature is of a serious and therefore newsworthy genre, or a sensationalist and therefore spectacular genre, chronicle or epheral. Truth and history are often ironically intermixed with spectacle, as when Thomas prepared for questions by watching videotapes of the Bork hearings. Spectacle, we might say in this case, allowed history to be produced by aiding the candidate to make clearly directed truth statements in reply to highly ideological questions. When the hearing was transformed into a trial on Thomas's professional behavior, two things occurred which turned a Senate hearing into a media event. In the first, when Professor Hill's defamatory charges meant that the carefully choreographed ritual of a Supreme Court hearing was no longer possible, Thomas found himself charging that the very spectacle that had aided him in preparing for the hearing was now "a hi-tech lynching." The second was that, when Hill decided to present herself as dispassionate and logical, despite her identity as a woman and as a former inferior to Thomas, then her concurrent decision had to be that she would not play to the cameras, which meant *her* truth statements were not believable to many *as* truth.

At face value, of course, the Thomas hearing was important in and of itself because it followed the rejection of Bork and the acceptance of Souter as Supreme Court judges under the self-acknowledged Reagan-Bush plan to load the Bench with conservative justices.[13] For the White House, it was important to act quickly in response to liberal Justice Thurgood Marshall's announced retirement since he would serve until a new confirmation took place. Judge Thomas seemed the ideal conservative appointee, able to turn Marshall's strenuous defense of civil rights back to the conservative philosophy he used at the EEOC, where he insisted race was not a class-actionable hindrance to opportunity, and that any instance of discrimination must be prosecuted on a case-by-case basis. But the irony of Thomas as (white) Moral Majority–supported and Ivy League–educated insisting that blacks make it on their own turned out not to be of as great historical import as Thomas's attitudes toward career women, nor as important as the gender makeup of the Senate committee that conducted his hearing. The *Encyclopaedia Britannica Annual 1992* lists the Thomas and Thomas/Hill hearings among the major events for 1991. With the weight of historical commentary behind it, the *Annual* attempts to determine the larger significance of events, noting that

After the hearings had ended and Thomas had been formally confirmed, prominent members of the mass media generally agreed that, if nothing else, the hearings and the discussions they engendered had awakened the American public to a new realization that sexual harassment is illegal, degrading, humiliating, and much more widespread than had been generally assumed. (25)

In this the *Annual* echoes not Republican Gergen's plea over racial divide, nor the general line of questioning followed in the *MacNeil/Lehrer* coverage, but instead the final segment of the *Newshour*, the essay by Roger Rosenblatt on the nature of harassment. The concurrence is important to note, since the *Annual* relies on "prominent members of the mass media" who have "generally agreed" for its assessment of the event's historical mark. Gergen, the Republican critical of Bush who argued "on the spot" with an emotionalism that contradicts his trademark rationalism; Shields, the Democrat who un-Democratically calls Thomas's use of "the race card" for what it is: together their anti-party positions cancel each other out because history—the *Annual*'s chronicle—demands that the assessment be "generally agreed."

Rosenblatt's editorial, on the other hand, contextualizes the hearing and its ramifications for sexual violence, and offers a well-constructed, single perspective analysis that is more acceptable to a chronicler's needs. In line with Rosenblatt's views, and with the hindsight available to the *Annual*, it was able to account for the sociological changes of the twelve months following Judge Thomas's confirmation: the phenomenon of women increasingly coming forward with reports and allegations of sexual harassment in the workplace, the dramatic increase in cases being brought to trial of harassment and abuse, and the unprecedented increase in women running for office in the 1992 electoral campaigns.[14] The ironic twist to Thomas's confirmation, although not part of Rosenblatt's essay, is clear now in that his role at the Equal Employment Opportunity Commission to diminish civil rights has demonstrably backfired once his views were revealed by one of his own workers.

Yet Rosenblatt gave his editorial at the end of the bitter Senate hearings, before any evidence of social reaction, or even any indication that women felt Anita Hill's ability to publicly give voice to her humiliation at the hands of her boss was liberating and enabling to other women. Rosenblatt's white male position of editorial power, aided by the placement of his essay as the final word of the *Newshour*, countered Clarence Thomas's position as boss of the EEOC; his opinions about the relations between men and women countered the allegations of Thomas's behavior in the workplace; his statement of ethics effectively laid out a programmatic roadmap for Thomas to take with him to the Supreme Court, or at least for others in positions of power to consider taking into the office. Such a program could not have been so concisely laid out by a woman for the important historical reason that to date, positions of power are still overwhelmingly held by men. The need for Rosenblatt to speak for women from the particular position of power that he embodies, became even more clear during the last stages of the 1992 electoral campaign. Even as polls and pundits agreed that the ramifications of the Thomas hearing far outweigh those of the Gulf War, the other great political event of 1991, "Hillary bashing" became the media's favorite pastime. It is perhaps worth noting that when Hill's charges were made public, President Bush did not consider them a serious threat, stating that he was "not in the least" worried about the allegations.

Worry over allegations can be dismissed only in an environment of trust or of ruthlessness. Part of Bush's trust in Thomas lay in the role of the EEOC during the Reagan agenda to destroy liberal legislation. Although Thomas did not feel comfortable with the "ruthlessness of the Reagan administration, which intended to hack down federal regulations and cut back on federal social programs," he did not protest and instead agreed to play the game (Phelps and Winternitz, 95). His loyalty against his race aligned him with those who thought, as he did, that affirmative action "was a narcotic of dependency." It also aligned him with a powerful front willing to fight on his behalf—not so much to repay his loyalty but to overload the Supreme Court with conservatives.

The administration's willingness to fight for Thomas is hardly anomalous; Bush demonstrated his militaristic stance when defending his role in the Iran-Contra affair, which was itself a conspiratorial operation in military guise. Parenti notes that when Dan Rather tried to interview Bush about his participation, "Bush just refused to answer and instead picked a fight" on the evening news. "For this evasive but belligerent performance Bush was hailed by his own public relations people as a hero for having 'stood up to the media' " (15). Bush's militarism was viewed as effectively countering the media's militaristic tactics, a portrayal that showed the single man as heroic when using the strategy of the larger body against itself. Yet the press was generally supportive of Bush, and during his first electoral campaign it was Geraldine Ferraro's husband and not Bush on whom the press descended like "a hit squad" (15). Bush's tactics against Dan Rather revealed how familiar the territory of militarism and conspiracy is to Bush, ex-CIA director: instead of answering questions about his own part in the arms conspiracy, he was able to imply through a show of personal force that Rather's own attack was not an individual, but a representative act by a media conspiracy to undermine Bush's presidential authority. The choreography of this incident underscores the same pattern of individual accused by conspiratorial group that became the conservative defense of Clarence Thomas during the hearings. Anita Hill began to be accused of attacking Thomas not as a single woman but as a representative of rebellious women who refused to support their men in front of other men. Thomas's defense of using "the race card" proved an effective counterattack because even though it seemed to transform him from an individual nominee into a member of a victimized race, it effectually turned him from secret-holder into victim; at the same time, it singled him out as a particular victim, particularly attacked by both the powerful white men of the panel and their conspiratorial ally Anita Hill. Like Bush with Rather, Thomas was able to imply that Hill's allegations reveal a deep conspiracy in order to make himself the heroic warrior.

The interrelation between policymakers, newsmakers, and the military is blurry at best, particularly because the rhetoric flows so freely that behavior gets transposed by allusions and metaphors. Thus the Thomas hearings, which were not a trial, could become a "hi-tech lynching" or a trial without jury. A trial without jury insinuates conspiracy, suspicious plots, and absolute distrust.

The next and final chapter examines feminism as an intellectual institution in the sense of an ideological and philosophical concept that engenders more disagreement and provocation than it does cooperation and concession. War resides here too, with feminists engaging in militaristic thinking and the conspiratorial and aggressive strategies that such thinking necessitates. It is not surprising that those at the heart of intellectual discussions about language, politics, and gender should find themselves speaking or facing violent contradictions and irrational argumentation. And yet, a discussion that thinks about the thinking about women's relation to politicized language provides a different space, a meta-arena, from which to reflect back on the issues examined in this book. Indeed, it is helpful to hear the different voices within the debate which are not sanguine about each others' positions, and cannot even always agree on the grounds of debate.

NOTES

1. See Benedict for an analysis of the language expressly used to report sexual crimes against women.

2. See particularly Faludi's chapter on "The 'Trends' of Antifeminism: The Media and the Backlash," 75–111.

3. The statement is by the chief organizer of the New Right groups, Paul Weyrich. Quoted in Phelps and Winternitz, 128.

4. See Gans, and Parenti. For a recent examination of how a particular kind of story gets determined as historical or ephemeral, see Klaidman.

5. Gans, 8. Gans analyzes the individuals reported in national news as either "Knowns," those with high visibility, and "Unknowns," or ordinary people. Of the Knowns, who make up the majority of the news, only a sitting president is constantly newsworthy both for his person and his office (9).

6. Multiperspectival journalism is less pursued than a single perspective that promotes the sense of homogeneity. It would require more reporters working from less accessible sources; the story format would change to reflect differences in experience, and more journalists would be required to collate and interpret this information, thus producing longer and longer stories. Personal and advocacy journalists would have to be added to the format. "In the process, the news would

become more ideological, with explicit ideological diversity replacing the implicit near-uniformity that now prevails" (Gans, 315).

7. See Besen et al.

8. *Boston Globe* (January 31, 1993): 1.

9. See Phelps and Winternitz for the implications of Thomas's support by the Moral Majority (126–41). His supporters are powerful, strenuously anti-abortionist, and ardently anti-feminist.

10. Wendy Kaminer interviewed the two current women U.S. senators about their response to the Judiciary Committee's role in the Thomas hearings. Both Nancy Kassebaum and Barbara Mikulski were invited to sit with the committee after Hill's testimony was to be heard, but both refused. Kassebaum only commented that "it would have been demeaning," but Mikulski said, "I was not on the committee. It was not my job to give an imprimatur to the hearings. It was not my job to prop them up or do a whitewash," making clear that the all-male committee was perceived as attempting to control gender politics both in terms of Thomas's detractors and Senate colleagues (59–60).

11. A special issue of *The Black Scholar*, devoted to the Thomas/Hill hearings, offers a variety of perspectives on the event as well as some primary documents. This collection makes it clear how difficult it is for even one community—let alone a nation—to take a single position on a divisive and rhetorically contradictory situation (Winter 1991–Spring 1992).

12. Phelps and Winternitz, 237: "Hill drove to Wiegand's nearby house and while the two women drank coffee and read the Sunday newspapers, the media began converging on suburban Norman. Television vans were parking in front of Hill's house. At nine, National Public Radio (NPR) broadcast an interview by Nina Totenberg with Hill as part of its morning news program, which aired across the country."

13. Phelps and Winternitz provide a concise summary:

When Clarence Thomas was nominated by President Bush, no Democrat had been appointed to the court in the twenty-four years since Marshall's appointment. By then, there were no true liberals left to challenge [Chief Justice] Rehnquist's leadership of the court. The only two moderate Republicans left on the court, Blackmun and Stevens, became its liberal wing by default. But two votes would have little influence in a court with seven conservatives. (163)

14. In a direct response to the Thomas/Hill hearings, Massachusetts State Representatives Susan Tracy and Pamela Resor filed a sexual harassment bill. An October 13, 1991 article in the *Boston Globe* reports that Hill's charges against Thomas "have caused an explosion of reactions over the issue of sexual harassment in the workplace . . . 67 [cases] have been filed with the commission [against discrimination] so far this year" (85). However, harassment is not limited to relations between male bosses and female employees. Women report humiliating pranks played by male co-workers, and a survey of 9,000 women in corporate management positions reported from a survey conducted for *Working Women* magazine, shows that 63 percent of those questioned had experienced sexual harassment (*Boston Globe*, May 18, 1992). Concern that the encouragement women are feeling to report harassment may lead to false accusations led Anita Hill to refute this notion in a speech given at Yale Law School on April 2, 1992. Hill noted that only 3 percent of harassment charges are unfounded. And, as a direct result of Hill's testimony at Thomas's hearing, both Carol Moseley Braun and Lynn Yeakel decided to run for the Senate in an attempt to change the gender ratios in that body.

Chapter Five

Gender Games: The Troping of Intellectual Debate

Now what should we answer to the question "What do light blue and dark blue have in common?" At first sight the answer seems obvious: "They are both shades of blue." But this is really a tautology. So let us ask "What do these colours I am pointing to have in common?" (Suppose one is light blue, the other dark blue.) The answer to this really ought to be, "I don't know what game you are playing."

Ludwig Wittgenstein, 134

Modernism is an age not of rhetoric, but of rhetoricality, the age, that is, of a generalized rhetoric that penetrates to the deepest levels of human experience.

John Bender and David E. Wellbery, 25

We have been examining rhetoric in its most politicized forms, but in doing so we have consciously set the terms of analysis around the *politicization of language* rather than around *language politics*. We could have connoted "rhetoric" in its traditional sense as language used in a political way to persuade an audience to agree with the rhetor's viewpoint. A good example of effective rhetoric is the Reverend Jesse Jackson's speech at the 1988 Democratic National Convention, which compared unifying diverse ethnic groups with his grandmother's handsewn quilts. Politicians have long practiced political speechmaking under this definition of language politics or use of language toward a political function. The reason I have steered away from this understanding of rhetoric is that it is highly formulaic both in its expression and its intention. Accounting for traditional rhetorical forms in contemporary culture cannot account for the complexity of motives, party struggles, and power hierarchies at work in language that does not seem political and that is not easily recognizable as such.

Yet the subtlety with which partisan warfare has veiled itself during the past two decades has invariably manifested itself in institutional language usage. The purpose of rhetoric is no longer sheer persuasion between two clear-cut positions; rather, it is to dissemble the rhetor's actual goal beneath a simplified account or defense or attack meant to divert the audience's attention. If rhetoric *enhances* real options to make one seem more effective or true, politicized language destroys the credibility of one option by *lying* about both its reality and the relation of the second option to it.

The positive and negative valences of rhetoric and politicized language too easily converge in our minds until we either believe politicized speeches because we think they are only rhetoric, or we disbelieve everything because we think all rhetoric is politicized speech. Thus the polarization of political language polarizes its audience too, and is performative in the same way as are the individual tropes we have been discussing. Whether we become, through the machinations of political language, believers or cynics, we cannot easily protect ourselves from the other operation language politicization performs: manipulation of constituencies for political ends. We have been examining the subtle ways in which this manipulation occurs for the constituent populations of children and women. However, the study of politicized language and culture is itself partisan—not only between conservatives and liberals, but also between believers and disbelievers in the ability of language to ever escape rhetoric and achieve a transcendent truth. Consequently, this book needs to examine the intellectual debates on language and on culture as they pertain to gender and power.

One caveat necessarily guides this chapter: once debates over intellectuality address gender difference, intellectuality itself becomes hystericized. In examining several participants in the current debate, it seems that whoever takes the position of conservative believer will also take on the role of the hysteric; alternately, whoever positions him- or herself as liberal disbeliever will be portrayed as hystericized by the hysteric. This operates between and among genders according to male-defined or female-defined goals with which participants identify. Finally, because intellectual debates rage both in academia and in the public sphere of the media and government, parts of the following discussion nod to prior chapters through analyses of the convergence of intellectuality with the arenas of pedagogy, public and private, literature, or the media.

MAKING WAR, OR HYSTERICIZED HISTORY

In *The End of History and the Last Man*, Francis Fukuyama declares an end to history, in the sense of a scripted or narrated phenomenon, with the teleological climax of the Cold War. Although his book may not at first seem to take part in the debate about language and gender, its politics are fully implicated in the terms of the debate and are overtly invested in the debate over culture; it therefore proves a useful proponent of the conservative-believer position.

Fukuyama's project politicizes the rhetoric of history in order to rewrite historiography so that it supports the conservative perspective. His goal is to shore up conservative culture as it encounters growing difficulties toward the end of the millennium; he provides a soothing assurance that the United States will not surrender its power in the new century, and predicts instead that the postmodern life will be boring and nostalgic for the past. Yet none of this is ever stated, for the politicizing rhetor must never reveal the truth of his goals even when he believes in the ability of language to convey truth.

Fukuyama borrows his philosophy of history from Hegel, or Alexandre Kojève's interpretation of Hegel. His historical teleology draws a line from the warrior state, in which class divisions are predicated on knighthood, valor, and prestige through self-risk, to the mercantile state, in which class divisions are erased in the name of liberal democracy. In the creation of a warrior aristocracy, recognition of the self's achievement by others becomes a symbolic wealth over and above material or landed possession. Those defeated become possessed by the victor because he valued life over recognition, and resorted to cowardice rather than valor.

The dialectic between the aristocrat who continues to desire recognition and the slave who, as a nonsubject, cannot deliver it, produces a history of the struggle to attain recognition by one's peers. History as the master-slave struggle should have ended with the French and American revolutions, when the production of a single-class society silenced the prestige dialectic. Fukuyama translates Hegel's interpretation of democratic revolution into a nearly worldwide legitimation of liberal democracy. And although Fukuyama plays with the notion of late twentieth-century international trade as a kind of bourgeois warfare, he continues to insist that the "end of history" has arrived, at least in Hegel's sense that the demise of the master-slave dialectic is the precondition for the "synthesis" toward which history has been striving. In the end of history there no longer exists the possibility of valorous warfare: a battle of the individual warrior against death-defying odds. Instead of a bare-chested bravery that risks all, Fukuyama characterizes the current culture as bored at the prospect of having already achieved all that counts.

However, there are at least four ways in which Hegel-Kojève's theory, or Fukuyama's interpretation of it, does not account for history as a specific rather than a theoretical process. First, it does not account for the historical ways in which valor has been accorded the less valorous side: the bare-chested Native American warrior tribes were viewed as cowardly in their battles with the better-armed pioneers and riflemen; George Washington's Provincial Army was viewed as ragtag and cowardly as they prepared for war with the British redcoats. Thus the valorous behavior that produced an aristocracy in the "beginning" of history, by differentiating victors from defeated and thus enslaved peoples, has become anachronistic in late history. It does so because it is not efficacious to bare one's breast in an industrial age (in the case of tribal warfare), and because warfare in the eighteenth century was no longer a test of individual warriors' or knights' wills, but was regimented and depersonalized (in the case of the volunteer colonists).

Second, in retelling history as the story of war and male prestige, Fukuyama takes from Hegel an understanding of gender warfare as the inclusion of women on the slave side of the dialectic, for woman's unequal ability in hand-to-hand combat as well as her proclivity toward protection of the young by *not* risking her life destines her for slave status. Yet this "history" cannot account for historical facts such as the successful reigns of Elizabeth I, Victoria I, or Margaret Thatcher of Britain, all of whom engaged successfully in strategic and symbolic warfare, and were awarded prestige for it. Third, during the early modern era—in the seventeenth and eighteenth centuries—warfare among the aristocracy, particularly in the milieu of court culture where the most prestigious warriors traditionally reside, began to turn from knightly jousts and other contests of valor to contestations of dress materials, wars of wit, wars of love intrigue, and other symbolic forms of physical warfare. The prestige won ensured aristocratic status over the rising challenge of the bourgeoisie; and the warfare was equally risk-taking, since failure could mean being ostracized from the court (exile to the country was the equivalent of social death). Because these transitional forms of warfare and prestige-garnering are symbolic and metonymic (the body's dress and loves as "dangerous liaisons") rather than literal and metaphoric (the bodily killing of other bodies), Fukuyama (and Hegel and Kojève) does not consider them within the historical dialectic. This is because, given the warrior-master/bourgeois-slave construct Hegel uses in his analysis of history, only literal warfare is pure masculine-masterful behavior because it is based on metaphorical ideations of risk and death as power and prestige: it transcends body. Symbolic and therefore metonymic activity, as we have seen previously, is always perceived as feminine-slavish behavior because the metonym makes meaning via embodiment: warfare as love intrigues or dress contests, death as social exile or loss of "face."

Finally, recognition, rather than obligation, contract, or consent, is the ground for bondage in the outcome of war: the slave is necessary to the lord insofar as he *fears* his own death or loss of identity and thus recognizes the lord's supremacy. Fukuyama's predication of human freedom from the ground of nature and death on male prestige battles (he who risks his life wins) assures that his conjectual history will be peculiarly slanted, since the only possible position for women to inhabit is that of slave. And even with the current post-historical class unity, women remain in a secondary and subordinate position to the male citizen.

With the entrance of the bourgeois into the political marketplace, the master-slave dyad was disrupted by this new third nonfeudal party; interestingly, the husband-wife dyad was only more insistently inscribed in middle-class domestic politics. Fukuyama validates the public-private split of political domesticity by claiming the private as only viable (or fully human) *because* of the public prestige act of gaining recognition. The private, then, is truly the site of slaveship and slave mentalities *because* it is not a site of freedom by risk. There can be no border disputes in this view of the world; connected to this is the fact that Fukuyama ignores the result of prestige battles, which is that the entitled prestige becomes the precondition of power as well as its product. Any power structure that constitutes itself on a basis of dominance or prestige works to reinforce or reproduce the conditions for entitlement and to jealously guard against diminishment.

What Fukuyama authentically denatures is the third-party bourgeois, "an entirely deliberate *creation* of early modern thought, an effort at *social engineering* that sought to create social peace by changing human nature itself," that is, by consolidating Hegel's warrior "first man" with the secondary slave to produce a nonman (Fukuyama, 185; emphasis mine). Further defined as "the human being narrowly consumed with his own immediate self-preservation and material well-being, interested in the community around him only to the extent that it fosters or is a means of achieving his private good" (160), Fukuyama's bourgeois is an anti-citizen as much as he is an anti-aristocrat. What is more, he is "liberal society's most typical product," an oddly communitarian claim for a neo-conservative to make. So, while the lord is not interested in community either, except when concern results in prestige as public-spiritedness, the correlation of self-interest *not* with the "first man" but with the "new man" provides us with another example of appositive thinking. Selfishness, embodied by the prestigiously wealthy new citizen known as the "yuppie," is a postmodern valorization. Yuppie self-interest, and its coming to power both in the marketplace and in the nation's capital, alarms Fukuyama's sense of history: the new man should be classless and self-liberating, the product of historical struggle. Instead he is a nonman, feeding appetites instead of valorizing values; to echo Madonna, he is "a material girl," feminized by his nonheroic, nonmasculinist desires. Fukuyama's alarmist argument intentionally blindsides because he wants to ground his claim that the bourgeois is artificial in a sense entirely different from the first man's *authentic* self-individuation from nature. To do so, he absents women from the picture and pits the effeminized and denatured man against his predecessor, the authentic and natural first man: Bill Clinton against Dwight Eisenhower, for instance.

Fukuyama's argument evinces the fear of conspiracy without agency, a takeover of the marketplace battlefield by nonmen who cannot be counted on to fight honorably. Any time real people are elided from the landscape by a critic who can see only men before him, and who sees those men as feminized because even they are not "real men," we have hystericized theorizing. Although Fukuyama's fears are not new, and indeed repeat a historical pattern of social critics who fear the new generation is morally and spiritually degenerate, he presents them as if unprecedented. Rhetorically, this is the most effective way to prod an audience into anxious unrest, while once again pointing to women as the destroyers of the new Eden.

Catharine MacKinnon's *Toward a Feminist Theory of the State* responds powerfully to a book such as Fukuyama's, particularly since where he disguises his use of rhetoric in order not to call attention to his partisan goals, MacKinnon deliberately deploys rhetoric in order to both make and to embody her argument. Even MacKinnon's title presents itself very differently from Fukuyama's: instead of nostalgia, endings, and the passivity of disappointment ("and the Last Man"), it presupposes agency, a movement forward, and a theory for participating in that movement from here to there. Tellingly, the last man is reconfigured not as Romantic authenticity but as positionality—feminist—and as in-relation-to (the state).

Positioning herself against reactionary politics, MacKinnon purposefully engages the tropes of politicized rhetoric—particularly appositive thinking—to earmark her work as a consciously worked-out political discourse. Her opening sentence reads, "Sexuality is to feminism what work is to marxism: that which is most one's own, yet most taken away" (3).[1] The formula for appositive thinking runs something like $a + b = b/a$ (a practice plus a concept equals a correlative truth), whereas it gives the impression that it is actually accomplishing $a + a = 2a$, or even magically, a^1 (= Marxist feminism). It is true that both feminism and Marxism labor against the state to free an oppressed class from the natural/physical attribute for which they are both valued and invalidated. But it is not true that feminist theory labors to free women's sexuality up to self-possession; it labors to free *women*, to validate them as fully human without being encumbered by body.

To insist that body is the habitation of women while men inhabit something else like work is to labor within patriarchal conceptual thinking. Taken thus far, MacKinnon could be read as misguided. But the conscious deployment of rhetoric tells another story: MacKinnon chooses the rhetoric and defining terms of patriarchal language in order to turn it back against itself. She will agree to define women solely in legal terms in order to argue the case: a woman is the embodiment of sexuality, without which she would be a man (or would not be). As the embodiment of sex, women are not fully human but are rather the repository of men's lust and the bearers of their children. By taking on the definition that has guided legal judgment and court decisions throughout American history, MacKinnon forces an argument on equal terms because she forces a consciousness that cannot be masked about the rhetoric involved in gender politics. As such, she is a formidable opponent for Fukuyama, since his argumentation depends on a prestige-maintaining vagueness.

However powerful a position MacKinnon achieves by arguing within rhetoricized language, some feminist theorists would claim that to be within the politics of patriarchal language at all is to be bound by its laws. That MacKinnon is indeed stuck becomes apparent in a later chapter when she comments that while Marxist critique needs class as much as feminist critique needs sex, yet each "as critiques of the real seek both an account of their approach to reality which differs from the dominant account and a lever for change" (107). What are work and sex but marks of difference? What is important is not the market but the political strength of that mark, its particular use to the dominant class. MacKinnon's work analyzes precisely this but by a different name, and naming peculiarly skews empirical evidence into unintended and horned bulls. Part of MacKinnon's stuckness is her feminist take on statist theory, a theory which understands agency as actual agencies or institutions. The populace must grapple with the resulting agentless or faceless nature of the state as a structure which produces, by ideological re-production, individuals as state officials, literal officeholders. Yet her statist take on feminism does not challenge the liberal notion of people as rights-possessing individuals. Thus she can discuss *the real* as if it were entirely possible to postulate a "real" in a statist world of ideologically produced reality. To give her "real" credence, she remarks that the basis for much of her thought comes from nonacademic thinkers, yet those she names are almost entirely academically based.

For MacKinnon to deny the nature of her sources is to create a tension in theory as unworkable because literally academic (unable at this moment to be put into practice). Her authority, she claims, is also "real" or experiential as to how she came to write this book, offsetting the theoretical nature of the book which "engages sexual politics at the level of epistemology" (ix). MacKinnon thus initiates a book based on beliefs formed by the women's movement of the seventies (that women, nature, experience, and the real are aligned against men, theory, culture, and the symbolic) by juxtaposing two seemingly apposite concepts: "Writing a book over an eighteen-year period becomes, eventually, much like co-authoring it with one's previous selves." With the first prefatory sentence, MacKinnon discovers the way out of appositive thinking by situating herself squarely inside two different feminist ways of thinking about the world: the liberal humanist, in which experience is authentic and authorizing, and the post-structuralist, based on the multiplicity of the cognitive self/selves. By posing Marxism as a third, but not a synthesis of $a + b$, she moves out of the bipolar field into a multiple one in which she is then free to posit a "Toward" or even the new theory itself. Indeed, her book "thus became a meta-inquiry into theory itself—Is it feminism or marxism? Is it relativity or quantum mechanics?" (xi). Refiguring liberalism as "relativity" and post-structuralism as "quantum mechanics" seems to equate by apposition feminism with the first but not necessarily, and Marxism with the second—again not necessarily. In this way she uses rhetorical thinking to *educate* rather than blindside by pointing out the relationship *between* the two correspondences. Political theory makes philosophy thinkable and vice versa. The difficulty is that she does not employ this alternate construct throughout the book, and so finds herself too often stuck by appositive thinking, and without the necessary lever.

The lever MacKinnon seeks is a method or theory that will pry feminism out of the public's perception of it as nonmethodical: "It has been perceived not as systematic analysis but as a loose collection of complaints and issues" (108). The difficulty with these complaints, of course, is that they come to represent appositively bodily/sexual/natural female complaints over against legitimizing political complaints. Against this misnaming MacKinnon sets empirical experience as productive of political theory. The centrality of sexuality in feminism arises not from male theories but from female practice "in diverse issues, including rape, incest, battery, sexual harassment, abortion, prostitution, and pornography" (109). What MacKinnon claims here, despite a misnomer of her own, is that feminist theory arises not from sexuality itself but sexual violence against women as a class, and not a body. MacKinnon negotiates the public/private split by viewing it as much a theory/practice issue as a rights issue or boundary dispute. The social practice of women's lives here is that of publicly private (or body as ground) as ruled by ungrounded "notions": "notions that women desire and provoke rape, that girls' experiences of incest are fantasies, that career women plot and advance by sexual parlays, that prostitutes are lustful, that wife beating expresses the intensity of love" (109). This reduction of women to the natural or sexual order "eliminates women's capacity for freedom." Feminism can reverse this order by revealing the politics of sexuality (or sexual violence); thus abortion is read as a statist and not a moral issue, incest is understood as a crime against the family rather than "mere" fantasy, rape and intercourse can be opposed rather than assimilated to each other, and sexual harassment can be differentiated from the normal/normative initiation into heterosexuality as a naturalized power imbalance (112). Feminism, for MacKinnon, does have an (empirical) theory: "sexuality is gendered as gender is sexualized. Male and female are created through the eroticization of dominance and submission. . . . This is the social meaning of sex" (113). Regardless of how one gets here, whether by pre- or poststructuralist intervention, theory *and* practice must map on to each other (Fukuyama would disagree here) to produce the irrefutable as a theory of power. To this end MacKinnon rejects liberalism as a polity no longer productive of change: "liberalism has been liberalism applied to women. Radical feminism is feminism" (117).

MacKinnon's rhetorical decision is to parlay the fact that the juridical state views society through male eyes, and that even as it positions itself as neutral, the state understands events by men's proclivities, resources, ambitions, and liberties. To win her case, MacKinnon rhetorically takes on the male perspective in the way she presents women under law as sexed, as primarily and only sexed, as no other. The verbal gestures of this argument, and the incisiveness, the refusal of demure eloquence, indicate a male audience to whom she addresses her knife-twisting truths. The rhetorical effect is to reverse women's experience in social issues such as pornography, battery, rape, and abortion, so that men feel the pain of exclusion, the shame of sexual blame. In inscribing experience into readerly interaction, MacKinnon refuses to allow the kind of abstraction she argues exists at the level of the state, in which women's experience can be abstracted past anyone's ability to see what has actually happened. In this way, regardless of the gender of the reader, the "mind fuck" MacKinnon ascribes to the legal system's dealings with women is materially available to those who need the tools to enact legislation.

Therefore, while MacKinnon's argument that feminism defines women by sex as Marxism defines society by class is ungrounded. It is a male legal point of view that women are defined by sex; thus what MacKinnon has done is to take the current state of affairs and say this is what *is*, and therefore this is how it is. She thereby refuses to differentiate between the perceptions that govern our rule-making, and the reality that offers up different ways of seeing. For MacKinnon, there is only one way of seeing, the masculinist way, because that is the only empowered perception available. "To the extent sexuality is social, women's sexuality is its use, just as femaleness is its alterity" (111), which is to say the social is male. But in terms of a critique of jurisprudence she is right in her assessment of the necessary tool for persuasion. This is an interventionist text of political theory for the purpose of enacting legislation in the negative state for the protection of women under patriarchy. MacKinnon's jurisitic masculinist rhetoric is both the powerful propulsion of her assertions (playing the game as if true) and her hardline dismissal of weak arguments (that women are fundamentally human, only secondarily sexed): The state represents itself as autonomous of class because outside class it cannot maintain this position in respect to sex. Which is to say, a nonevolving liberal polity must be refuted by a reform-oriented politics, a jurisprudential reform that revises liberalism against itself.

MacKinnon presents an anti-rights-based argument in that she deems rights as available to legal weasling; when the abortion right is argued as a right to privacy (as it is under the Supreme Court ruling), its distinctive relation to women is articulated only in terms of their bodies and their domestic lives, without reference to their right to live without coercion. Because the negative state views individuals as primarily male, women's rights become confused as "special interest" issues despite women's majority presence in the population. If the Constitution does not speak for women because women are treated like men from the perspective of male privilege under law, but inherently different because they are less capable, "why is upholding legislation to give them a voice impermissibly substantive and activist, while striking down such legislation is properly substanceless and passive?" (166). The body provides the basis for an argument of the personal as antidote to the abstraction of a rights-discourse. MacKinnon forces this connection to take the form of pain, or violence to the (female) body, as the only way in which the body can emerge in the reading procedure. That is to say, her rhetorical strategy is to make words hurt; male readers, whether liberal or conservative regarding gender rights issues, attest to the pain her words cause their readerly (male) sensibility. It is interesting to consider that MacKinnon's strategy of rhetorical attack wounds the male-identified ego, while documentary writers like Susan Faludi, who records an astounding array of damning facts about the systematic violation of women's rights in contemporary American culture, wound female-identified readers. Women readers, whether liberal or conservative regarding gender rights issues, attest to the pain of Faludi's book, and to the difficulty they experience in finishing it. MacKinnon writes to readers accustomed to seeing their experience validated; she employs a rhetorical strategy that denatures this expectation. Faludi writes to readers accustomed to seeing their experience ignored and deleted; she deliberately accosts this expectation, and so denatures the accustomed erasure.

FIGHTING WORDS

Feminist thinkers engage words as pain in order to take the abstraction out of reading, and like MacKinnon they turn their texts into an embodied rhetoric. Faludi's *Backlash*, for instance, provides extensive journalistic research to narrate a conspiracy theory of staggering proportions perpetrated by conservative officials on the American people. Faludi's argument is rhetorically persuasive, her facts overwhelming. It is rhetorically interesting that her critics counter by claiming that she has skewed facts with the help of her co-conspirators at NOW, while at the same time she claims funded (and therefore covertly politicized) gender studies distort the evidence.[2] But Faludi should be seen, as some critics have informally suggested, as a conspiratorial theorist; that is, as someone who sees conspiracy

everywhere and uses it to account for otherwise unaccountable phenomena. In our common imagination conspiracy theories occupy the space
between paranoia and unbearable truth: that which we prefer not to know.
But to label Faludi a conspiratorial theorist is to dismiss her data. Indeed,
the strongest message we can take from Faludi's research is that we need
to renegotiate liberalism's individual rights *as agency*—that is, convert
women's presence from passive into active rights—instead of engaging in
real conspiratorial thinking, which tropes secret brotherhoods as agents
while the individual can only be a passive victim.

The process of acceptance where conspiracy is involved requires dig-
ging beneath the layer of media representation and appropriation. We can
do this with Faludi's work by examining one of the parental organs of
popular journalism, *Time* magazine. The March 9, 1992 issue of *Time*
presents as its cover story, "Fighting the Backlash against Feminism: Susan
Faludi and Gloria Steinem Sound the Call to Arms." The militarism of this
title, as discussed in chapter one, overtly implies conspiracy through the
metonymic linkage of overt and covert battle. The actual story title reverses the paradigm: the war, in fact, is being fought against feminism.
The photos of Faludi and Steinem repeat this inversion of agency: the
cover photograph is a studied positioning of Steinem in a masculine pose
on a metal chair while Faludi leans passively, uncomfortably against the
wall behind her. Both women are dressed in black or jeans; the space they
inhabit is dark as well, although they are suggestively placed by a sunny
window. They are, the image implies, either in an imprisoning domestic
space or a conspiratorial interior (empty, in either case), but they will make
use of the window both to let in light and to escape out of it. Conversely,
the photo used to grab readerly attention on the contents page revises this
symbolism. The second image depicts a sunny, light, and equally empty
room. This time the two women are dressed in feminine, more colorful
clothes, the stiff pose of the cover replaced with a conversational stroll
through the room. This, the photo seems to say, is an intellectual space of
reason and calm strategy. However, no photo of Steinem and Faludi
together accompanies the actual story, so that the bond is a manufactured
one, an intrigue.

How can one read the discrepancies in the titles and images, especially
when the story and accompanying stories reveal the criticism launched
against the militant and/or intellectual weapons/books of these two
writers? It is helpful that within the cluster of surrounding stories there is
a piece on Steinem alone, entitled "Steinem: Tying Politics to the Personal."
Its presence underscores the public/private battle scripted on the cover,
and suddenly the choreography of inner spaces in the two photos collides
with the divisive rhetoric of the two titles. To complicate this postmodern
media dance, a cluster of photo images occupies the central space of the
article spread, photos of recognizable women in popular culture: Candice

Bergen, Madonna, Roseanne Arnold, Jodie Foster, Susan Sarandon, and Geena Davis. Conspiracy is confused with community in a kind of visual version of appositive thinking which undercuts the seriousness of the issue; as Steinem reminds the interviewer, "This is a revolution, not a public relations movement." That is to say, to "repackage" (the interviewer's term) feminism as a family rather than political issue is to hide women's concerns as individual behind "family values" in another appositive move.

"All family issues should not be women's issues," Faludi responds to the same question. "What bothers me is the implication that women have to prove they are good mothers before they can ask for anything else." What bothers in the misequation is that if women are only mothers, only body, only sexuality in MacKinnon's terms, then they can never be completely separated from the private sphere which they culturally embody. Without this last freedom, women will never be fully integrated into public life. And, to use Fukuyama's terms, women cannot escape the slave or bourgeois position if they are not allowed to engage in battle, particularly political battle. In "Crashing the Locker Room," Wendy Kaminer researches the trials and tribulations of women politicians.[3] Kaminer begins her essay anecdotally: "In her thirteen years as a senator from Arkansas, Hattie Caraway, the first woman elected to the U.S. Senate, made only fifteen speeches on the floor. 'And they say women talk all the time.' she wrote in her diary, after listening to her colleagues' orations." Kaminer notes that only fourteen women have ever served in the Senate, most having inherited their husband's seats or having been appointed through special connections. Only 117 have ever served in the House, out of 11,230. The reasons for such discrepancies are many, but one is particularly relevant to our discussion of public/private bonds. According to Senator Barbara Mikulski, politics is complicated for women: "If you're married, you're neglecting the guy; if you're divorced, you couldn't keep him; if you're a widow, you killed him; if you're single, you couldn't get a man" (Kaminer, 61). Which is to say, women are not allowed out of the kitchen or into the brotherhood. Feminine conspiracy, the notion goes, occurs among all-women groups in the kitchen, and is always directed against men. Men's conspiracy is also always directed against men, but metaphorically enacted on the female body; this is the stuff of James Bond, not marital or domestic bonds. Women's conspiracy is witchcraft, men's conspiracy is militaristic derring-do.

Step one out of such liberal bondage, of course, is to emulate Senator Mikulski and locate the double binds; step two is to discover the appositive thinking almost assuredly located therein. The third is to use the advice given in the epigraph above: to ask, "What game are you playing?" And although game-playing is usually conceived to be of the political realm, game-playing as Wittgenstein uses the term refers to the rituals of discourse that direct cognition, rituals that are differentiated according to arena and discipline, or that can hold sway across social registers. The battle-game over rhetorical power in academia tends to differ very little from the legalistic, journalistic, and political game-playing described in this chapter so far.

SEXUAL WORDS: THE CASE OF CAMILLE PAGLIA

Camille Paglia entered the discussion in chapter two as one of several conservative thinkers responding to the current intellectual movement of "political correctness." She upholds the same values as Fukuyama and attacks the values of academic feminists like MacKinnon because she believes the first to hold verities and the second, ironically, to sustain establishment power illiberally. But she provides a curious hinge to a discussion of MacKinnon, Faludi, and Steinem in relation to Fukuyama because all these thinkers are concerned with the aggressive commerce in society and aesthetic culture. Academia, like government and business and any other ideologically implicated structure, is susceptible to the negative forces of the market. All of these figures have managed to sell themselves through the commercialization of academia in the popular imagination, and so where they intended to critique they also succeeded in exploiting. Their publications, lecture tours, and wide media coverage are markers of their ability to manipulate the very system they attack.

But what Paglia achieves over and above the others is that she has recreated herself as a sexualized academic within popular culture, a "Madonna-wannabe" as at least one commentator has noted.[4] Her contentious appeal as she rides the rapid waves of pop culture lies partly in a cultural malaise with intellectuality and elite institutions. Audiences are captivated by divides within these cultural forces, which ironically are argued to be ineffectual and uninterested; they are even more captivated by those who offer to bodily represent these divides.

Paglia's second book, *Sex, Art, and American Culture* (1992), is a loose collection of unpublished writings that revealingly includes the transcription of an unscripted public lecture as a kind of performance art. The essays are loosely allied with the concepts explored in her scholarly book, *Sexual Personae: Art and Decadence from Nefertiti to Emily Dickinson* (1990), and include the cancelled preface to that book. However, although most of these essays assume that the reader is familiar with both *Sexual Personae* and the controversy Paglia has raised, without this background coherence is lost. The essays are too sketchy to do justice to her critiques, and when they resort to reiterating in brief the broad arguments and generalizations of her first book in place of argumentation, there is too little for the reader to work with beyond the persuasiveness of her rhetoric. But the rhetoric and its emotionalism is really the point in the end; argumentation is displaced by sheer emotional display. The style is hystericized not out of fear but for effect: the sentences are extremely short and rapid, the connections are lost or unclear, thoughts jump or depart, and emotion reigns. "I smiled with admiration," "I actually shouted 'Yay!' and 'Hurrah!,'" "I relished her scornful trouncing" (84–85; Paglia is reviewing another scholarly book). Even the arrangement of essays in this book is hystericized, lacking any logic of inclusion or sequence. And why are there three appendices, all of which document Paglia's presence in the cultural consciousness: the media's reaction to her, the cartoonists' response, and a long list of articles, reviews, and interviews of her and her work? What would such detailed chronicling have to do with a book of cultural critiques, except that they prove that Paglia has understood academia as war and commerce in the same way that Fukuyama has, with his lecture tour to universities to promote his ideas.

In order to sell her ideas Paglia must market herself, proving her importance to the academic institution and her salability to the public. Her self-positioning relative to her chosen profession includes flouting the rules of intellectual argumentation, making outrageous and unsupportable claims, being flatly self-contradictory, and at the same time virulent in attacks on others. This hystericized and yet calculated spectacle production is at once self-serving and self-vindicating; at the same time it works to support the stronger institution that underwrites academia, patriarchal misogyny.

The system of thought pervading Paglia's words is that the mythical archetypes at work in Western culture have historically been imagined in terms of culture (art, reason, Apollo) or nature (body, emotion, Dionysus). Thinkers like Rousseau, who have tried to artifice a different relation between these poles, are wrong thinkers for Paglia, self-deceived and engaged in deceiving others. Right thinkers are those who, like the Marquis de Sade, embrace and attempt to embody the poles through sexual experimentation. This allegory (questionably) substantiated by historical proofs, allows Paglia to declare that academic feminists and others of the "politically correct" are wrong thinkers, while sadomasochists and others who deal in pain as an aesthetic are right thinkers. Paglia identifies herself as a sadomasochist bisexual who considers enlightened men benighted:

A woman simply is, but a man must become. Masculinity is risky and elusive. It is achieved by a revolt from woman, and it is confirmed only by other men. Feminist fantasies about the ideal "sensitive" male have failed. Manhood coerced into sensitivity is no manhood at all. ("Alice in Muscle Land," 82)

The essay this quote comes from is a response to one young man's odyssey through the pain- and steroid-filled world of bodybuilding. That the man was the son of famous academics made his return from a world of "Roid rage," "shotgunning" growth hormones, crash diets, and relentless transformations of the body, all the more "disappoint[ing]." "I was rooting for [his] rebellion, his alienation from establishment values and mores" (81). But the life of the body, used by this man to rebel against the life of the mind, is perhaps more exploitative and more saturated with establishment values, and more punishing than anything the man had left. He had not become an athlete working toward Olympic trials; he had signed up for war in order to become a hero only to discover the surrealism of battle. Paglia, however, applauds the image of his body, "[g]aunt, haggard, skin blotchy and pitted," as he wins second place in a competition. "For me, [his] punishing iron adventure belongs to the noble tradition of warriors, athletes, and ascetic monks and yogis" (82). However, her title shows that she believes his adventure to belong to the order of Lewis Carroll's Alice, who also underwent enormous body transformations in order to "fit." Both were escapists as well, seeking something fantastic to put in the place of the mundane. But whereas Alice achieves an integrity in the end, Paglia's almost-hero succumbs to the greater powers of parentage, therapy, and survival. Still, she believes his narrative should be taught in classes, where it would "smoke out the rabid feminists and pious do-gooders, who would beat their breasts over [his] self-abuse. I myself," she continues, in order to contrast herself with these wrong thinkers, "found this an inspiring book, since I identify not with those who seek comfort and contentment but with those 'who strained and starved for the saber,' the 'glorious' silver prize that eludes [his] grasp" (82). It is not this man's escapism that matters, only his vision—a bodybuilding trophy, a metaphor for self-worth and godhead and mastery. Similarly, what little he does achieve is sufficient to negate the loss his parents and friends feel when he departs on his quest for self-glorification. Paglia feels an attraction to the same impulse as does Fukuyama: the warrior's quest for glory and recognition, an impulse that defines the self as superior against others. This is the impulse that also drives artists and geniuses of all kinds, Paglia argues, and she and Fukuyama applaud that it is the product of a masculinist schema that opposes self to others and sets self above nation. Yet it is this schema that divides democratic systems by pushing individuals to isolate themselves from their group as group leaders, and to therefore see themselves as superior to the laws that govern others. What Paglia is attracted to, then, is the very drive that would strike her down, the saber whose phallic intent is *against* her and which would enslave or rape her.

Were Paglia serious about her attraction to masculine sexuality, violence, sadomasochism, death or deformation, and the importance of self-seeking, she would have to justify why she did not support extreme examples of sexual acts such as the brutal, repeated rape of imprisoned Bosnian women by Serb soldiers. Like most violence against women, these war acts literalize a sociopolitical metaphor in which men's aggression is carried out against men's women. While these were acts so horrible that the West found itself unable to imagine them until the reports were too numerous to ignore, yet they simply replaced murder with sex, and death with new (Serbian) infants. They were also a strategic action of war designed for conquest, humiliation, torture, and genocide. Brutal and relentless, they contained none of the ritual and mystery of fifty-century B.C. Dionysian rites, none of the sensuality or religious importance of mystical scapegoating. Their acknowledged purpose was to eradicate one population by killing its men, and impregnating its women with the seed of another. MacKinnon's rigorous analysis of rape, its meaning, and its consequences is far more informative and far less "breast-beating" than Paglia's assumption that acts of sex upon the body are always sexual, always erotic acts for both parties involved.

What this analysis reveals is that the difficulty with reading Paglia is that she equates words with deeds, emotions with realities. She assumes, for instance, that intellectual argument is the same as ideological struggle, that wordplay and vitriol equal political battle. For this reason her critical strategy is essentializing and humanist, precisely because she believes that pronouncement displaces enunciation or enumeration. But displacement underwrites tropes of division and displacement: hysteria, appositive thinking, and conspiracy. Not surprisingly, all of these are important to her writing and thought. Displacement is also a psychological, political, and ideological tool that deafens the listener to what is being promised: loss, so that those already in power may gain. To attack theories used by feminists (e.g., "the stale cliché of 'the male gaze,' that tiresome assumption of feminist discourse") is to reassert woman's place as separate, divided from her own consciousness, objectified, and beneath the law. Paglia wants none of this for herself: she has claimed a voice and shows no sign of giving it up. Like Phyllis Schlafly, she is willing that all women should be enslaved so that she may be free. This is not only a bid at establishment thinking and acceptance by the powers above, but it is also self-centered. And since selfishness is exactly what Paglia accuses feminist academics of being, it is contradictory as well.

Paglia's attack on academic feminists is simply her version of D'Souza's attack on post-structuralist academics or Hirsch's attack on multiculturalists (discussed in chapter two): all three are jumping on the anti-political-correctness bandwagon by selecting their own particular target. Paglia's attack on academic feminists, however, focuses somewhat perversely on Harvard feminists. Her December 15, 1991 review of the sexual scholarship of Marjorie Garber's recent *Vested Interests*, for instance, begins with rejection:

The publication of a book on transvestism by a high-ranking woman professor of English at Harvard University should be the occasion for us to rejoice in the cultural changes in America over the last twenty-five years. . . .

But Marjorie Garber's *Vested Interests*, which examines real and fictive examples of cross-dressing from the Renaissance to the present, is too often a demonstration of what is wrong with academe rather than what is right . . . when one begins to take a closer look, it's downhill all the way.

Paglia's review, however, does not then proceed to demonstrate "what is wrong with academe," or even what is wrong with Garber, but rather reconstitutes all that characterizes her own discourse and thought. For instance, the generalized time period of "twenty-five years" makes the reader stop to ask what 1967 signifies in academe, but Paglia never lets on. The answer is the advent of French poststructuralist thought in the United States, through a conference on deconstruction held at Johns Hopkins University. This conference inaugurated a widespread exploration of post-structural thought in American academic circles, and was an important event because poststructualism is perhaps one of the most significant challenges to the traditions of American or Anglo-American thought in this century. Its main precepts are that the mind cannot know objective truth for two reasons. First, truth per se is ultimately unknowable because language and other signifying systems operate through political interest or ideology; second, the mind cannot even fully know itself since it thinks through language and since the self is constantly in flux. These are clearly the precepts of Garber's book, which discusses transvestism as a signifying system, or a meaning-making code that we read familiarly but subliminally, barely even conscious of its existence or of the ways in which it works on us to produce particular kinds of behavior in us. Even though these are so clearly the reviewed book's precepts, Paglia does not say so; she thus creates a double-bind situation in which we are doubly removed from the reviewed book and instantly prejudiced against it without any clear reason why. Yet elsewhere, Paglia dismisses poststructuralism outright, and she criticizes its uses harshly here; one is thus hard put to imagine why she holds the ensuing "cultural changes" so dear. The second generalization, that nonheterosexual practices "are now legitimate subjects of scholarly inquiry," fudges the issue: such inquiry has been legitimate for more than a century as long as it was medical, anthropological, or scientific research. Finally, the full description of this book's physical appearance is placed so as to answer "what is wrong with academe rather than what is right," as if the book's "juicy, piquant sexual details about famous people" or "appeal-ing package," or even its handsome illustrations, are a metaphor for Har-vard itself. Spend your money on tuition and books and you will be given the deal, yet "it's downhill all the way." The appositive thinking of the book/institution metaphor is continued in the review when Paglia implies that the book has been infected by the poststructuralist jargon of Harvard intellectuality: "it's a hard slog through lumpish patches of tedious Lacan jargon, which has infested Garber's formerly clear, plain prose, presumably through toxic contact at Harvard." How ironic then, that Paglia's own *Sexual Personae* was published with Yale University Press, Yale being the bastion of deconstruction—a particular school of poststructuralism—in the United States.

The greatest complaint Paglia has of the "Harvard" book is that it never defines the word "culture," from which Paglia deduces that "Garber's grasp of intellectual history is weak." In light of the fact that the author runs a vast array of scholarly seminars at the professional level for the Center for Literary and Cultural Studies at Harvard, seminars that cover every historical period and specialty of current literary studies, it is hard to imagine making such a statement. After reading *Vested Interests*, it is even harder. What, then, is actually at stake for Paglia in attacking a book that takes on a subject so complementary to her own?

The radical discrepancies Paglia displays in her critical thinking about Garber's book are provoked by a scholarship too close to her own yet stemming from an opposite ideology. While Paglia's theory of art argues for the supremacy of nature over culture, the scholar she attacks argues that a certain pattern of artistic representation is the result of social pressures and anxieties. But in her review, this opposition is never actually identified, and is instead reduced to an exemplar of the conspiracy trope—in which Paglia imagines that academe has set out to regain control of both popular and high culture by taking it back into campus enclaves. There art will be overly theorized without any feeling for its true merit, merit which Paglia has herself theorized but from a sensualist rather than rationalist perspective.

Like all conspiratorial thinking, Paglia's attack has the scent of desire, a yearning for what the privileged other has produced. It is a yearning she yields to the same Sadean treatment prescribed throughout her books, and the attack is vitriol, "pleasure-pain," a coercive intermingling with the desirable other. How can Paglia not angrily attack, like Schlafly, those feminists who have or do what she wants to have or do, since this too is the mark of the conspiratorial thinker? But at the same time, how can the *reader* differentiate between Sadean desire and hate? And how can this be a viable theoretic stance when it all looks the same, and produces the same effect on the sensation seeker, the voyeur, the consumer? At the same time, it was the Marquis de Sade who experienced all the thrill, not his victim. Power is a "glorious saber" in the hands of the power seekers, but the question of what the saber means to the community at large is one both Paglia and Fukuyama push aside as irrelevant to the individual questor. It is a question Garber, Gilligan, and MacKinnon push to the forefront—despite the differences in their approach, theoretical positioning, and even worldview—because they value the group over the one, or rather, the group of ones.

Beyond the basic problem of whether one values the individual over the group, or the reverse, there is another problem of political intent. Paglia's attack on Garber and on academic feminists at large is more than sadistic desire, and more than the individual quest. Paglia, like D'Souza and

Fukuyama, is invested in critiquing the political correctness movement and poststructuralist thought because she is frustrated that higher education has failed to live up to its stated goals. Critics like Paglia take the promises promulgated by elite education as truth statements—about liberalism, equality, knowledge—and they are incensed to discover the pledges are historically and continually mere political platforms. When D'Souza and Paglia respond hysterically to the rhetoric of the intellectual establishment, condemning it for *being* politicized speech that upholds establishment power, they display their belief in language as a truth vehicle. The difficulty is that in order to criticize the language of academia which they have not understood as rhetoric, or are surprised and horrified to discover is rhetoric, these critics implement their own rhetorical wars without understanding that their language is political rhetoric as well. The hurt that they feel at being too far outside the power monopoly would not be articulated in business, where monopoly is undisguisedly romanticized as the only possible form of success. But academia, ironically enough in terms of the popular perception of academic ivory towers, pretends to a transcendence of this romance.

Thus the clarity of an overt declaration of war on academic politicization is refreshing to intellectuals who are confused by the hidden politics of a highly ideological institution that hides behind a face of open-minded liberality. Thus Fukuyama enthusiastically admires the aristocrat warrior as the true hero, while Paglia glories in the romance of the warrior, athlete, and muscleman—the "true man." And thus both revel in a nostalgic love for masculine glory shored up by feminine subservience, as a solution to the current confusion of rhetorics and political goals. It is telling that the man Paglia longs for—a kind of transhistorical Heathcliff—is the historical product of a late eighteenth-century cultural hysteria in which the sadomasochistic Byronic hero was adored by both men and women precisely because he detested women and could not admit his love for men. Too, Paglia admires the sensibility of another author who dabbles in Byronic heroes, Jane Austen, because she writes about love stories very sensibly. What Paglia does not acknowledge is that Austen's heroines can fall in love with their Byronic suitors precisely because these men agree to be changed by the women they love just as the women agree to learn from their lovers. Mutual love and growth is a feminist, not a sadomasochistic, model of human relations; it is the very touchstone of the feminist intellectual thought Paglia deplores and hystericizes in her attacks as illogical, self-interested, and politicized.

Against the romanticized concept of sexuality that Paglia would use to "radically" displace feminist conceptions, MacKinnon offers a strong intermediary voice. Although many feminist thinkers find fault with MacKinnon's ideological base, her rhetorical argument clarifies the appositive moves in Paglia's thought. The difficulty with the legal definition of sexual difference, she writes, is that for the law, "[s]exuality remains largely pre-cultural and universally invariant, social only in that it needs society to take socially specific forms" (132). One of these forms is pornography, a form Paglia assumes to be normative, transhistorical, and aesthetically valuable. For MacKinnon, however, pornography not only allows for a systematic representation of all things as sexual, it also "connects the centrality of visual objectification to both male sexual arousal and male models of knowledge and verification." Similarly, the proximity of the pornographic object to the rape victim is not an extension of the sadomasochistic erotic energy of art; it is a similarity in political power. At the same time that pornography endangers women by making the conceptual fantasy too easy to literalize, to trope, it is also not true that pornography is a necessary, almost medical aid to men's emotional health. That is, it *becomes* sex to the extent that male medical professionals fear barring its access, for without it men would become " 'erotically inert wimps' " (139). The appositive thinking MacKin-non thus locates translates aphoristically: "No pornography, no male sexu-ality." MacKinnon's rhetoricized analysis of sexuality reveals the irony of women thinkers romanticizing and sensualizing dangerous sexual prac-tices, pain and humiliation, masculinist rule, and other "warrior" motifs. On the other hand, in examining Paglia's own rhetoric we might think about that other romanticized category, the witch, a figure MacKinnon does not account for but which has intrigued French feminists. Witch and warrior square off against each other in American and French masculinist and feminist thought as figures walking out of our historical past and across historical boundary lines. They are invoked as the vessels of power legiti-mated by their historical presence, and as harbingers of the future order. But when Paglia recalls the sexuality of the historicized warrior figure, she applies the same conservatism to considering the future as do D'Souza and Fukuyama: all three insist that because the past has produced us, the future must continue in the same mode, a mode worth celebrating and fighting for. What none of these critics consider is that none of them could write what they write, would be allowed to write as they do, if history were the glorious legacy they insist it is. None of these three are of the dominant culture they write about—indeed, it is their outsider status that practices their anxiety and hysterical writing about the institutions of that culture.

Paglia can critique academia and academic feminism precisely *because* the masculinist history of the warrior-athlete culture has not held. She has the space to speak and the ears to hear because she is employed in an academic institution as the result of an elite education—a position impos-sible in the Romantic age of the Byronic hero. She could have no place in the intellectual and cultural world of her hero Michelangelo, in the intel-lectual and cultural world of Renaissance Italy of her forefathers. Her Roman Catholic heritage, her church, would have condoned—had she lived in the Renaissance—her forcible marriage and her husband's legal

right to imprison, murder, or otherwise harm her. This is real sadomasochism, legitimized by historical argument predicated on biblical authority,
not a titillating aesthetic theory. Unlike Hirsch, who is mainstream and
successful, and therefore has something at stake in preserving the status
quo, Paglia's support of a conservationist agenda has, like the agendas of
D'Souza and Fukuyama, nothing to do with history. It has to do with taking
power oneself, with claiming a right to the power hierarchy through
arguments about tradition that do not themselves partake of tradition. That
is, Paglia could not say what she says about the sexuality of male art and
against the Apollonian ideal if she truly partook of tradition—truly took
Grecian values of reason over sensuality to heart, truly believed in the
inferiority of women and of the only possible meaning of women to be
bodily, truly believed in conservative humanist values over the intellectual
play of continental thought. That she allows herself poststructuralist-style
play within the academic setting, that she writes books *as* an academic and
intellectual despite what she claims to be writing as, shows that Paglia
would have her cake and eat it too. Like Dan Quayle, she would willingly
confuse the literal with the literary, fact with fiction, but would not reap the
consequences of such blurring, only the rewards.

WITCHERY, OR FRENCH FEMINISMS

In the introduction to *Eminent Rhetoric* above, I mentioned the work of
Catherine Clément and Hélène Cixous, who view the witch and hysteric as
"the end of a type—how far a plot can go." Witches combine anti-romantic
spells with female power, while hysterics play out male fantasies on their
bodies. The two variations—power and passivity—reveal just how disem-
powering Paglia's sexual theories would actually be to women. But
Clément and Cixous are more interested in following the witch to discover
her source of power and how she deploys it. Her ability to cast spells (like
Austen's charms) can be viewed in the terms of this book as the production
of anti-tropes; or in Clément and Cixous's terms, her mystery is that she
spells differently from men.

In addition to this position, French feminists evince a variety of political
stances. One such stance, for instance, is that stepping outside institutionalized divisions of gender and power is presently impossible, especially in
terms of linguistic divisions. This view is foregrounded by Luce Irigaray:
"How can women analyze their own exploitation, inscribe their own
demands, within an order prescribed by the masculine?" In her *Language
and Sexual Difference* (1991), Susan Sellers employs the quote to illustrate the
paradox French feminists have pointed to at the center of debates on
language, gender, and ownership or subjectivity, but Irigaray's words
exceed the use to which Sellers puts them, asking two different things: How
can we feminists think our way out of this box; and how can we be in the

box and still be thinking our own thoughts? These opposing positions (possibility versus impossibility) formulate the debate in France between women intellectuals, and although in the late 1970s the lines of demarcation were fairly clear, they are now far more intricately implicated in each other, and complicated by intervening voices of feminists from outside France.

Claudine Hermann is a French feminist who wrote her *Les Voleuses de langue* (*The Tongue Snatchers*, 1976) out of her experience of living in the United States. In that book she works out the implications of Hélène Cixous's statement in "Laugh of the Medusa" that "*Flying* [*stealing*] is a woman's gesture—flying [stealing] in language and making it fly [steal]. . . . It is no accident that 'voler' frolics between flight and theft, taking pleasure in both, and thus throws the agents of sense [the Sense Patrol] off its trail" (49). In Hermann's hands this theft becomes a meditative analysis of writing oneself into and out of meaning. Women's writing style itself takes part allegorically in this process: "In the immense totality of culture, woman appears to have been placed between parentheses, emerging unexpectedly in connection with other things, when she can't be stopped, traversing texts like a shadow, to be eliminated as quickly as possible so that one may go on, without wasting time, to more important matters" (6). The only way out for Hermann is the flight that is simultaneously the theft of tongues, for "the woman who wants to become educated is forced to let a little man grow inside her," yet "[i]t is not true liberation to accept the beliefs of one's masters" (6–7). Hermann, who is a lawyer, novelist, and feminist thinker, has shaped herself into an intellectual voice of stature whose contribution to the American feminist debate might be best imagined from her concluding thoughts: "I have tried to record here certain of the stupefactions that were mine when I attempted to initiate myself into virile knowledge and culture . . . it strikes me as particularly enriching for the two sexes to try to learn each other's language, instead of declaring one official language" (135–36). Which is to say that tongue snatching is not the same as establishing powerful voices through group identity, the strategy Sellers writes into her own book; rather, it is the assertion of an *écriture feminine* that already exists within parenthetical structures, and which needs to be given space and voice.

RHETORICALITY

While French feminists argue for reconfiguring linguistic systems in order to escape masculinist constructs, or what we have been calling tropes, scholars like John Bender and David Wellbery are arguing that the history of rhetoric can explain the current condition of language exchange in our culture. Because their work is grounded in historical patterns rather than cultural myths, Bender and Wellbery cannot produce anti-tropes as do the French feminists, but they can produce insights into where rhetorical systems are headed. And although anti-tropes are an effective immediate weapon against rhetorical tropes, they cannot enable us to do precisely what it is French feminism struggles toward: to get out of the language game altogether.

In their essay "Rhetoricality: On the Modernist Return of Rhetoric," Bender and Wellbery (3–39) rehearse the invention, study, and practice of rhetoric. Rhetoric in its classical sense is

an art of positionality in address. Audiences are characterized by status, age, temperament, education, and so forth. Speakers are impersonators who adapt themselves to occasions in order to gain or maintain position. . . . The cultural hegemony of rhetoric as a practice of discourse, as a doctrine codifying that practice, and as a vehicle of cultural memory, is grounded in the social structures of the premodern world. (7)

This is rhetoric as a highly stylized system for keeping people—speakers and listeners—in their place. Although we have been saying that contemporary political rhetoric accomplishes the same end, it does so secretively, in an age where the use of rhetoric as a ritualistic convention contradicts our modern assumptions about class and truth.

Bender and Wellbery divide rhetoric's historical trajectory into three main phases: the classical and medieval phase, the Enlightenment and Romantic phase, and the Modernist phase. The first represents the age in which oratory was the main form of political activism, legal procedure, and class enforcement; the second, an "enlightened" period in which the written word superseded the oral, marked the "end" of rhetoric in that the new belief in an objective, scientifically abstract, reasoning self necessitated a discourse unmarked by rhetorical form and intent. In addition, Romanticism translated the discourse of a knowing self into the literary, where the artist was now viewed as self-authoring, original, and arhetorical because spontaneous. Finally, the Modernist period, which began with a belief in the pure language of Enlightenment thought—where science and nature match up in a pure correlativity so that words mean precisely what we intend them to—has seen the return of rhetoric. This return is not in the form of classical rhetoric, however, but as what Bender and Wellbery call "rhetoricality."

Rhetoric can only return because the conditions that determined its demise are now no longer dominant: "objectivism, subjectivism, liberalism, literacy, and nationalism." These conditions were necessary to the perception of self as abstract, objective, scientific, "enlightened." But since the 1960s we have begun to question these conditions: science is no longer trustworthy, objectivity works to marginalize women while subjectivity works to marginalize ethnic groups and extra-nationals, and the printed word is being superseded by screens. The return of rhetoric, however, does not signal a renewed intellectual interest in regaining a structural power-hold, although this does seem to be George Bush's aim.[5] Rather, intellectuals have seized on rhetoricality because of a self-consciousness about language itself, about its paucities and its potentials. Rhetoricality "is a transdisciplinary field of practice and intellectual concern, a field that draws on conceptual resources of a radically heterogeneous nature and does not assume the stable shape of a system or method of education" (25).

We have already seen that intellectuals representing a variety of disciplinary interests are engaging questions about language systems and usages—rhetoricality. And although many of them are concerned about the relation of such issues to our cultural future, discussion of educational systems remains at the level of critique and anxiety. This is because while rhetoric in the classical age was a system one learned at school in order to take one's place as a citizen in society, rhetoric today is hidden and taught only informally through the daily exchange of politicized language. It cannot therefore be systematized as a pedagogy because its reactionary ideology cannot be thus openly acknowledged. This raises the question, then, of how to think about pedagogy effectively in terms of language use and its ideologies.

CONCLUSION: TALKING BACK

In order to think toward a discursive pedagogy, we must begin with embedded culture. Nearly twenty years ago Sherry Ortner examined the gendered problematic of nature versus culture to expose a cultural system which contains women in the "natural" sphere of femnized nature, and promotes men to the "cultural" or technological, artificial, and therefore masculine sphere. In Simone de Beauvoir's version, women are "immanent," inhabiting and embodying nature, while men are "transcendent," drawing on nature to sculpt culture. Thus, when in the eighteenth century science intervened in the dominance of economic and religious thought to bring on modernist culture, the discipline and language of science understood itself as "same": as disinterested, objective, clinical. Its object, nature, encompassed all that was self-interested, subjective, and embodied: different. Although we have recently become aware of how rhetorical scientific discourse actually is, the myth of its arhetoricity continues to inform our understanding of science's modernist role in relation to nature as one of male to female, sameness to difference. Once the making of laws, *the* fundamental mode for artificing culture, became accessible to women through the vote, overt systematic changes in the nature/culture, sameness/difference ideology could begin. But as MacKinnon's book shows, this is still a very contemporary struggle toward change.

In the end, discussions of women and language—whether these relate to art, politics, law, education, or cultural myth—do come down to sameness and difference. The problematic depends on whether a thinking woman sees herself as a thinker, and therefore the same as all other thinkers, or whether she sees herself as a woman, and therefore the sexually different one who must see through her sex. Both positions reflect the modern condition in which we understand ourselves and our world through others' words. Many deny that there exists any current inability to own our language, or that women experience more difficulty than men. Those who decry our (women's and men's) lack of representational mastery and refute it, hystericize the current condition by refusing its historical presence. These critics, men and women, insist that those who talk do so simply because they can, and that those who are silent are so because they are weak. Moreover, those who talk about being silenced or being unable to represent their reality accurately through language are assumed to be hysterical, verbal exponents of the weak, who must be exposed before their hysteria spreads to the strong. Against this position, which is best illustrated in this chapter by Fukuyama and Paglia, we can pit those who do speak out despite their awareness of linguistic alienation. These thinkers, men and women, break the silence, refute the hystericization, and "talk back" against the tropology of those who want to insist that historical breaks have not occurred and that we do still live in an age capable of representing itself to itself as continuous and whole.

Foremost among these thinkers are French feminists such as Cixous, Clément, and Hermann. But also included here are American feminists who do not take up the philosophical question because they are engaged in the social practice of representation: MacKinnon, Faludi, Steinem. The intellectual debate engaged here is between those who use tropes while insisting they are speaking only naturally, representational, and representatively, versus those who use every word to call attention to such representational disorder. Yet there are other voices to be heard, including those who hear tropes through more than one level of differentiation such as class, race, ethnic, sexual orientations, and so on. A speaker like bell hooks, who inhabits several of these registers of difference and still speaks out, provides a clearer position for action than does the anti-tropic witch of Cixous, the thief-bird of Hermann, or the revisioning camera-eye of Patricia Rozema.

Hooks's position metonymically brings into focus the multiple dislocation of our lives in the current moment—whether that is postmodern or beyond. She persuasively argues that the classroom is a pivotal arena for claiming a space from which to speak because the classroom is a space of generation. "My classroom style is very confrontational . . . based on the assumption that many students will take courses from me who are afraid to assert themselves as critical thinkers, who are afraid to speak" (*Talking Back*, 53). In this space, students who assume sameness *or* difference can be challenged to articulate the representative value of their positions, and to coerce these positions into meaningful terms for the self. Hooks concedes both the difficulties of women's self-representation and the difficulty of convincing new generations that any such divide exsists. Or, alternately, that any such divide can be addressed. The question of generation is not a question of rights or of privilege; rather, it is one of intellect. Will the coming generations allow themselves to be troped out of history, or will they think the problem through, refute tropological politics, and practice for themselves a political and social discourse that respects their person and that of others? As hooks might say, one can begin the process of social transformation by talking back, by calling a trope a trope, and by insisting on a discourse that must disclose its designs upon us.

NOTES

1. For an alternative treatment of feminist statist politics, see Brown; and Fox-Genovese. While Fox-Genovese criticizes MacKinnon's argument, her book is in many ways fundamentally like-minded.

2. For an interesting critique of Faludi's work, see Lehrman.

3. Kaminer's work is suspect however, since she is both a Harvard faculty member and the author if *I'm Dysfunctional, You're Dysfunctional,* a work whose unsympathetic critique of twelve-step groups does not take into account her own position of privilege.

4. A 1991 political cartoon by Tim Gabor depicts Paglia in Madonna dress— leather corset, panties and garter, fishnet stockings, stiletto heels, and whip—for *The American Enterprise.*

5. Interestingly, MacKinnon's book offers a rhetorically crafted juridical argument that is a singular return to classical rhetoric in that it seeks to use formalized language in order to construct women as property owners (of their own bodies) and therefore as citizens. While the construction of men as property owners and thus citizens was the original purpose of rhetoric, Bender and Wellbery claim that this usage was outmoded by the eighteenth century. MacKinnon's calculated resurrection of the language system used to form community and consensus in the classical age of democracy reveals just how long women have been absent from models of legal recognition and privilege.

Bibliography

Altick, Richard. *The English Common Reader: A Social History of the Mass Reading Public 1800–1900.* Chicago: University of Chicago Press, 1957.

Armstrong, Nancy. *Desire and Domestic Fiction: A Political History of the Novel.* New York: Oxford University Press, 1987.

Auerbach, Nina. *Romantic Imprisonment: Women and Other Glorified Outcasts.* New York: Columbia University Press, 1985.

Austen, Jane. *The Works of Jane Austen: Minor Works*, vol. VI. Ed. R. W. Chapman. London: Oxford University Press, 1965.

_____ . *Persuasion.* Oxford: Oxford University Press, 1991.

Auster, Bruce B. and Gloria Borger. "Shape Up or Ship Out." *U.S. News and World Report* (April 5, 1993): 25–29.

Baron, Dennis, *Grammar and Gender.* New Haven: Yale University Press, 1986.

Barrie, J. M. *Peter Pan.* Harmondsworth, England: Puffin Books, 1986.

Bender, John and David E. Wellbery, eds. *The Ends of Rhetoric: History, Theory, Practice.* Stanford: Stanford University Press, 1990.

Benedict, Helen. *Virgin or Vamp: How the Press Covers Sex Crimes.* New York: Oxford University Press, 1992.

Berlin, James. "Rhetoric and Ideology in the Writing Class." *College English* 50 (1988): 477–94.

Besen, Stanley M., Thomas G. Krattenmaker, A. Richard Metzger, Jr., and John R. Woodbury. *Misregulating Television: Network Dominance and the FCC.* Chicago: University of Chicago Press, 1984.

Bourdieu, Pierre, and Jean-Claude Passeron. *Reproduction in Education, Society and Culture.* Beverly Hills: Sage Publications, 1977.

Brand, Dana. "From the *Flaneur* to the Detective: Interpreting the City of Poe." In *Popular Fiction: Technology, Ideology, Production, Reading*, 220–37. Ed. Tony Bennett. London: Routledge, 1990.

Briggs, Le Baron Russell. *To College Girls, and Other Essays*. Boston: Houghton Mifflin, 1911.

Brown, Wendy. "Finding the Man in the State." *Feminist Studies* 18 (1992): 7–34.

Bryson, Norman. *Vision and Painting: The Logic of the Gaze*. New Haven: Yale University Press, 1983.

Carroll, Lewis. *Alice's Adventures in Wonderland: Through the Looking-Glass and What Alice Found There*. New York: Random House, 1965.

Clément, Catherine and Hélène Cixous. *The Newly Born Woman*. Translated by Betsy Wing. Minneapolis: University of Minnesota Press, 1986.

Connolly, William E. *Identity/Difference: Democratic Negotiations of Political Paradox*. Ithaca: Cornell University Press, 1991.

Culler, Jonathan. *The Pursuit of Signs: Semiotics, Litrature, Deconstruction*. Ithaca: Cornell University Press, 1981.

de Man, Paul. *Allegories of Reading: Figural Language in Rousseau, Nietzsche, Rilke, and Proust*. New Haven: Yale University Press, 1979.

Denison, D. C. "The Interview: Camille Paglia." *The Boston Globe Magazine* (December 1, 1991): 8.

DeVore, Frances. "Women Reporters Fight Wars in, Out of the Newsroom." *Ocala Star-Banner* (March 31, 1993): 7C.

Douglas, Ann. *The Feminization of American Culture*. New York: Knopf, 1977.

Dowling, David, ed. *Novelists on Novelists*. Atlantic Highlands: Humanities Press, 1983.

D'Souza, Dinesh. *Illiberal Education: The Politics of Race and Sex on Campus*. 1991; New York: Vintage Books, 1992.

Dyhouse, Carol. *Girls Growing up in Late Victorian and Edwardian England*. London: Routledge & Kegan Paul, 1981.

Easthope, Antony. *Poetry as Discourse*. London: Methuen, 1983.

———. *Poetry and Phantasy*. Cambridge: Cambridge University Press, 1989.

Edelman, Murray. *Constructing the Political Spectacle*. Chicago: University of Chicago Press, 1988.

Elbow, Peter. *Writing with Power*. New York: Oxford University Press, 1982.

———. "Reflections on Academic Discourse: How it Relates to Freshmen and Colleagues." *College English* 53 (1991): 135–55.

Eliot, Charles W. *Education for Efficiency and the New Definition of the Cultivated Man*. Boston: Houghton Mifflin, 1909.

Elliott, John. "The Ethics of Repression: Deconstruction's Historical Transumption of History." *New Literary History* 23 (1992): 727–45.

Evans, Mary. *Jane Austen and the State*. London: Tavistock, 1987.

Faludi, Susan. *Backlash: The Undeclared War Against American Women*. New York: Crown Publishers, 1991.

Fasold, Ralph W. *The Sociolinguistics of Language*. Oxford: Basil Blackwell, 1990.

Fox-Genovese, Elizabeth. *Feminism Without Illusions*. Chapel Hill: University of North Carolina Press, 1991.

Freire, Paolo. *Pedagogy of the Oppressed*. Translated by Myra Bergman Ramos. New York: Herder and Herder, 1970.

Frug, Mary Joe. *Postmodern Legal Feminism*. New York: Routledge, 1992.

Frye, Northrup. *Anatomy of Criticism: Four Essays*. Princeton: Princeton University Press, 1957.

Fuchs, Cindy. Review of "I've Heard the Mermaids Singing." *Cineaste* 16 (1988): 54–55.

Fukuyama, Francis. *The End of History and the Last Man*. New York: Free Press, 1992.

Gans, Herbert J. *Deciding What's News: A Study of CBS Evening News, NBC Nightly News, Newsweek, and Time*. New York: Vintage, 1980.

Garber, Marjorie. *Vested Interests: Cross-Dressing and Cultural Anxiety*. New York: Routledge, 1992.

Gates, Jr., Henry Lewis, ed. *"Race," Writing and Difference*. Chicago: University of Chicago Press, 1985.

Gibbs, Nancy. "Fighting the Backlash against Feminism." *Time* (March 9, 1992): 50–57.

Gilbert, Sandra and Susan Gubar. *The Madwoman in the Attic: The Woman Writer and the Nineteenth-Century Literary Imagination*. New Haven: Yale University Press, 1979.

Gilligan, Carol. *In a Different Voice: Psychological Theory and Women's Development*. Cambridge, MA: Harvard University Press, 1982.

———. *Making Connections: The Relational Worlds of Adolescent Girls at Emma Willard School*. Edited by Carol Gilligan, Nona P. Lyons, and Trudy J. Hanmer. Cambridge, MA: Harvard University Press, 1990.

Giroux, Henry. *A Pedagogy for the Opposition*. S. Hadley, MA: Bergin and Garvey, 1983.

Goodman, Ellen. "Changes Find Conservative Towns." *The Washington Post* (March 31, 1993): A17.

Grimshaw, Allen, ed. *Conflict Talk*. Cambridge: Cambridge University Press, 1990.

Grundmann, Roy and Cynthia Lucia. "Gays, Women and an Abstinent Hero." *Cineaste* 19 (1992): 20–22.

Harrison, Barbara Grizzuti. "P.C. on the Grill: The Frugal Gourmet, Lambasted and Skewered." *Harper's Magazine* (June 1992): 42–50.

Hermann, Claudine. *The Tongue Snatchers*. Translated by Nancy Kline. 1976; Lincoln: University of Nebraska Press, 1989.

Hirsch, Alan. *Talking Heads: Political Talk Shows and Their Star Pundits*. New York: St. Martin's Press, 1991.

Hirsch, Jr., E. D. *Cultural Literacy: What Every American Needs to Know*. Boston: Houghton Mifflin, 1987.

Holloway, Karla F. C. "The Legacy of Voice: Toni Morrison's Reclamation of Things Past." In *New Dimensions of Spirituality: A Biracial and Bicultural Reading of the Novels of Toni Morrison*, 21–28. Edited by Karla F. C. Holloway and Stephanie A. Demetrakopoulos. Westport, CT: Greenwood Press, 1987.

———. "Response to *Sula*: Acknowledgement of Womanself." In *New Dimensions of Spirituality*, 67–81.

hooks, bell. *Talking Back: Talking Feminist, Talking Black*. Boston: South End Press, 1989.

———. *Yearning: Race, Gender, and Cultural Politics*. Boston: South End Press, 1990.

Irigaray, Luce. *This Sex Which is Not One*. Translated by Catherine Porter. Ithaca: Cornell University Press, 1985.

Jaehne, Karen. Interview with Patricia Rozema. *Cineaste* 16 (1988): 22–23.

JanMohamed, Abdul R. *Manichean Aesthetics: The Politics of Literature in Colonial Africa*. Amherst: University of Massachusetts Press, 1983.

Joyce, Joyce A. "Black Woman Scholar, Critic, and Teacher: The Inextricable Relationship between Race, Sex, and Class." *New Literary History* 22 (1991): 543–65.

Kaminer, Wendy. "Crashing the Locker Room." *The Atlantic Monthly* (July 1992): 59–63.

Keller, Evelyn Fox. *Reflections on Gender and Science*. New Haven: Yale University Press, 1985.

Klaidman, Stephen. *Health in the Headlines: The Stories Behind the Stories*. New York: Oxford University Press, 1991.

Kramarae, Cheris and Paula A. Treichler. "Power Relationships in the Classroom." In *Gender in the Classroom: Power and Pedagogy*, 41–59. Edited by Susan L. Gabriel and Isaiah Smithson. Urbana: University of Illinois Press, 1990.

Kristeva, Julia. "A New Type of Intellectual: The Dissident." In *The Kristeva Reader*, 292–300. Edited by Toril Moi. New York: Columbia University Press, 1986.

Krug, Edward A., ed. *Charles W. Eliot and Popular Education*. New York: Teachers College, Columbia University Bureau of Publications, 1961.

Langbauer, Laurie. *Women and Romance: The Consolations of Gender in the English Novel*. Ithaca: Cornell University Press, 1990.

Lehrman, Karen. "The Feminist Mystique." *The New Republic* (March 16, 1992): 30–34.

Lerner, Gerda. *The Creation of Feminist Consciousness: From the Middle Ages to Eighteen-seventy*. New York: Oxford University Press, 1993.

Lewis, Anthony. Editorial. *New York Times* (September 7, 1992): 19.

Locke, John. *An Essay Concerning Human Understanding*. Vol. 2. Edited by Alexander Campbell Fraser. New York: Dover Publications, 1959.

MacKinnon, Catharine. *Toward a Feminist Theory of the State*. Cambridge, MA: Harvard University Press, 1989.

Mailloux, Steven. *Rhetorical Power*. Ithaca: Cornell University Press, 1989.

Meyer, Charles F. *Apposition in Contemporary English*. Cambridge: Cambridge University Press, 1992.

Morrison, Toni. *Sula*. 1973; New York: Plume/Penguin Books, 1982.

Nyhan, David. Editorial: "Clinton's Stumbling, Bumbling Start." *Boston Globe* (January 31, 1993): 69.

Ortner, Sherry. "Is Female to Male as Nature is to Culture?" In *Woman, Culture, and Society*, 67–87. Edited by Michelle Z. Rosaldo and Louise Lamphere. Stanford: Stanford University Press, 1974.

Paglia, Camille. *Sexual Personae: Art and Decadence from Nefertiti to Emily Dickinson*. New Haven: Yale University Press, 1990.

———. "Ninnies, Pedants, Tyrants and Other Academics." *New York Times Book Review* (May 5, 1991): 1, 29, 33.

———. *Sex, Art, and American Culture*. New York: Vintage Books/Random House, 1992.

Parenti, Michael. *Inventing Reality: The Politics of News Media*. New York: St. Martin's Press, 1993.

Paretsky, Sara. *Burn Marks*. New York: Dell Publishing, 1990.

Pateman, Carole. *The Problem of Political Obligation: A Critique of Liberal Theory*. 1979; Berkeley: University of California Press, 1985.

Phelps, Timothy and Helen Winternitz. *Capital Games: Clarence Thomas, Anita Hill, and the Story of a Supreme Court Nomination*. New York: Hyperion, 1992.

_____ . "Getting the Story." *Newsday* (June 2, 1992): 51.

Randall, Marilyn. "Appropriate(d) Discourse: Plagiarism and Decolonization." *New Literary History* 22 (1991): 525–41.

Rother, James. "Face-Values on the Cutting Floor: Some Versions of the Newer Realism." *American Literary Realism* 21 (1989): 67–96.

Sedgwick, Eve Kosofsky. "Jane Austen and the Masturbating Girl." *Critical Inquiry* 17 (1991): 818–37.

Sellers, Susan. *Language and Sexual Difference: Feminist Writing in France*. New York: St. Martin's Press, 1991.

Shakespeare, William. *Hamlet*. In *The Complete Works of William Shakespeare*. Cambridge: Cambridge University Press, 1966.

Sharrett, Christopher. "Debunking the Official History: The Conspiracy Theory in *JFK*." *Cineaste* 19 (1992): 11–14.

Smith, Barbara. "Beautiful, Needed, Mysterious." In *Critical Essays on Toni Morrison*, 21–22. Edited by Nellie Y. McKay. Boston: G. K. Hall, 1988.

Snead, James. "European Pedigrees/African Contagions: Nationality, Narrative, and Communality in Tutuola, Achebe, and Reed." In *Nation and Narration*, 231–49. Edited by Homi K. Bhabha. London: Routledge, 1990.

Steedman, Carolyn. *Landscape for a Good Woman: A Story of Two Lives*. London: Virago Press, 1986.

Stierle, Karlheinz. "Studium: Perspectives on Institutionalized Modes of Reading." *New Literary History* 22 (1991): 115–27.

Tannen, Deborah. *Talking Voices: Repetition, Dialogue, and Imagery in Conversational Discourse*. Cambridge: Cambridge University Press, 1989.

_____ . *You Just Don't Understand: Women and Men in Conversation*. New York: Ballantine Books, 1990.

Walker, Alice. *The Color Purple*. 1982; New York: Washington Square Press, 1983.

_____ . *In Search of Our Mothers' Gardens: Womanist Prose*. New York: Harcourt Brace Jovanovich, 1983.

Waugh, Auberon. "Princess Monster as a Model for the New Britain." *The Spectator* (January 30, 1993): 8.

White, Mimi. "Representing Romance: Reading/Writing/Fantasy and the 'Liberated' Heroine of Recent Hollywood Films." *Cinema Journal* 23 (Spring 1989): 41–56.

Williams, Patricia J. *The Alchemy of Race and Rights: Diary of a Law Professor*. Cambridge, MA: Harvard University Press, 1991.

Wittgenstein, Ludwig. *The Blue and Brown Books: Preliminary Studies for the "Philosophical Investigations."* New York: Harper & Row, 1958.

Index

About the Author

ELIZABETH A. FAY is Assistant Professor of English, University of Massachusetts at Boston. She is co-editor of *Working-Class Women in Academia: Laborers in the Knowledge Factory* (1993) and a contributor to *Constructing and Reconstructing Gender: The Links among Communication, Language, and Gender* (1992).